Memories: real or imagined

My life & times

an autobiography by

Bernard Kessler

The author in mid-life

My parents in Krakow, Poland under Nazi occupation, 1940

Dedication

It is customary to dedicate a book; In my case, since it is the only book I wrote – and will write – I have to dedicate it to a number of persons.

My parents – who perished in the Holocaust – Avraham Hirsch and Sima Yochwet (Selma) Kessler

My siblings- Bezallel; Sara Susi; Dvora Dorle

Both my Wives – Marion Hilda (who died in 1973, aged only 45) and Ilana whom I married in 1978 and who is with me to this day

My children: Simone, David, Naomi and Yael

And last but not least my five grandchildren. Eitan aged 28; Tamir aged 25; the twins Mai and Shir aged 15; and their sister Romi aged12

They are all partially responsible for my writing this Memoir.

Contents

Foreword

In 1923 just five years after the end of the First World War, Germany was subjected to an attempted putsch in Munich which became known as the Bier Halle Putsch. This was, I believe, the first indication of the shape of things to come, and probably led to World War II and the Holocaust. The instigators and leaders of this attempt, among them Adolf Hitler and Rudolf Hess, were sent to prison. During his imprisonment, Hitler dictated his autobiography, *Mein Kampf*, to Hess, who also edited the work. The book contained all the elements of Hitler's beliefs – national, social, economic, political – as well as his ambitions. Above all, the book made clear his racial prejudices – in other words, his hatred for the Jewish People. He started to dictate the book in 1923. The first volume was published in 1925, the second in 1926.

This was the Germany into which I was born in 1927.

These events, and those that followed, are most certainly what influenced my attitude to life from birth to the present. It surely made of me what used to be referred to as 'The Wandering Jew', since the circumstances of my life have taken me from my birthplace, Leipzig, in Germany, to Krakow, Poland, then to London and Ely in England and eventually to Jerusalem, Israel where I have lived since 1974. Here I can finally feel at home.

The thought occurs to me that taking Hitler's book and subsequent actions as the example, does it not follow, logically, that the world at large – and certainly we in Israel – should *believe* our neighbours when they declare their feelings concerning us? If they *openly* boast of their hatred and their declared intentions to destroy us, would we not be foolish, even self-destructive, to doubt their word?

I was 84 years old when I started this project. I am a little older now and have reached the 'venerable' age of 91 plus; the date at present is the end of March 2019. It is now more than 73 years since the end of World War II and 71 years since Israel's Declaration of Independence. Having finally our own State again has certainly changed the situation for Jews everywhere dramatically. In the years leading up to WWII no country was prepared to open its doors to large numbers of Jewish refugees. Such is not the case today for fleeing refugees and those seeking better living conditions who flood the more affluent and peaceful countries, often to the detriment of the indigenous, local, residents. If only we had our own State in the 1930s, just how many lives of our people would have been saved, including my own parents, and many other family members – both close and not so close!

I realize now, or rather was told by those around me, that I should document my past and present life for those who follow me. I cannot easily document my past since I never kept a diary to record my regular life. I have no one alive still to ask and have no recorded history of my ancestors. Hence mine is not an easy undertaking. Memory is a tricky thing at the best of times; how much more so as one grows older. Nevertheless, I have tried to remember my childhood, my youth, my young and not-so-young adulthood and to describe my life as I remember it (or imagine it) – and sometimes as I was reminded by those who shared some of it. If I have erred in some detail, those who will read these lines will know to make the appropriate allowances. Just know the time covered is from 1927 to near the end of March 2019 so far; a not uninteresting slice of human existence.

Leipzig - Germany

The date is July 13^{th,} 1927. I, Bernard (Bernhardt) Kessler, am about to embark on my life's journey... and *what* a journey – at times long, often weary, sometimes terrifying; too short at other times; sometimes exciting, even exhilarating; never really dull.

Being the third child born into a religiously orthodox Jewish family, at this time of approaching economic, as well as social and political, mayhem in Germany, did not exactly make the life of my family financially easier. This did not, however, inhibit or limit the family's joy at this happiest of events. On the contrary; at least, so I would like to imagine.

I must confess that to me the event of my birth did not make a particular impression – at least not until much, much later, if at all. On the positive side, my earliest vague memories are of starting to attend the "Cheder" (Jewish religious supplementary school) at the age of 3-4 years, as was the custom for all boys from orthodox Jewish families. On the negative side, I have dim but lasting memories of roaming bands of thuggish Nazi youths in my hometown.

There is, however, one event which I particularly remember. It concerns the arch-terrorist, Adolf Hitler, *Yemach Shemo* (the Hebrew expression meaning "may his name be obliterated for ever" – or in other words "may he burn in hell"). After his party's election victory at the end of 1932 – itself partly due to his thugs' hyper-activity during the run-up to the election – he was appointed Kanzler (Chancellor) by the German president, Field-Marshal Paul von Hindenburg.

This was at the beginning of 1933 when the Prussian aristocracy – both military and civil – thought they could control this 'upstart', as they called him. I was a few months short of six years old at the time and can't claim that his election made any sort of impression on me. *Our parents did not make a practice of discussing such matters in our hearing. In any event, I would not have understood what it was about at that tender age.*

However, the specific event that stands out in my memory is that Hitler paid a visit to Leipzig at the time. Clearly this was part of his tour

11

throughout Germany, either during his election campaign or as a triumphant victory journey. There were huge crowds everywhere and I remember being out in the street. I do not remember with whom. I would surely not have been alone at that age, and it must have been near my home. I recall finding myself, at some point, in the middle of an enormous throng. Indeed, all the streets along Hitler's route were packed with wildly, deliriously, chanting crowds of people – who were not necessarily Nazis or members of that accursed party – just ordinary Germans, if one could call them 'ordinary'.

As the 'Fuhrer' – he was so termed by all – came by, the whole multitude raised their right arms in unison, and shouted at the top of their voices: *"Heil Hitler!"* I was terrified, not just overawed but absolutely petrified. So, out of fear, I could not decide whether to join the throng and also shout, with raised arm of course. I fervently hope that I didn't.

Round about that time, perhaps a year or so later, another event occurred which made an everlasting impression on me. I fell prey to a fairly severe case of tonsillitis. I recall that the doctor placed a mask over my nose and mouth, poured a few drops of chloroform on that mask and asked me to count backward from 100 – 99, 98, 97 and so on. I don't remember what number I reached before I woke a little later to the most solicitous attention I recall ever receiving till that day, with the possible exception of my circumcision. (However, I don't really remember that event; I was, after all, only eight days old at the time).

However, when I awoke on this occasion, it was explained to me that while I had 'slept', the doctor inserted a wide clip to hold open my mouth. He then inserted a long, thin glass tube to draw out a sample of the mucous substance attached to my tonsils. This confirmed that the substance was not toxic. Strangely enough, while it was customary at that time to remove the tonsils of children at the slightest sign of a throat infection, our doctor – for reasons I could never fathom – decided against the operation. Although I did suffer from tonsillitis frequently for a good many subsequent winters I am glad to have avoided what turned out to be an unnecessary operation.

After the medical procedure, the very friendly doctor informed my parents, deliberately *in my hearing I tend to believe,* that I was now *required* to eat ICE CREAM, since that would facilitate the healing process in my throat. This, of course, was much to my liking, as can well be imagined, and I took an immediate 'shine' to the doctor who, in my childish mind, became my everlasting, bosom friend.

Another event which made a lasting impression on me at that time was that my big brother, Bezalel, five years my senior, who had not paid too much attention to his younger brother till then, decided to present me with his own mouth-organ (harmonica). What is more, in order to make the gift more meaningful, he decided to teach me how to play it. The instrument, a coveted Hohner (which company manufactured the best quality instruments), had engraved on it numbers for each note in the musical scale. Zal – this was the shortened form of his name – wrote out for me some tunes, noting the appropriate number, and indicating whether to inhale or exhale.

In this fashion I soon mastered the art and proceeded to become the Larry Adler of the family. (Larry Adler was at that time the acknowledged master of the harmonica. He even performed with some of the major orchestras of the day, classical pieces of music which lent themselves to this particular instrument, as well as specially composed pieces of music for harmonica and orchestra.)

What greater joy could there have been for a 6/7 year old boy? I tried my darndest to imitate Larry, with only very limited success, I am sure. But it was fun trying and it stood me in good stead later when I was 11 years old. (Wait for it: we'll get there in due course.) I may add here that I still own a harmonica and try to persuade myself that it is the actual instrument given me by my brother, but it probably isn't. Anyway, I try now to teach Shir, one of my granddaughters, to play this instrument, writing out some tunes and indicating with noughts and crosses when to inhale and when to exhale. She shows some signs of success, but it is early days yet.

I think this is an appropriate place to introduce you to the composition of my nuclear family – that is, my parents and siblings.

My father, Abraham Hirsch, was born in Jaroslav in 1895 in the province of Galicia, Poland, at that time part of the Austro-Hungarian Empire. He was the second-born of seven sons. He came to Germany in 1905, together with his parents and five brothers. One brother, Moses, was born and died in 1898 when he was only 9 months old The family first settled in Munich. I will elaborate on this later when I also expect to mention other members of the family, particularly my uncles and their wives and families, as these reminiscences develop.

In 1927, when I was born, my father was 32 years old. He was neither strict nor lenient – he was always fair and straightforward in all his dealings. In other words, he was a very good father – an example to be emulated with only very limited success on my part, I fear.

My mother, Sima (Selma) Yochwet, born in Zalubincze, Nowy Sacz, Galicia, Poland, in 1898, was 29 years old when I was born, having come to Leipzig, Germany, with her parents, and four of her sisters, in 1899. Her fifth sister, the youngest in the family, was born after the family had moved to Leipzig in 1900. Here, too, I will elaborate as the tale continues. My mother was kind, thoughtful and, above all, most

14

loving – always ready to extend a helping hand where and when
needed. A very good mother and much loved by all.

My brother, Bezalel, was born on the 25th of June 1922. I imagine he
felt a great sense of responsibility. As the eldest of us four children, he
himself must have assumed that it was expected of him to set an
example, in due course, for his younger siblings to follow. It pains me
to realize that I have absolutely no recollection of my brother's Bar-
Mitzvah; true – I was only 8 years old then, but still feel great regret
now that I was unable even to be present at my brother's wedding in
Israel many years later.

My sister, Sara (Susi) was born on the 28th of September 1925.As I
recall she was always the calm and reliable one; quiet and composed,
and very practical. Here, I need feel no regret about not remembering
my sister Susi reaching the age of 12 when girls become Bat-Mitzvah
since it was not the custom in those days, if I recall correctly (certainly
not in our circles), to celebrate such an event, except within the family

15

circle perhaps. However, I don't remember any special celebration here either.

I'm next in the 'pecking' order – as they say. My birthday, as I mentioned when starting to record this story, was the 13th of July 1927. What can I say about myself? I'm the one who always got into trouble – there has to be someone like me in every family. I suppose I can only describe myself as a little 'volatile'. Like most young boys I expect I was thoughtless and concerned mainly with myself and my friends; playing football and such-like and thoughts of what mischief I could get up to. Rethinking the past, I realized long ago that the family *did* mean very much to me even then, as indeed it does to this day.

Last, but from any point of view by no means least, was my little sister, Dora (Dorle), born on the 19th of April 1929. She was the straightforward one. No, that's not right. We were all straightforward.

16

Rather she was the *outspoken* one, stubborn, nay, tenacious and persevering to a fault – if fault it be – a trait which is with her to this day. She was, and still is, always most lovable and loving.

Let me only add that I don't recall any birthday celebrations for any of us although surely those occasions must have been marked in some way. Although I don't feel it, either or mentally, old-age does put some limits on a person – in my case, at this moment - limits on what I remember of my childhood. However, I still take longish walks, when I don't feel too lazy, and enjoy going to a concert every now and then – about once every 3-4 weeks. Nor do I shirk travel on vacations, mainly to Europe. After all, age is very much of an attitude. It also helps to have a young wife! I will certainly write about her later in this memoire.

But, to return to my siblings, I know that we played all sorts of games together, often mental games, like naming the capital cities of not well-known countries, the lengths of rivers all over the world. Names of Prime ministers all over the world, and similar items.

My two sisters and me, in Leipzig - 1937/8 - are displayed in the photo above.

I am sure we often quarrelled as children, as most siblings do - even ganging up on one another. For example, when Susi came to my aid, Zal supported Dorle, and every conceivable other combination. However, when there was strife between us and our cousins, or with children outside the family, we four Kesslers were as one (at least, I like so to remember it). But we always loved one another.

That is a brief summary of my nuclear family. There is, of course, much more to write about each of my siblings and I hope to do so in due course – if I can jog my memory. It is quite marvellous what one remembers once one starts to record events on paper or – as in this case – on the computer. Other members of our wider family will also enter this recital when I record further events. This may not necessarily be in the order in which the events occurred because, as science has proved, time bends and warps. And, in this narrative, things do overlap, certainly in my memory. I apologize in advance if I mention some events more than once.

As mentioned before, having been born into an orthodox Jewish family, I was enrolled into a Talmud Torah or as we called it, a *cheder*, when I was about three or four years old. This was as far back as 1930/1931, and even then, the gangs of young Nazi louts were already roaming the streets. Thus, as a little child, I learned very early in life what dangers the world holds for us Jews – not that I really understood it at the time. Anti-Semitism was always rife, but I did not yet realize or anticipate what was to happen in the not-too-distant future. In any case, as a young, very young, orthodox Jewish boy, I had no occasion to mix with others not of my religion. I met very few non-Jews, as far as I remember.

Thinking back to those most formative days of my life, I believe that it was those early years that impressed themselves most upon my consciousness and shaped my character, my social and political attitudes, and my outlook on life. I suppose that my suspicion of the world around me, my distrust of the non-Jewish communities, my aversion to our present neighbours in the Muslim world who surround us here in Israel and my apprehension regarding their intentions towards us, can all be traced back to that critical period of my early childhood.

18

That is not to say that I remain unchanged over my more than ninety years of life. Indeed, over the years I have, inevitably, changed in many ways.

Most crucially, and in many ways to my regret, I am no longer orthodox in my practicing Judaism, although I still like to keep some of the traditions – to an extent, at least. For example, I no longer go to the synagogue regularly, as we used to do in Germany, although I continued with the tradition for many a year after being so forcibly separated from my family. The reasons for the separation will become clear as this memoire continues. When I first arrived in England, I continued attending the synagogue on a regular basis, not only at the hostel in Ely to which I was evacuated as a child, but also after that in my adult years.

Indeed, even as a married man living in Central London, I was a regular fee-paying member of the Central Synagogue which boasted the superb tenor Shimon Hass as its resident Chazzan (cantor). That regular synagogue attendance lasted at least until Marion, my first wife, died (more of that later) and I finally made 'aliyah' (emigration to Israel) and came to settle in Israel with my children. Since our *aliyah* in 1974, I have attended the synagogue on only rare occasions, such as on *Rosh Hashanah* (the Jewish New Year), *Yom Kippur* (Day of Atonement), *Simchat Torah* (at the end the Feast of Tabernacles) and the *Bar-Mitzvah* of both my grandsons. I also might attend occasionally on a particular *Shabbat* or one of the other festivals.

I feel strange and a little guilty about this at times. As a child in Germany, I would not only wear the *Arba Kanfot* (an undergarment with fringes, called *ziziz,* attached to the four corners) but would not even remove the garment at night. I would also insist on going to sleep wearing my *yarmulke* (skullcap) also known as a *kippa* in Hebrew. Today I don't usually wear a cap or hat at all, donning one only when required – principally when going to synagogue or another religious event. I was taught at the time that the hair and fingernails grow particularly on Thursday mornings. One must, therefore, avoid hair and nail cutting at those times. Naturally I adhered to that 'ruling' for many years.

Oh! How times have changed.

My grown-up grandsons, Eitan and Tamir – the sons of my daughter
Naomi – both attend Tel Aviv University, where Eitan is studying both
General and Jewish Philosophy while his younger brother, Tamir,
studies Psychology and Economics. They used to read the *Ma Nishtana*,
the four questions that are traditionally asked by the youngest present at
the Seder.

Now they have passed the torch to their cousins, the children of my
adopted daughter, Julia – Yael. Our three granddaughters – the twins,
Mai and Shir, who were born in April, 2004, and their younger sister,

20

Romi, who joined them, and us in December 2006, are now well able not only to ask the four primary questions (*kashot*), but participate fully and actively in the ceremonial service. They take their share in reading parts of the *Hagadah* and singing the many songs at the conclusion of the Seder - with great gusto.

What is of more importance, as far as they are concerned, they now require not only reasonable answers but expect suitable recompense in order to return the *Afikomon* (described later); but they are not avaricious – far from it - I am glad to say.

A few years ago, we moved to a new home in East Talpiot, the same Jerusalem district as that in which we first chose to live. Our new home is blessed with a fairly large patio-garden and so we are now the proud owners of our own Succah, the traditional temporary booth assembled for the festival of Succoth. Our grandchildren enjoy the *bruhaha* of all this very much, putting up the Succah, furnishing it with table and chairs and decorating it. Before coming to Israel it was not possible to erect a Succah in the street as one can in Israel.

I am very conscious of my Jewish identity and I have to say that living in Israel makes it easier to fulfil our traditions. However, I felt the same identification and closeness when still in the Diaspora; perhaps even more intensely.

This, quite naturally, leads me back to my earliest life, which is the object of the exercise – to place on record the life and history of Bernard Kessler up to this time. I fervently hope I can get my life's story recorded in time for my progeny to enjoy, reading it and understanding from where I, and they, came. After all, the past is the present is the future!

Now where did I leave us – ah yes. Me, Bernie, a little short of six years old in 1933 when Hitler rose to power and the real trouble for the Jews began. Not that we hadn't encountered Anti-Semitism before, both overt and covert. But it was nothing compared to what was in store for our poor, persecuted people. In those days, there was no State of Israel – no potential haven to which we could flee. Palestine, as this land was called at that time since, the Roman conquest some 2000 years earlier, was governed by the Colonial Office of Great Britain. They had put an almost complete embargo on Jewish immigration to that country by

21

their White Paper of 1939. This amounted to reneging on their undertaking to the League of Nations in 1919, upon being granted the mandate, to create a Jewish Homeland. Their reason, or should I say excuse, was the Arab revolt here in Palestine in 1936, which had cost the lives of a not inconsiderable number of Jews already living here. Thus, in the nineteen thirties, there was no place to which Jews could go to escape the fate which Hitler had prepared for us. Indeed, the nations of the world at large were not very eager, to say the least – and I am using the British form of understatement – to open their doors to Jews from Germany or elsewhere in any significant numbers, with the exception of the Kindertransport referred to later.

How different these days is the 'open door' policy of Britain and, indeed, many other countries around the globe, which makes a mockery of any sort of immigration policy, to the detriment of the indigenous population, Especially their open doors enabling people who are brazenly hostile to the very countries which are giving them shelter . In fact, instead of integrating into their host country's way of life – while practicing their own religion – they try to impose their way, particularly their religious practices, on their hosts. In many cases even the police cannot enter the areas occupied by them to impose law and order or investigate crime and criminals.

I don't really remember, if ever I knew, what had been my father's occupation but I think the Germans had him registered as a merchant, a term covering so many things. For a time, he was in partnership with two of his brothers in some business enterprise or other. This, apparently, came to an abrupt end for reasons unknown to me but which, I was given to understand, led my mother to warn my brother (it is rumoured that she made him take an oath, I was too young at the time) never – but *never* – to go into partnership and/or business with close family.

There is always an exception to the rule as I can only recall that later my father first helped my grandfather in his grocery shop and eventually took over the running of the shop. My grandfather had, in fact, offered to make my father partner in the ownership of the shop. But events in Nazi Germany moved swiftly and the intention remained an intention – at least as far as I know. My mother also helped when necessary (which was quite frequently).

I remember times when I went to my grandfather's grocery shop and had to pass a Jewish butcher shop which sold on one side of the shop kosher meat and on the other side non-kosher meat. It may be, most likely, that the shop had a kosher butcher on one side and a non-kosher butcher on the other side. I used to cross the street tens of meters before that shop, run past tens of meters as fast as I could, and cross back. I just could not even bear the smell of treifa (non-kosher) meat. I still can't.

At Jewish festival times, especially for Pesach, we children also were mobilized - to our utter delight. At that time, we often went into the basement of the shop, where all the *Kosher for Pesach* groceries were kept. We helped to weigh and package the different items. We then delivered them to the customers. Principally it was my brother Bezalel who did the deliveries, using a bicycle which had a front built specially to hold the cartons filled with the ordered groceries.

My class in Leipzig – 1937/8: If anyone reading this recognizes any one in the photo please let me know

23

We did all this, of course, during the time we were not in school. We all attended the Judische VolkSchule (the Jewish Primary School). I still have a photo – see above - taken in one of my classes, with all my classmates and our form master, Herr Joffe, in the back of the class. He was a rather forbidding figure, tall, as far as I remember, and dressed formally, as was the custom in those days. We never used the teachers' first names, of course, unlike the custom in Israel. I don't think I ever even knew his first name. To my regret, I also have no knowledge of what became of him.

I do remember, at the tender age of 10 or 11 years, having a crush on a girl in my class who I thought was rather lovely *She* was the daughter, I vaguely remember, of the owner of the bakery which was situated some 100 or so meters from my grandfathers' grocery which, therefore, I passed on my frequent visits to the grocery. Was my 'crush' due to the secret hope of receiving a favourite cake or other sweetmeat from her father's bakery? Who knows - or cares for that matter?

My frequent visits to the grocery, however, were usually marked by a quick 'nosh' of a little 'sauerkraut' to which I was rather partial (there was always a barrel of this tempting and delicious item in the doorway to the shop and I just 'swiped' or scooped a bit on entering and/or on leaving. I made sure, I thought, that my grandfather was not watching – I did not want him to catch me and give me a good 'telling off' – but I now believe he just pretended that he did not see me and turned a blind eye to my youthful, 'criminal', behaviour.

The next several years were spent routinely, for us children especially. Thinking back to those days I realize again what a frightening time it was. There were variations, of course - anxious times and less anxious ones that I recall, some distinctly, others more vaguely, contradictory as this may sound. Even now I recall a few examples.

My father was 'recruited', involuntarily – i.e. compelled – to clear snow (in a very harsh winter) from the runways at Leipzig airport, as I recall, in addition to other public places considered of special importance by the Nazi authorities – without pay, *of* course. We were never sure when he would come home nor, indeed, *if* he would come home. The Nazi authorities were already arresting and sending people to Dachau and other concentration camps (sometimes euphemistically

24

referred to by them as 'Correction Facilities'). (My sister Dorle does not recall this and thinks this may have been the case in other cities in Nazi Germany but was not the case in Leipzig. If it was the case in other cities in Germany why would it not have happened in Leipzig? To this my sister had no answer.

My brother, all of 14 or 15 years old, leaving home and going to what I was told was a kind of "hachshara" – a training course in which one trained to work on a kibbutz in what was then the British mandate of Palestine – now Israel. He left home twice in the course of two years or so to go on this hachshara. I think – I am not really sure - when and where he went but it must have been in the years between 1936 and 1938 – before our deportation to Poland, mentioned in detail later.

I know that at that time he learned carpentry (one of the hachsharot) and crafted a big wardrobe-like box for his belongings such as clothes, books and I don't know what else, which he eventually had sent to him on his aliyah, (immigration to Palestine – now Israel). I remember seeing the wardrobe, actually serving as a wardrobe again, at my sister Susi's home, when in 1951 I took my wife Marion on my first visit to Israel, described later. The other hachshara, more in line with tradition, was a gardening (agricultural) hachshara which, I imagine, was the beginning of his interest in agriculture which, eventually led to his studies in agronomy. He earned his title of Professor in that subject in due course.

On another occasion my parents sent my brother to Milan in Italy. It must have been in the first half of 1938. They gave him a suitcase to deliver to our aunt and uncle containing valuables including, among other items, a Leica camera and various other items of value. I don't really know what else was included but it was hoped these would help them in Palestine when they reached those shores.

I may have the timing wrong here but I am told this delivery to my aunt and uncle in Italy may have included sums of money which were to be used to purchase certificates to enter and settle in Palestine, both for my parents and for us children which, at that time, was still possible. The amount of money mentioned in one of the letters from our parents which are still in our possession – of which copies are also held by Yad

25

Vashem – is 2000 Lira. We, I at least, were never sure if Lira stood for Italian money or referred to UK pound sterling.

After delivering the suitcase Bezalel returned to Leipzig.

Some things are so rooted in your mind that one wishes they could be forgotten - such as coming out from 'Cheder', being met by a band of Hitler Youth thugs. They must have been at least 15 or 16 years old, whilst our ages range was between three years and a maximum of 13 (the Bar-Mitzvah age). They always congregated at the entrance to the cul-de-sac where the 'Cheder" was, waiting to bait us or attack us, and this was a regular occurrence. My blood always almost froze and I usually ran for kilometres, or so it seemed at the time, turning into a building I mistakenly thought was where my aunt, Fanny Zimetbaum, lived. Not finding her, I usually ran to the very top floor, terrified that the thugs who were running after me would catch me. This happened on more than one occasion. At other times I just ran, terrified, as fast and far as I could. Fortunately, they either tired of the 'sport' and did not bother to chase me for long or they found someone else to bait, which was more than likely and much more to their taste.

I remember playing in the street outside my aunt Regina's home with our two closest cousins, Bezalel, (we had a number of cousins named so) and Harry (later called by his Hebrew name – Zvi) both in age and in relationship. We were the children of two brothers (our fathers) having married two sisters (our mothers) and were thus particularly close. We were fortunate in that we also happened to live close enough to one another to enable us to meet frequently.

On one occasion I pushed the younger of the two, Harry, who was three years younger than I. He fell, and apparently hurt his knee. Bezalel, his older brother, all of three weeks my senior, wanted to protect him or maybe 'avenge' him, by hitting or pushing me. Bezalel, (as I mentioned we had a lot of so-called members in the family who were all named after our paternal grandfather) ran towards me. Naturally I had to run away and try to avoid him. I looked around to see if he was close to catching me, and when turning my head back ran, smack, into a lamppost thereby splitting my eyebrow. Blood streaming down my face, I was brought to the doctor who had to put at least three stitches in and said I could now be like a German student who, in his younger days, used to duel and always had cuts like mine to boast about. At the time I was rather proud of my 'duelling' cut above my eye. (But who wanted to be a German student – certainly not I).

During the summer one of the three rivers at the confluence of which Leipzig stood was frequently so shallow and narrow in the summer – at least in the part near our home - that we were able to jump over it on our way to and from our aunt Regina. There must have been some 60-70 meters between the stairs going down from near our street, *Berliner Strasse,* to the stairs going up to *Nord Strasse,* the street where Tante Regina lived. We jumped back and forth all the way, going and coming back. This was great fun - a game we played at every opportunity.

We also loved to play football, (I don't remember where we played), my friends and I, so much so that not infrequently I played 'hooky' from Hebrew classes (Cheder).Obviously we were usually found out and suitably punished for it: which reminds me of a popular Yiddish song, a particular excerpt of which goes:

Oy, Tatte, hod doch nit kan moiré far mir,

di ganze welt is nor a blotte,

as ich el sein asoi alt wi di

el ich sain a soicher unt el lernen toire!

In a free translation this means:

Oh! Dad, don't worry about me,

The world is just a load of mud,

When I'll be your age,

I'll be a merchant and will study the Torah!

At home one of our favourite games was climbing up to the top of the wardrobe. My brother reminded me that our bedroom, which we four children shared, was next to the bathroom which had a window between the two and through which we climbed on to the top of the wardrobe. We then jumped down onto the bed below which happened to be Bezalel's bed, but he didn't mind. He rather joined us in the fun. We did this over and over again. I'm trying to remember what happened to the bed. Ah, well! One can imagine.

My brother also reminded me the other day that in 1937, when our cousins, Alla, Bezalel and Harry, Regina's and David's children, were living with us for several months (I will elaborate on this later) we also played at being animals in the Zoo. I am a little embarrassed now to record that this usually involved us undressing completely and running around the flat stark naked, probably on all fours, making what we thought were the appropriate animal noises. (I remember that my two nephews, Eitan and Tamir, *when they were very, very little,* used to love to run around naked in their home. Mind you, they were *very* young then – but could this be something genetic? I wonder!)

For a very orthodox family my parents were pretty modern and 'cool', as they say in young peoples' slang nowadays. We were not deprived of music – both classical and popular, as well as liturgical. I remember particularly going to the theatre, with my family, to see a play – or was it a musical play or opera – called *Das Wolkenkind.* This was, in fact, an opera composed by the Austrian composer Franz Xavier Told (1792 to 1849) which was described as "*Gesungen, Gesprochen, und Gezaubert*" (Sung, Spoken and Bewitched – if it can be so translated). I think, when performed in Leipzig in the 1930s, it was adapted for a children's audience. Other than that, the plot escapes me after all these years.

I do recall that we also were taken to the Zoo several times as well as to the circus at least once. Furthermore, Leipzig, as is well known, was the city in Germany where the annual international "Messe" (Trade Fair) was held. This was an event where manufacturers from all over Europe, and even further afield, were able to display their wares, bringing them business in great measure, as well as bringing prosperity to the city. The Fair was established way back in the Middle Ages, in 1165, and has been an annual event since, barring times of war and strife. Sometimes it was even held twice or even three times in a year.

Much can be told of the development of the fair, which made a major contribution to the increased importance of Leipzig. Jews, who had settled in Leipzig hundreds of years earlier, contributed their share to the development of the town and the Fair brought more and more merchants from many places, including Jewish merchants. This led to the construction of one of Europe's most significant Moorish Revival buildings, the 1855 Leipzig synagogue - architect: Otto Simonson. Since I have not returned to Leipzig for so many years after being forced to leave it in 1938, I could only assume that this beautiful building had suffered the same fate which so many other synagogues suffered on Kristallnacht in 1938.Indeed, my subsequent research on the internet has confirmed that this synagogue was one of the first targets of those Nazi barbarians who left it in ruins.

At the time of my childhood in Germany, the Trade Fair was accompanied by a *Kinder Messe* (Children's Fair). Naturally we had to participate. There were roundabouts, mini-cars (?), a strong man, bearded lady, sweet-sugared cotton (candy floss), the big wheel, trapeze artists, animals, and all the usual hu-ha of a children's fair. Usually a good time was had by all, at least while Hitler and his barbarians still allowed us to attend such events.

Our flat, of which I can only give a very general description, was situated in Berliner Strasse – no. 4, to be precise. I think we lived on the first floor, or was it the second? Does it really matter? It was quite sizable, 7 or 8 rooms, as well as two kitchens, toilets and bathrooms in addition – I hope I have remembered this correctly. Two, or maybe three of the rooms, together with the smaller of the two kitchens and facilities, were arranged as a separate flat, which we rented out to another family. We occupied the remaining five rooms and large kitchen as follows: My parents occupied the main bedroom; we four children all shared one bedroom, as mentioned above already; our paternal grandmother, Bluma, came to live with us at the beginning of 1935, having lived in Munich with her son, my uncle Yisrael, from 1932 until 1935. When he and his family moved to Berlin in 1935, she came to us and occupied bedroom no. 3. Our maternal grandfather, Yehuda Leib, moved into bedroom no 4 in 1937 which, prior to that, must have been our lounge where we received visitors. Till then he had lived with our aunt Regina and her family until she and Onlel David

29

left for Italy, leaving their three children with us. I expect to write about this a little later.

The last room was the dining room (and eventually also the lounge) which we used for meals on Shabbat and Festivals only, except when we had guests. On all other occasions we ate in the large kitchen which served not only for the preparation of our meals – cooking, baking etc - but also as our eating area on weekdays. At least, that is how I remember things.

I may also mention that our flat fronted the street. There was a fairly sizable courtyard behind the house and a rear building after the courtyard. In that rear building there was a *shul* (synagogue). But although more convenient, we did not pray there (I believe it was a Sephardi congregation and we were – and still are, of course – Ashkenazi).

I recall that my brother used to 'bribe' me to go to the library to change his books; (I think the 'going' rate at the time was 10 pfennig per visit). If my memory still serves me, I think the books were usually Karl Mai stories which were then very much in fashion for youths as well as adults – looking for books of adventure.

My brother, and maybe my older sister too, belonged to a Zionist youth movement: *Brit Hanoar Shel Zeirei Mizrahi* (I think that this was the correct name) which is referred to nowadays as *Bnei Akiva*. This organization was the youth section of the religious Zionist party called *Mizrahi*. They prepared young boys and girls to join the organization's kibbutzim in Palestine. (A *kibbutz* is a communal settlement where the members owned and worked the land and marketed the produce communally). I couldn't wait to be old enough to also join the Youth Movement.

From what I have written and hinted at till now, it will be clear – or should be - that our family was not only very orthodox but also absolutely and fervently Zionist oriented. the developments in the immediate future prevented my parents from realizing their dream to settle in what was then Palestine. *Fortunately*, and due to their foresight, all four of their children reached the holy land after all, eventually – some sooner, some later.

Food, family and festivals

Back to Leipzig…

My brother sang in the synagogue choir of what I always considered the main synagogue which, of course had the principal Chazzan (Chazzan Wilkomirski) who was very, very good, with an international reputation. Here, too, I could not wait to be old enough to be accepted into the choir. However, as a Chazzan, I always preferred Chazzan Kupfer of the other big synagogue. I think I found his voice more mellow and lyrical. (I had the same feeling with the two opera singers, Caruso and Gigli, preferring what to me was the more lyrical interpretations of Benjamino Gigli to those of Enrico Caruso).

It had always been my intention to join my brother in the choir, at least until I became a famous Chazzan myself – regretfully an unfulfilled ambition, and *oh, what a loss to the known world!* Once I accompanied my brother to the choir, which, as is well known, was always located above the Holy Ark. The choirmaster sat me on his knees and promised that I could join the choir when I was somewhat older. He did not specify when that would be. I must have been about seven or eight years old at the time. That, too, was the reply I received when I petitioned the 'madrich' of the Zionist youth group to join them. What a reply to give a young boy, *almost on the threshold of adulthood?* It was very frustrating, to say the least, but I could do little about it!

In the meantime, in order to prepare myself to become the famous Chazzan I was sure to become, I practiced in front of the mirror, with a towel for my *tallit* rapped round my shoulders, the prayers – 'nigunim' – of the famous Chazzanim of the time, particularly those of Yossele Rosenblatt. He was always my favourite, at least so my sub-conscious remembers. My eldest daughter Simone, however, tells me that I had expressed, on occasion, that I imitated Chazzan Berele Chagy, and that he was, at that time my favourite. She may well be right, having it so fixed in her mind, that on one of my birthdays she scoured Jerusalem for a disc of that Chazzan because the lack of anything – record or disc - from this Chazzan left a gap in my collection of Chazzanut music discs.

Since those days, and with my son David's encouragement, I have become rather partial to Mordechai Hershman, to such an extent that in my wife's absence from home – not her cup-of-tea, as they say – I frequently 'warble' his melodies, although not too much in tune these days.

I mentioned above that my father's mother (Bluma Berta) and my mother's father (Yehuda Leib) both came to live with us at some stage, not necessarily at the same time, but in both cases after they were widowed. Prior to that, Yehuda Leib had resided with his youngest daughter, Regina, in a flat which, I am now told, he actually owned in Nord Strasse. Be that as it may, when Regina and David left for Italy in 1937 (which is reported elsewhere in these memoirs) he came to live with us, being eventually deported to Poland together with us in 1938.

In fact, when the Gestapo arrived at our flat at the time of the mass deportation, he was not actually on the list of those to be arrested and deported. He decided nevertheless to remain with us. I expect that since there was not one of his daughters with whom he might remain in Germany, his choice was logical. On arrival in Poland, he chose to go to his family in Nowe Sacz rather than come with us to my father's brother. That was, in fact, the last time I saw him. To our great sorrow he too did not survive the holocaust, and I have not been able to establish the circumstances of his fate – not when, or where, nor even *how* he died. Indeed I know nothing really about that side of the family, and there is no one still with us whom I may ask about their lives or fate - but one can imagine. I would at least like to know if he had siblings or cousins or any relations left in Poland who may shed light on that part of our family.

My maternal grandfather (Yehuda Leib) was not only the owner of the grocery shop to which I referred earlier, and of the flat just mentioned, he was also a 'Rebbe'. He had his own 'Shtiebl' – a small and intimate prayer and Talmud study establishment. To describe him in words is not easy. If my memory serves me he was of average height, slim as I recall, but since he sported a beard I am unable to describe his complexion. I can however relate that his beard was full, long and white and that he had what to me were piercing eyes. To the best of my recollection, we sometimes went to his Shtiebl, especially on some Shabbat or Chag. But my recollection is vague. In any case, I preferred going to the big synagogue which always had the best Chazzan whom, as mentioned above, I tried to emulate at home. Mostly we went to our regular *Beit Hamidrash* which, I think, was situated somewhat nearer to at least two of my aunts' residences. I am sure that my late brother (G-d Rest his Soul) remembered the place and I wish I had asked at the time.

My paternal grandmother, Bluma Berta, on the other hand, continued to live in Munich, alone, since the death of her husband in 1921. In his life-time he, like my maternal grandfather, also sported a long white beard. To me, seeing the photos side by side, they did not look dissimilar. In 1932 Bluma Berta, having lived alone for eleven long years since the death of her husband, moved in with her son, my uncle Yisrael, who, together with his family still resided in Munich. Because of continuing Nazi pressure Bluma, as well as Yisrael and his family, left Munich in 1935. Yisrael and his family moved to Berlin while Bluma Berta came to live with us in Leipzig , as I already mentioned earlier.

I remember her as being a little rotund, if I may put it so without being disrespectful, with a round face. Not being of any noticeable height, no doubt emphasized the fullness of her figure. She was eventually deported to Poland together with us. Here too, to our regret and sorrow, we have no knowledge about her fate – not what happened, not when and of course not how. As she came with us to Krakow when we were deported to Poland in 1938 and lived there when the Nazis invaded, it can be surmised that her fate was sealed. There can be no doubt that she was murdered by the Nazis quite early on in the war. She was, after all, an old lady and would not have been considered useful by them for any kind of forced labour.

On Friday night and Shabbat, we always had festive meals, on returning from the synagogue, as well as on all our festivals. On Friday evening, my mother lit the Shabbat candles, as did my grandmother, after she came to live with us. We, the men folk mainly, went to shul, and when we returned, the festive table was laid and ready to receive us in the dining room reserved for such occasions. It had a shining white tablecloth, sparkling silver cutlery and the best china. In the centre of the table, was a multi-pronged, highly polished, silver candelabrum. It had five branches and a centre piece – one for each member of our nuclear family. There were also two more silver candlesticks for my grandmother. The candles were lit early, before sunset, as was required by Jewish law and custom, while we were in shul.

I still feel a thrill running through me, when I suddenly remember all these things, now that I am writing my memoirs. We all sat down to our festive meal. Before Kiddush was recited we all sang together the introductory liturgy שלום אליכם (peace be to you) and my father recited the prayer in praise of my mother, the lady of the household –

אשת חייל - (a woman of worth, who can find).

Both my father and grandfather then recited the *Kiddush*, as did my brother also, on reaching Bar-Mitzvah. We all stood up for this, of course. Then we all ritually washed our hands and recited the blessing over the chalot which my mother had baked, two of which lay on the table, covered with the customary embroidered cloth. This was a reminder of the Shewbread at the Temple – as instructed by the Almighty. A portion of the chala was given to everyone present at the table, dipped in salt, and eaten after reciting the appropriate blessing: "Blessed Art Thou, Oh Lord, Our G-D, King of The Universe, Who Bringeth Forth Bread From The Earth."

My mother encouraged us to help in the kitchen. For instance, when she baked the chalot for Shabbat she gave each of us some of the dough so that we too could fashion (braid) our own small chalot These would then be baked together with hers. If they turned out reasonably 'respectable' they were also put on the table, each by his seat.

Our Shabbat and Festival meals were invariably rather extended occasions. In between courses we all sang the usual *Zemirot* – in harmony of course, since all of us had been blessed with fine voices which we were always prepared to demonstrate, even if only to each other. These were the liturgical hymns for the occasion, in thanksgiving

36

and praise of the Almighty for his bounty to us all. We also told each other about our activities during the week just ending. Usually some part of the week's Torah portion was discussed, as well as the happenings in the wider family circles during the week just ending – including political, communal and general items. Not that I understood much of this, nor took any particular interest in such serious matters. What, after all, did all this have to do with football?

Also, since my grandfather came to live with us he made it a point to have me sit on his knee while he tested me on what I had learned that week in the Cheder (what a terrifying experience, although he was never unkind to me and I greatly respected him).

I recall also that my mother was wont to not only cook for Shabbat. The festive meal called for much more than mere cooking. She also prepared egg and onion salad or chopped liver. And then there was real 'gefilte' fish. Carp, of course. What else could it be? And that was just the first course! Then came the second course, which invariably was chicken soup with lokshen (noodles) and bebelach (white haricot beans) – except for Pessach when it always was kneidelach (matzo balls).

This was followed by the main dish consisting of roast or boiled chicken, sometimes stuffed or '*eingedempt*'. I don't know how to describe this word in English – stewed, maybe. It included not only the meat or chicken but also potatoes, carrots, onions and garlic. The potatoes were baked or roast potatoes or similar and sometimes we had rice for a change. Finall there was always some sort of dessert – fruit or other. Having started the meal with a benediction, we naturally concluded the meal with the appropriate prayers of thanksgivings – vocally and musically, of course – for the bounty we had received and of which we had just partaken.

Being basically a cheerful person and having a lovely voice, my mother frequently went around the flat singing some favourite song or other. I think she may have done so especially when we went to bed. I particularly remember two of the songs. One of these was Schubert's well-loved song: *Am Brunnen vor den Tore da steht ein Lindenbaum*. The other was a Zionist–oriented song, not composed by the same person who composed the National Anthem of the Zionist Movement and eventually of the State of Israel. This song, *Dort wo di Zeder*

37

schlank die Wolken Kuesst, indeed was the song which almost became the Zionist Movement's and The State of Israel's National Anthem. How we loved to hear her sing these, and other songs, but these two just got rooted in my memory. Sometimes I just sit back when I am alone and think of her singing – I can almost hear her. Thus, she is still very much alive for me.

As I mentioned already my mother usually baked at least two chalot, while we children not infrequently worked with her and fashioned one or two miniature chalot for ourselves. Our mother also baked two or three (sometimes even four) yeast/cinnamon and raisin cakes. My mouth still waters at the thought of those cakes which I loved so much. I got into the habit of lifting the cloth with which my mother covered them to keep them fresh and when no one was about, cut a piece from the centre, push the cake together, cover it with the cloth again and think nobody noticed what I did.

These were happy occasions, when the family sat down together to celebrate Shabbat, Festivals or other family gatherings. Even the prevalent oppressive feeling which the Nazis caused Jews to feel throughout the country could not dampen our joy on these occasions. The family was, after all, still together and we could not know yet, or even imagine, what really awaited us. Furthermore, I was still very young; what did I understand except the unexplainable apprehensions which I felt every time I left the flat on my own. Naturally I felt more secure when out and about with other members of the family, especially with my parents. My parents tried not to burden us young ones with remarks about what really was going on but, of course, we overheard conversations and tried to understand what it was all about. We could not help noticing the parades, the Nazi flags everywhere, the looks of hatred and the 'thrown out' insults, especially the slogans painted on shops owned by Jews. All these happenings no doubt had their insidious effect on us. Yet our family gatherings were, for us children at least, joyful occasions. I think our elders, parents, aunts, uncles and grandparents, strove to make them so.

Since this is, by its very nature, confession time I must be absolutely frank and truthful. To my great regret now, I must own to frequently being a 'trial' to my mother. Why, and how? Well, I was something of a 'sheygitz' or 'lobbus' – as it was called in English/Yiddish. In Hebrew we would say a *shovav*. In other words, I was a little uncontrollable at times – perhaps even frequently. As a result, I was the 'resident' receiver, regularly, of my father's disciplinary measures. At the time I had the impression that, rightly or wrongly, any punishment meted out at home seemed to target me for the misdemeanours of all four children. I am, however, reminded by my brother that when I was not in the immediate vicinity my 'little' sister, Dorle, was the inevitable 'victim'. Whenever I protested that on that particular occasion, I was not the guilty party, as I was wont to do frequently, my father's inevitable response invariably was that I could 'chalk' it up to the next time I would merit the punishment.

My mother, may her soul rest in peace, had occasionally, and with great reluctance and regret, to resort to the 'threat' of "surely, Bernie, you would not wish me to mention this (whatever it was on that occasion) to your father on his return home." Not that my father inspired fear in me; on the contrary. I greatly respected and loved him but I did not want him to think badly of me. Nor did I feel any pleasure in having brought my mother to such a point to even make her mention that she considered such a possibility. The possible punishment was also a factor, I tend to realize now, which may also have been taken into consideration by me.

Another incident I recall relates to our custom of 'walking-up' an appetite on Shabbat morning when we took a lengthy stroll in the park nearby - it was called, I think, The Rosenthal (Valley of the Roses). This took place after the Shabbat morning service (prayer) which was frequently followed by a *kiddush*. Wine, slivovitz, pickled herring (how this makes my mouth water just remembering it), cakes of one kind or another, and fruits, of course - in celebration of some event such as a Bar-Mitzvah, engagement, *brit mila* (circumcision) etc. We then returned home for our Shabbat meal which, incidentally, frequently was *cholent* the way my mother made it. I wish I had paid more attention to how she made it so I could have taught my children. I didn't even ask my older sister, while she was still alive; perhaps she had learned how to make it.

While on this Shabbat - after morning prayers - walk I often started to 'wail and moan' that I was tired and could not walk anymore. My father's standard reply to this: "Bernie, you sit on this bench and rest, when we come by next Shabbat, we'll pick you up on our way home." Of course, this promptly helped to galvanize me into action, shed my tiredness and enabled me to walk on with the rest of the family.

I am pretty vague about how we celebrated the various Jewish festivals and holy days in Leipzig but will try nevertheless to put together a small picture of these events while I was very young.

Shabbat, I have described already, except to add that it really *was* a day of rest for us. No running around, no TV - there was none anyway - and no radio. Switching on a radio was forbidden on that holy day. Even switching on the *light* was forbidden. It was an *'aveira'* - transgression. I should point out to those unfamiliar with Judaism, that the Ten Commandments are only a small portion of an observant Jew's religious obligations - albeit the main foundation. There are, in fact, 613 *mitzvoth* (commandments). Some are the do's and some the don't dos. No noise was one of the rules of the day, as my parents had to rest from the week's labour. This was referred to as *'Shabbes nuch Tisch'* – the period of rest after the Shabbat lunch.

After a suitable rest we, the men folk again, returned to the synagogue for *Mincha* - the afternoon prayers, followed by 'Shale Sheedes' (*seuda shlishit*), as it was called, or as is more likely, we called it "Melave Malke", "escorting the Shabbat Queen" out till the following Friday. The *seuda* ("feast") consisted of chala, pickled herring, 'bronfen' (which usually was slivovitz, or other strong alcoholic beverage), cakes and biscuits. This was always accompanied by community singing of other liturgical hymns - sometimes with a solo performance of one or another of the participants. This went on till the time when Ma'ariv, the evening prayer, had to be recited, on the conclusion of the Sabbath.

We then went home. My father pronounced the *Havdala* ("Distinguishing") prayer over a beaker of wine to signify that we had returned to a normal weekday - till the next Friday evening. (For *Havdala* it was even permitted to use milk instead of wine.) Let me add here that, not infrequently, we did not return to the shul for the Seuda Shlishit. Often, we children stayed at home and sat in the lounge singing liturgical melodies and Zionist songs, while it was getting darker and darker outside. This was termed "Oneg Shabbat" – which the Zionist Youth Movements also held on Friday evenings (Erev Shabbat) and on

40

Shabbat afternoons and evenings, indoors in winter but frequently outdoors on the much longer summer afternoons and evenings.

I may add that although my father was not able to attend synagogue on a daily basis - that is, every morning and evening – he never failed to put on the obligatory *tefilin* (phylactories) for morning prayers, as did my brother, Bezalel, on becoming Bar-Mitzvah. My grandfather did too, as was usual for all males on reaching the age of 13.

Since I mentioned earlier that my father, although very orthodox, was 'cool' (modern in outlook), I may mention that unlike the older generation, neither my father nor any of his brothers let their beards grow, nor did they sport *payot* – the side curls which the ultra-orthodox let grow. All were clean-shaven except for the moustache on my father's upper lip. (I think some of my uncles also sported moustaches.) How was this 'miracle' achieved, bearing in mind the injunction that no sharp metal object may be used to remove facial hair? I don't know about others but my father - and my brother also – used a wooden spatula instead of a metal shaving knife with which to shave.

As very observant Jews we all recited the afternoon and evening prayers at home – and did not overlook the night-time prayers before going to sleep. Festivals were celebrated similarly, although somewhat differently. As on the Sabbath, *tefilin* were not put on - these were required only on regular work - days. Normally we attended our own synagogue (that is, when not 'visiting' another, obviously). Particularly on the *Yamim Noraim* – the Ten Days of Penitence, which lasted from the first day of *Rosh Hashanah* (New Year) till *Yom Kippur* (the Day of Atonement). How proud I was to fast on that day for as long as possible. The biblical injunction was "and ye shall afflict your souls." We spent the whole of that day in the synagogue. My father, therefore, always took with him provisions for us young ones, which my mother had the foresight to prepare for us, so we would not feel ill by fasting too long. When obliged to, because of being overcome by hunger, he gave us a sandwich, or something else, and sent us out of the Synagogue, to eat and regain our strength.

Succoth (Tabernacles) was a very happy occasion. Everyone blessed the *Lulav* (palm branch) and *Etrog* (large citrus fruit) every day, for the eight days this festival lasted - although not everyone possessed them individually. Neither did we put up our own *Succah* - we were after all 'strangers in a strange land' and were unable to use the street, as people do here in Israel. Prayers called *Hakafot* were recited daily while the festival lasted, and we all joined in the liturgy. The name was derived from the translation of the meaning – going round and round the Bima while holding the lulav and etrog and musically reciting the relevant prayer,

On the last day of the festival (*Simchat Torah* or Rejoicing of the Torah) all the males over the age of 13 were suitably honoured. It was our custom to take out all the *Sifrei Torah* (scrolls of the Torah) and circle round the synagogue with song and dance until every male over 13 years old had the opportunity to hold the Torah scroll for a 'whirlaround'. (In Israel, they even do this in the streets!) Then came the Reading of the Law. Over the course of the year we read one portion or "*parsha*" of the Five Books of Moses, every Shabbat and had now reached the end. On this day we would repeat the final parsha of the Torah (*Vezot Habracha)* and recite the *first* parsha (*Bereisheit*), thus symbolizing the restarting of the cycle.

Again, every male over the age of thirteen was 'called-up' to a reading of a sub-portion, and this was repeated till all had been 'called'. Before the final, short sub-portion (called "*maftir*") all children under 13 were called together to stand on the *bimah* (raised platform) A *tallit* (prayer shawl) was spread over us, like a canopy (or *chupa*) at a Jewish wedding and we said the blessing in unison. This is known as an *aliyah* ("ascent") to the Tora. Then a portion of the parshah was recited by the Baal Koreh (the Reader), usually a prominent member of the congregation. After we children recited the concluding blessing for our *aliyah*, the very last section – the maftir – was blessed by the person designated as the *Chatan Torah* ("Bridegroom of the Torah") and recited. This honour was always allocated to one of the more affluent or learned personalities in the congregation.

Thus, concluded the reading of the very last portion of the Torah. The scroll was then wound up, while the 'Chatan' was pelted with almonds and raisins and sweets. The second *Sefer Torah* was then hoisted on to the *bimah*, having been rolled to its beginning already. The Chatan Bereshit then went through a similar procedure as his colleague when the congregation was expected to acknowledge vocally the reading of each day of the creation. The Sifrei Torah were then returned to the Holy Ark – with song and dance – and the congregation waited, impatiently I always thought, for the Mussaf (additional) service to begin.

Now, finally, we get to what I have been waiting to record. This was my father's moment of the year - or rather that of us four children, the children of Abraham Kessler. At the Mussaf service on Simchat Torah, in our Beit Hamidrash, it was my father's honour and privilege regularly to officiate as *Shaliach Zibbur* (Chazan/Cantor, in other words) for the service. He had a fine baritone voice, as I recall, and we always enjoyed listening to him. This particular service, on this particular festival though, had its "dangers". It was after all Simchat Torah, and ANYTHING – well almost ANYTHING - was permitted.

And needless to say it did. The congregation almost went wild with ecstasy. They threw, at the *Shaliach* Zibbur, small and light cushions, paper curled into balls, folded socks etc, as well as sweets, nuts, raisins and the like, all in order to confuse and distract him – such was the custom. We children took it upon ourselves to be the defence shield for this valiant person - he was, after all, our own father! The whole congregation always faced east, in the direction of the Holy Land. The Chazzan, in front of the congregation, also faced in that direction so that his back was to the congregation and he could not, of course, dodge the 'missiles' aimed at him from behind. We children stationed ourselves strategically between the Chazzan and the congregation, facing them all - BRAVELY.

As the objects were thrown so we caught and threw them back. We diverted as many as we could. Invariably one or another of the 'assailants' managed to outflank us, reached my father and managed to tie his shoelaces together. Since at the end of the *Mussaf Amida* (the standing prayer) the *Shaliach Zibbur* takes three steps back, this would invariably cause him to trip unless the laces could be untied in time. Whenever possible we managed to untie the laces before this happened – but not always. I can only relate that a really good time was had by all.

There were other occasions in the synagogue of great satisfaction.Nothing unusual to describe. There were the usual spate of bar-mitzvas, engagements, pre-marriage celebrations, births, *britot* (circumcisions), *pidjot-ben* (redemption of the first-born son), and other occasions for celebratory kiddushim at the end of Shabbat services. At home, however, there was much more about which to write.

My father and grandfather both wore a snow white *kittel* for synagogue on Rosh Hashana and Yom Kippur. This was the practice also on *Leil Haseder* (Seder night – the first evening of *Pesach* or Passover). Needless to say, the whole of the liturgy – the complete Haggadah - was recited from beginning to end. Nothing was left out, as we tend to do now. And after singing all the songs at the end of the Haggadah we all retired to bed with a great feeling of joy.

I mentioned the Afikomon before. This is a half of the middle matza on a ceremonial plate of three, that is set aside to eat at the end of the meal. It is a tradition that the children of the household should try to "steal" the Afikomon before the end of the meal and then hold it to "ransom" – bargaining for a present from the head of the household. This is to encourage young children to fully participate in the festivities. The afikomon must be returned in order for those present to fulfil the requirement (*mitzvah*) to finish the meal with a piece of the Afikomon. I can't really remember what presents we were given in exchange for returning the 'stolen' Afikomon. I am inclined to think the gift was not the expensive sort which children expect nowadays. Our youngsters are not greedy – I must confess.

Most of the songs too were left to the end so that young children, as we were at that time, would stay awake till the end, if possible, even as late as midnight. Needless to say we made every effort to do so, not always successfully.

I don't remember our going on holiday as a family when we were children. I do remember my father going to Karlsbad in Czechoslovakia to rest for a short time. This spa was one of the Health Resorts in Czechoslovakia, inviting visitors to 'take the waters', as it is said. The spring waters there were considered to be therapeutic – definitely beneficial to a person's health. I don't remember if he had been really ill, but he had for some time shown signs of problems with his stomach and the waters in that spa seemed to ease his pains.

I also remember that on one occasion, at least, he took my sister Susi with him on that journey – I even have a photo of them walking down the street in Karlsbad (Karlovy Vari) or was it Marienbad, on this occasion? Perhaps my sister needed to recover from an illness. I don't really remember, except that I was a little jealous at the time thinking: *why she, not me*? My father loved us all, but Susi really was the apple of his eye – or so my brother tells me now. Anyway, it is all WATER UNDER THE BRIDGE, as the saying goes.

Thus, endeth this chapter of The Bernard Kessler Saga – unless my subconscious allows other memories relating to this period to come to the surface by the time I have completed these, my memories.

Well, what comes next?

Our Clan

This would appear to be the appropriate place to expand a little about my wider family circle – at least as far I can remember or was reminded recently. If there are some repetitions of what was already written, I can only ask for the reader's indulgence.

My paternal grandfather was Bezalel Salomon Kessler, who was an Austrian national, although he was actually born in Jaroslav, Galicia, on the 16th of December 1866. I did not know him personally because he died before I was born; in fact, even before my father married. I must point out that Galicia, at the time of his birth, was surely part of the Austro-Hungarian Empire.

Since my grandfather was considered a relatively well-to-do businessman in Munich, I must assume he was such also before he came to Germany. Anyway, I am not aware of anything else concerning his occupation. I was, of course, too young to query my father about this before we were forcibly separated in August,1939. Because of the circumstances of the political situation, my parents anticipated the imminent outbreak of hostilities and they wanted us away from the danger zone. Genealogy was not uppermost in my mind at that time, as can well be imagined, but it is a pity and more than sad that circumstances made it impossible to have any sort of more adult discussion later on – there just *was* no later on…

On the 12 of January 1893 my paternal grandfather married, in Jaroslav, Bluma Berta Krieg, born on the 12th of December, 1866 in Lancut, Galicia, one of two daughters of Natan and Frieda (Assel) Krieg. As the Kesslers were, so family Krieg too must have been very orthodox.

The happy couple was blessed, over the coming years, with seven sons, (as mentioned already one – Moses – died aged 9 months) all of whom became Polish nationals when, at the end of the first world war, Marshal Jozef Klemenc Pilsutski returned to Poland from his captivity in Germany and took control of the areas, which included Galicia, which were declared the reconstituted Polish State by the newly established League of Nations.

The remaining sons, in order of their births, were: Naftali (1894), my father Avraham Hirsch (1895), David Mendel (1896), Yisrael Leizer (1899), Chaim (Heinrich) (1902) and Efraim (Franz) (1905). I can't say with any degree of certainty whether Efraim was born while the family was still in Poland or if he was born in Munich after the arrival of the family in Germany, the year of his birth. But in June 1905 the whole family Kessler – Bezalel, his wife Bluma, and their sons – came to live in Munich, Germany. It appears that they lived in Munich continuously until 1915, in rented apartments.

My paternal grandfather was considered well-to-do, as I already mentioned, a businessman, dealing in furs, leather, cloth, and other items. My grandmother, Bluma, as was the practice in those days, looked after the household and the raising of the children.

I was told only recently that at the outbreak of World War I Bluma invited her young sister Rachel Sonnenblick and family, who still lived in Poland in very difficult conditions, to join her in Munich, to live with them until they were able to establish themselves. After World War I, in 1920, this family left Munich and moved to Berlin. The family comprised Rachel Sonnenblick nee Krieg or Kruk, her husband Elimelech (his parents were called Moses and Tova) and their seven children: Moshe (1900), Sara (1901), Naftali (1903), Frieda (1905), David (1907), Lea (1910) and Shmuel (1913). Upon arrival Elimelech went into business and relatively soon became the owner of a clothing factory. I have no recollections about this family or any details about their move to Berlin.

In 1915 Bezalel and Bluma bought a five-story house in the centre of Munich which was registered in my grandmother Bluma's name. We have not been able to establish why in her name, what became of the house, and its subsequent ownership, although one of my nephews, Avi, and his sister Yochewet, conducted research concerning this for a while. Unfortunately, the German Authorities have not been able or willing to establish my grandmother's ownership – following the Nazi removal of Jews from Munich – which they considered their particular domain.

In 1916, my father and my uncle David were both recruited into the Austro-Hungarian army in which they served until the end of the war, it would seem. Very little, if anything at all, is known (to me, at least) of their military exploits. Suffice it to be thankful that both returned safely to the bosom of their respective families.

On the 14th of April 1921, at the age of 54, my grandfather Bezalel died, of what I know not, and was buried in Munich, where he had lived since 1905. That, too, was the year (in June of that year) of my parents' marriage in Leipzig. My paternal grandfather lived to participate in few only of his sons' marriages, if in any. However, in the passage of time, all of Bezalel's and Bluma's sons married and left Munich. Naftali, Avraham and David settled in Leipzig. Chaim, and Yisrael eventually, moved to Berlin while Efraim returned to Poland to settle in Zawiercie.

The other side of the equation is the Berggruen family. My maternal grandparents were Yehuda Leib, born in September 1862 in Nowy Sacz, the son of Berl and Sima, and his wife Sara Hindel nee Weissberger, who was born in Nowy Sacz in 1859. They, too, were blessed with six children – this time all girls: Esther Ilse (1885), Chava Eva (1889), Fanny Feigel (1893), Marie Maayan (1897), Sima Yochwet (Selma) (1898) my mother, and Regina Rivka (1900).

The whole family Berggruen, husband, wife, and five of the six daughters, came to live in Leipzig in 1899. The youngest of the six daughters, Regina Rivka was born in Leipzig the year following their arrival – I don't know if Sara Hindel was pregnant on the journey to Leipzig or not; it is really of no great moment whether yea or nay.

We now have two Jewish, very orthodox families, both originally from Galicia, living in Leipzig not far from one another. I have no information of how the families came to know each other, but the community was not that large, especially those from Galicia. They all lived in the same areas of the town and prayed, presumably, in the same synagogues. They probably bought their necessities in the same shops. In some way contact was established. As I have said already grandfather Berggruen owned the one really kosher grocery store which served not only the whole Kosher-eating community in Leipzig, but also the orthodox Jews living in small towns and villages all around Leipzig. We can safely assume that family Kessler came to buy their groceries at Yehuda Leib's grocery shop. Then, one thing leading to another, the younger generation met, probably in 'shul' first, and at least two Kessler scions fall in love with two Berggruen 'princesses'. The other young males also find their brides in the community in Leipzig, and elsewhere.

Esther, the eldest of the six sisters, married Tanchum Kernkraut (born 1876). They were blessed with five sons and their livelihood was based in the fur trade. Neither of the parents survived the Holocaust, nor did their eldest son Gavriel, 1908 to 1942. He left Leipzig in August 1939, first going to Belgium, as did his parents, before the deportation. When the Germans invaded Belgium, he went to France. Here he was caught and spent some time in Drancy concentration camp outside Paris. I don't know what happened in the camp, but he was eventually transported to Auschwitz, on the 12th August, 1942, or at least so we believe since he appears, as I have been made aware, on the Beate Klarsfelt lists of transports from France. However, contrary to this information, I was told recently that he died, in fact, of starvation while still in Drancy Concentration Camp. I have not been able to establish what really was his fate. His parents, Ester and Tanchum who had remained in Belgium were arrested there shortly after the Nazis invaded Belgium. Here they were confined to a holding centre and presumably made to work until they too were sent to their deaths in Auschwitz on April 19th, 1943.

Fortunately, the other four sons reached Palestine, as it then was called, in the years before war broke out; that is between 1935 and 1939.

Zvi-Herman was born in 1909, came on aliyah in 1935 and died in 1980.

Benno-Dov was born in1910, came on aliyah in 1939. I am not sure when he died – I believe it was on November 15, 1985 - and I recall we still met him when we came on aliyah in 1974. We certainly saw him on our earlier visits to Israel. His wife Miriam who, until her death, lived in Jerusalem leaves two daughters, Hadassa and Neomi, and their lovely families who all live in Jerusalem.

Jonas was born in 1912, came on aliyah in 1937, and died in 1981. He remained unmarried.

And, finally, Adi who was born in 1916. He came on aliyah in 1936 and died in 1995.

The only things that stick in my mind about my cousins Kernkraut are (1) we saw them only infrequently although we lived in the same town and (2) that in a time when ownership of a working radio was rather rare - we apparently, were the proud owners of one (as well as a telephone I was reminded - although I, myself, do not remember this). Two of my cousins Kernkraut constructed a crystal-powered, working radio which we all applauded as a marvelous achievement. What they all did in Palestine, later Israel, I don't know, except for Benno who became a Banker and for Adi, who found employment in the security division of Israel's Aircraft Industry. Here one of his daughters, I think it was Ilanit, also found employment. She never married. The other daughter, Ariela, became a Nutritional Therapist, married and has two sons. Benno's, and Miriam's, two daughters – Hadassa and Neomi – as recorded already, both married and had families of their own. Zvi-Herman, who worked on Israel's Railway, married and also had two children, Shulamit and Nahum.

Apart from the Holocaust victim, Gavriel, three of the four Kernkraut offspring married and had families. I have few details here but some of those I have are given in the previous paragraph; one can get an inkling of the family's expansion.

My aunt Eva, the next in line, married Meier Scheiner In December 1914. I have no recollection of his trade or occupation. It is reasonably safe to assume that he, too, was a businessman of one sort or another. They lived in the same street as we did in Leipzig. Naturally we saw more of them, but not too much. She, Tante Eva, had three children: -

Esther, born in 1917, who was much older than we were, reached Palestine, but I don't know when exactly. She married someone named Zurabel or Zuravel (I don't remember his first name) and left for Holland with him. I think he was sent on some sort of *shlichut* (from "*shaliach*" – emissary) on behalf of one of the Zionist organizations. Then, when World War II broke out, she and her husband came to Scotland. Here she gave birth to a son. However, some time after that, she divorced her husband and returned to Israel, leaving her son with his father. I don't know if that was by choice or if she was obliged to do so in accordance with the divorce settlement. On her return to Israel she settled in Givat Brenner. Here she remarried and had three children with her husband Mario, - Rivka, Meir and Chava,. She lived here *happily*, as far as I know, till her demise in 1980. I rather liked her. Mario, her husband, was, to my recollection, quiet and unassuming, a kind and very friendly person. From the little I remember of their children they too were of similar disposition.

I am not sure about whether to include gossip in this history of my family recollections, but here goes, since it is somewhat piquant. Rumour in the family had it that one of the uncles, although married and a family man either had or attempted to have an affair with my cousin Esther (before her marriage I believe). She was, I understand, a very attractive girl, with very long, thick hair – really her crowning glory.

As with most of my cousins, our contact with them was almost non-existent; perhaps because we were separated for so long. I lived in London, boy and man, they all in Palestine (later Israel). We were completely out of touch all this time which made close relation almost impossible. They were all immersed and influenced by their lives in the Middle East, while my sister, Dorle, and I were subject to, and influenced by, our lives in Britain. We, therefore, on our arrival in Israel many years later, had very little in common other than our distant past in Leipzig.

Nettie, Tante Eva's second, was born in 1920. I don't remember much about her 'doings' in Leipzig. She reached Palestine with her family by illegal immigration in 1938/9, I think. I think also that she and her family were part of the families who hid in our flat in October/November 1938 following our deportation until they were able to escape to Italy. I have since been told that Tante Eva and her family, in fact, first 'escaped' to China, and returned from there to Italy, on their way to Palestine. I really don't know how much credence to attach to that story; for example, how long were they in China? Where and what did they do there? After we were deported to Poland, I had no contact with her until I came to Israel on my second or third visit. I visited Israel in the spring of 1951, again in the spring of 1961 and once more at the end of 1970 and/or early in 1971.

On that occasion I also met Nettie's husband who considered himself an expert chess player. I think it must have been our third visit – 1971 – when my son David was almost 14 years old. He was a member of his school's chess team. I don't know who challenged whom. Nettie's husband – Abrasha - and David sat down to play chess. The match was tense and exciting. We all stood around the two contestants and watched - until Nettie's husband lost patience because he could not defeat David, who took his time over each move. Eventually he actually lost his temper a little and stopped the game. Ah, memories, memories! Nettie, who died in 2001, also left behind three children – Ruti, Adina and Itamar - and I don't know how many grandchildren.

The youngest in this family – Mottel – was just a year older than I. His birthday was June 23rd, 1926. We did meet from time to time, not too often though. He, too, reached Palestine/Israel via illegal immigration in 1938/9 – he was then 12 or 13 years old and, no doubt, attended school here. I am not sure what his life was like at that time – completely different to mine, to be sure. I was alone while he had a lot of family around: mother, possibly father – I am not too sure about that - sisters, aunts, uncles, cousins and so on. I can only imagine what his life was like.

There are happenings of which I have no direct knowledge – let those who have such knowledge relate them if they wish. I can only add that Mottel also married, moved to Ashdod, went into business with members of his wife's family and was quite successful in his endeavors, becoming a pillar of the Ashdod business community. He fathered two children – a boy, Baruch and a girl, Chava – who both also married. I don't know how many, if any, grandchildren resulted from these unions.

The one item I can mention concerning my cousin Mottel relates to the packing and dispatching of a lift from Leipzig to Palestine in 1938. As I mentioned earlier some of my mother's sisters with their families hid in our flat after our deportation to Poland until they were able to escape to Italy and eventually to Palestine. Before escaping to Italy, they managed, apparently, to put together a lift, containing many things from the various families, and had it sent to Palestine. Included in the lift was my brother Bezalel's precious and valuable stamp album. No doubt there must have been many other items belonging to my family although to my knowledge none of us ever received anything from that lift. Even the precious stamp album was, I was told, appropriated by my cousin Mottel who, it seems, steadfastly refused to return it to my brother. There are a number of these snippets to relate, but I don't know if I will. After all, as I said earlier it is all WATER UNDER THE BRIDGE.

I don't know what the count is by now, but it is becoming pretty clear that the clan which should surely be termed the Kessler- Berggruen clan is growing by leaps and bounds.

The next in line is Fanny Feigl who married Herman Zimetbaum on July 3rd, 1919. Herman, like Tanchum Kernkraut, was also in the fur trade and on a very big scale, my brother told me. They also lived in Leipzig, not far from us, not far from Tante Regina also in Nord Strasse (theirs was the house to which I ran, or thought I did, when bolting from the young Nazi thugs – as I wrote earlier). We saw each other

53

occasionally. I imagine that the brothers and sisters – our elders, I mean – saw one another more frequently but without the presence of us young ones. Tante Fanny and Onkel Herman had two children.

Raphael Ralph was born in 1920. I am given to understand that on leaving school he joined his father in their family business.

The other son, Yeshayahu Jesse, was born in 1923, also in Leipzig, as was his brother. Apparently, he too, on leaving school, joined the family business.

In 1936 Herman, realizing earlier than others, the direction in which Nazi Germany was moving – applied to migrate to the USA. Since it was taking too long for permission to enter the USA to reach them, the family left for Italy first. This was an interim measure, of course. While in Italy, Onkel Herman decided to take his family to Cuba and attempt to enter the USA from there. They did reach Cuba and while waiting for visas to America, Herman used his knowledge and contacts to deal in furs and other commodities. Whiling away the time prompted the younger son, Jesse, to write to the President of the USA, Franklyn Delano Roosevelt. He poured out his heart to the President telling his tale of woe, about all they had suffered, all they had lost and pleaded for permission for his family to enter the United States to rebuild their lives in a free and democratic country.

Nothing happened for a while. I don't know if Jesse wrote again, but suddenly he received a letter from one of President Roosevelt's assistants granting him, Jesse, and only Jesse, an entry permit to the USA. After much 'humming and hahing' it was decided that Jesse must not miss this opportunity. The rest of the family would continue to try and hope. So, Jesse was off to the United States. He settled in New Jersey, I believe, and found work and a place to live and decided to, once more, impose on President Roosevelt's time. He wrote him again, pleading to permit his father, mother and brother to join him. Surprise! Surprise! The necessary permission to enter what was then often referred to as 'The Promised Land' – the *'goldene medine'* in Yiddish – was granted.

Family Zimetbaum was again united. They went into business and fulfilling the American Dream became quite successful. The only blight on the complete happiness of the family of which I am aware was when it became apparent that Tante Fanny, surely as a result of what had befallen the family (who knows?) had fallen prey to a mental illness which plagued her, and them, until her death in 1966.

One other incident pops up in my mind. Onkel Herman came to London on business after the end of WWII. He, naturally, made it his immediate concern to visit both my sister Dorle and me, to see how we were faring, as any good uncle would. After satisfying himself about my welfare and seeing that in me he was dealing with an adult after army service, he invited Dorle to come to the USA, to stay with them there and assured her that he would see to all her needs and provide for her future. But Dorle declined most vehemently. She always was a very determined, even stubborn, person. She explained to our uncle that, much as she appreciated the offer, the only move she would undertake would be to Israel where most of her relatives were – especially her brother and sister. She would thus fulfil not only her own dream but also that of our parents.

Ralph and Jesse both married and had children. Ralph meanwhile died in 2003; Jesse, in July 2011 when I started this journal, was still with us but died in December of that year. I may add more about my cousins Zimetbaum, if I remember more of them - if not now then maybe in the second edition of this memoir – if there is one.

We now come to the only one of the Berggruen sisters who, although married, regretfully had no children – I don't know, of course, if from choice or otherwise. Marie Maayan was born on January 17th, 1897. In January 1917, 10 days after she turned 20 years old, she married Zudik Gleitman. The young couple also lived near us in Leipzig and we were not infrequent visitors to their home. Perhaps to compensate for their being childless we were always fascinated by the variety of caged birds in their home: canaries, papageis (is that how it's spelled?) and others. I have it also in my mind, and don't think that it is wishful thinking about the past, that we were always greeted with something sweet – biscuits, chocolate, sweets etc. The love of personally caring for one's own living creatures is strong in most humans, and so it must have been in my aunt Marie and uncle Zudik. We went to visit them, Marion and I, on our first visit to Israel in 1951. Yes – they too managed to reach the Holy Land via Italy in the late 1930's.

If my memory is not going completely haywire I must include in this tale the information that we found that my uncle Zudik harboured a goat in their home in Israel which they kept in their bathroom. Apart from that, I think there was also the usual, expected assortment of birds.

My own mother, Sima Yochwet, is next in line. She was born in Zalubince, Nowe Sacz, Galicia, Poland on June 4th, 1898, the year before the family moved to Leipzig. As already mentioned in the earliest parts of this story she married Avraham Hirsch Kessler in June of 1921 and settled down in Leipzig. I know nothing, really nothing, of her life in Leipzig before her marriage to my father and the births of us, her children. That is a good chunk of life – after all she was born in 1898, came to Germany at the age of one, must have gone to school. Did she graduate? Did she have further, advanced education? What did she do till the age of 23 when she married my father?

While writing these lines I only now begin to really understand my loss. When I left her, I was much too young to think of such things and now I cannot talk to her about her past life, cut short when she was only 46 years old. I am convinced that this is a major reason why I decided to put in writing what I remember of my own life and surroundings so that my children, and those following them, who may want to delve into their past history, have where to look for some of the information.

The same holds good for my father who was just three years older than my mother. Whereas we know, with a reasonable amount of certainty, the date of my mother's murder in Auschwitz – Iyar 21, 5704, 36th day of the Omer, corresponding to May 14, 1944 – we have absolutely no information about my father's fate, neither date nor even approximate, nor method, nor location, or under what circumstances. The only thing about my father's childhood of which I can be sure is that he was 10 years old when he and his family left Jaroslav and came to Germany. What school did he attend in Jaroslav? What school in Munich? What did he study and till what age? What did he do after he left school? I know none of this and, regretfully, there is no one left to ask.

I do have a photograph of my father in overalls washing down a car which surely must have belonged to a Nazi officer in one of the camps. Was it still in the Krakow ghetto? Was it in the Plaszow concentration

camp or elsewhere? We just don't know with any degree of certainty –
not where, not when and under what conditions.

I also mentioned earlier briefly that my brother, Bezalel, was born in
June 1922, almost an exact year after our parents married. He will
feature in other parts of this memoir.

The older of my two sisters, Susi, was born in September 1925. She was
a sweet, warm and loving child with whom it was almost impossible to
quarrel. Her personality was such, as far as I recall, that when asked to
adjudicate in an argument between family members or friends she
would reply – as her aunt Regina is reported to have done on occasion –
"you are right" to one and then say the same to the other party involved.

When it was pointed out by someone that they can't both be right that person too was told: "you too are right."

My younger sister, Dorle, was born in April 1929. She, too, was all of the above but her sharp mind and sense of justice and fairness, as well as her phenomenal memory, constrained her to 'give judgment' rather than avoid showing support for one side or another. This trait not infrequently caused her some anguish, but she is a strong character, well able to cope with such a burden.

I, Bernard, was born in July 1927. I don't really know what to say about me. Let others, if they so choose, sit in judgment of me.

We are all Leipzig born of course. I may elaborate more on this later. Suffice it here to say that she, my mother, was the fifth in line of the Bergguen girls. I must add also that my mother, and this was very rare at the time – we are talking of the late 1920th - was granted an official certificate by the German authorities authorizing her to act as an agent of some kind in business or travel – not that I ever noticed her acting as such.

The sixth daughter, bringing up the rear, was Regina Rivka. She was born on May 9th, 1900, the only one of the sisters to be born in Leipzig, Germany. Regina married Avraham Kessler's brother David in October 1922, thus cementing the close association between the two families – The Kesslers and The Berggruens.

Regina and David had three children:

Adele Alla, their first child was born in Leipzig in 1923 and died in 1994 in Tel Aviv. The whole family managed to leave Germany for Palestine in the mid-1930s - and thereby hangs a tale. We'll see how it goes later. Alla – short for Adele, whose Hebrew name was Adina - married Feri Ronen formerly Rosenbaum who worked, I think, for one of Israel's security services. She, Alla, settled down as a housewife and bore three children. The whole family continued to live in her parents' home in Tel Aviv 's Mazeh Street. They, in turn, had three children with whom, to my great regret, we have practically no contact these days – not from our choice.

The first, Gadi, now has a family of his own and probably also grandchildren. I think he and his family are resident in one of the settlements over the 'green line', as it is termed.

Dalia, is also married. She has several children – I don't remember how many. She most probably has grandchildren too. She and her family moved to a kibbutz in the Beit Sha'an valley where she lived for a good many years. She left the kibbutz, I believe, some years ago. Where she and her family have settled meanwhile, I don't know. Our country, Israel, is small but everyone is busy with his/her own affairs and it is difficult to keep track of everyone – except for happy or sad events – and these meetings are brief and passing.

Yael, the youngest of Alla's children, lives in Tel Aviv in the flat which had been her home with both her grandparents and her parents. I don't really know if she married and/or had children. On one occasion she visited us in London together with Nurit. It must have been in late 1972 or at the very beginning of 1973, shortly before Marion , my first wife, died.

Regina and David's second child is named Bezalel (we have a lot of Bezalels in the family,all named after our paternal grandfather). He was born in June 1927, one year to the day after our cousin Mottel and just thee weeks before my birth. This Bezalel, who died in 1987, became a musician. He played the violin and taught this instrument to both young and older aspirants, first in Israel, then in Holland and eventually in Germany to where he had returned after two unsuccessful marriages. I believe he left behind three children from both marriages, but I'm not really sure of this since for reasons beyond my comprehension we have no contact at all with any of them. We did invite them, as I recall, to both my childrens', Naomi's and Yael's, weddings but had no reaction from any of them. What a pity!

The last one of Regina's offspring, perhaps the most successful one according to today's criteria, is Zvi (Harry). He is the one I wrote about earlier, the one I pushed in the street outside his home where we played, when his brother, Bezalel (see above), chased me and indirectly, and I am sure unintentionally, caused the injury over my eye.

Zvi was born in Leipzig in 1930. He, too, managed to reach Palestine with his parents in the mid -1930's. I have yet to enlarge on the flight

59

from Germany to Palestine, via Italy, of various members of the family but will endeavour so to do later. Suffice it meanwhile here to write a few words about my cousin Zvi. As my WWII years, as well as my post-war years, were spent in England I can't say much about Zvi's early years in Israel. We didn't see each other much from 1937/8 until my visit to Israel many years later, except for a few occasions when Zvi visited London.

I believe that when he left school, he was an ardent supporter of the Etzel resistance movement and of Menahem Beigin, its leader. In the years that followed, inevitably, he changed his political views. He studied economics and became a senior editor and economics journalist with the popular *Yediot Achronot* Newspaper. He also served as consultant to various companies as well as to the German Restitution Claims Conference. He married twice. His first wife was Diana, who bore him his daughter, Cigale. Cigale is now married herself and has two grown daughters of her own.

Zvi's second wife is Yael. She was, and maybe still is, the spokeswoman for the Meretz political party, whose politics are diametrically opposed to the Etzel organization which went through various changes, eventually becoming the Likud party. Zvi and Yael had two sons: David and Eliav; the latter died of leukaemia not long after his Bar Mitzvah. David is now married and has also started a family. *"Kein Yirbu"* So may they multiply!

About Zvi's first wife I may say just a little more. At some point in their lives they, at least Diana and Cigale, lived in London for a year or more. (I am not really sure.) During that time we did see them not infrequently. My son, David, had a little red car when he was very young. He used to ride in it at the local 'Adventure Playground' with which his mother had so much to do, having helped to raise the funds to establish it. At some point he, with our full consent and encouragement, decided to present this car to Cigale so that she should also have a nice present from him. She was absolutely thrilled by her present. (We had to have the car repaired first since the steering wheel had come off on one occasion causing David a rather unpleasant wound in his cheek and wanted to make sure nothing similar would happen to the young girl)

My daughters also wanted to bring joy to Cigale – so they presented her with a dancing doll, which was also much appreciated. We saw Cigale again in her home and garden not long ago – our contact with her is most irregular, especially since she lives a good distance away from us. She arranged a get-together of what she termed the Berggruen clan of those in Israel, where we met again members of our family whom we had not seen for a good long time (or ever). Nor have we seen almost all of them since – everyone being concerned with his or her own affairs. Life is neither simple nor easy, especially in our "neck of the wood."

Having recorded those details which I remember, although there may be much more to tell, of the Bergguen side of the equation, let me now return to the Kessler side of the coin.

Naftali, the first born, saw the light of day on January 7th, 1894. He married Esther in Munich in 1919 having found his bride, who was born in 1899 in Nurenberg to family Henig. He took his bride to Leipzig two months later and found accommodation near Marie and Zudik. Here, presumably, their two daughters were born: Frieda-Julia on December 31st, 1920 and Elisabeta – date of birth unknown, to me at least. My knowledge here, as in many other cases of our family history is, to my great regret, very skimpy. We do know, however, that they lost their lives in Poland in the Holocaust – but have no information how,

The next in line was my father who appears in the sequences of my story whenever appropriate and need not be elaborated on here.

Then came David, and here too nothing need be added at this point since I already expanded on this family when writing about Regina.

The other three brothers, in order, were Yisrael, Chaim and Ephraim.

Yisrael was born on December 12th, 1899. He married Frieda (Yuta) Sonnenblick, his cousin from Berlin, six years his junior. They had two children, Bezalel (again) and Moshe. I know very little, practically nothing, about their lives. I do know that whereas Naftali, Avraham and David, the three eldest of the brothers, moved to Leipzig in the early twenties. The two next in line, Yisrael and Chaim, after remaining in Munich for a while longer, settled in Berlin.

Yisrael stayed in Munich until 1935. His mother, my paternal grandmother, who had lived alone since her husband died in 1921, moved in with him, in 1932. When Yisrael and his family moved to Berlin in 1935, his mother, Bluma, came to us in Leipzig. I am not sure when Chaim moved to Berlin but apparently, he lived in the German capital from late 1929 until the early 1930's into the start of the Hitler regime. Fortunately, he too reached the shores of the Holy Land early in the nineteen thirties.

In October 1938, Yisrael was deported to Poland from Berlin, as we were from Leipzig. Unlike the deportations from Leipzig, from where whole families were taken, the men only were deported from Berlin, leaving the women and children in Germany. Shortly after that the men were permitted to return for one month to settle their affairs. Yisrael apparently did not heed the instruction to limit his time to one month. He was still found in Berlin in September 1939, after the outbreak of WWII, was arrested it appears, on September 13th of that year and sent first to Sachsenhausen, then to Ravensbruck, and found his death on May 23rd, 1942. His wife, Frieda, Yuta, was forced to work in the Berlin branch of one of the Siemens factories until, on March 4th, 1943 when she, together with her two sons, Bezalel aged almost 12 and Moshe aged seven, and other Jewish women forced labourers were deported to Auschwitz where they all found their deaths.

What may also be of interest here is that Yisrael and Chaim also married two sisters, this time their cousins actually – daughters of Bluma's sister Rachel, whom Bluma had brought to Berlin at the beginning of WWI. Chaim, in the early 1930s, felt stifled in Germany. There is also the tale of his falling in love with his cousin, Golda (Gusti) Sonnenblick, renouncing the promises given to another young lady to whom he was already engaged, and being forced to flee the anger of her family. He went first to Italy and then to Palestine on a tourist visa issued by the British consul in Berlin which he obtained before he bolted, I imagine. In September 1936 Golda reached Tel Aviv in order finally to marry her beloved Chaim. They eventually had a son in October 1937 who was also named… you've guessed: Bezalel.

The youngest, Efraim, returned to Poland, and made his home in Zawiercie where we, eventually, in 1938, on being deported from Germany, found temporary shelter. Efraim, who was born January 1st, 1905, married Tiebel nee Rosenbaum in Poland. The couple had four children – Shmuel, Moshe, Gitl and Boris of whom I know absolutely nothing – to my enduring regret. They are, after all, my cousins in the first degree. How did it come about that I have such a limited knowledge of what is my close family? Although we triumphed over Hitler by just being alive, this monster still left a gaping hole in our existence by so limiting our knowledge about our family. Yet, the tale continues. The whole family – six souls – all fell victim to the holocaust. If in the time left me I can glean more information about them I will insert whatever may be necessary into these lines.

The Deportation

The year is 1938 – October 28th of that year, to be exact.

The Nurnberg Laws have not only been enacted. They have been rigorously applied for some considerable time. Since Hitler's rise to power – *all legal and democratic - after all the so-called 'cultured' German people had elected his Nazi party to lead them* – his anti-Jewish laws have caused numerous outbreaks of violence, perpetrated by his thugs, not a few supported and encouraged by large sections of the local population.

Jewish shops and stores were vandalized and looted. Jews were attacked and beaten-up in the street. Not just a few of their menfolk have been frequently sent to forced labour, such as clearing the snow from areas like airport runways, main streets and approaches to buildings the Nazis considered important. Although my younger sister doesn't recall this and is of the opinion that such horrors were not prevalent in Leipzig, I remember, distinctly and very clearly, my father being one of those forcibly conscripted for such labour.

Others were rounded up and sent to Dachau, outside Munich, and other concentration camps. All this before Kristallnacht – the nights of the 9th and 10th of November 1938 - when between 1000 and 2000 of the synagogues and thousands of Jewish-owned shops all over Germany and Austria went up in smoke. Almost 100 Jews were murdered in the streets of this so-called civilized country and hundreds or thousands more injured by rampaging Nazis, lusting to 'avenge' the desperate act of a Jewish youth – aged 17 – who, in his despair at his own family's misfortune in Germany had attempted (with little success) to shoot and kill a junior German diplomat from that country's Embassy in Paris.

Coming back to October 1938, the 28th of that month, if my recollections are correct. This was the day Jews in Leipzig, the city where I was born, of Polish nationality, were rounded up by the Gestapo, ably assisted by the regular police. We were assembled first in a huge hall close to the central police station – actually, I think it may have been the gymnasium of the Carlebach High School. It mattered not if you were born in the city, married in the city, lived in the city for many years, owned property there, conducted your business there and contributed to the social, cultural, business and industrial life. If you were a Jew and a Polish national that was all that mattered! This was the situation in general that year. I will try to describe how this affected us, that is my family, and me in particular. I was now eleven years old, and like many another 11-year-old my head was full of 'friends, football, and playing 'hooky' from Cheder.

The day the police and Gestapo came to our home most definitely made a tremendous impression on us all and no doubt left its mark on me. I will try to recount the events of that fateful day as it is imprinted on my mind.

It was very early in the morning, a Friday, Sabbath Eve. My mother had risen at dawn, I think, as usual, to start preparations for the Sabbath before getting us children ready for school. My father had already left to open grandfather's grocery store, which he, with my mother's help, ran. I don't recall where my sister Susi was, but my brother, Bezalel, had already left for school. My younger sister, Dorle, and I were still at home, getting ready to go to school also. Suddenly, there was a loud knocking- more like pounding - on the door. On opening the door we found two men, both in civilian clothes – as far as I remember – of whom one at least must have been a member of the Gestapo. I think the other was a regular policeman although I am not too sure of this. He may have been in uniform, after all – I was confused then and still am, I suppose. When they realized that my father and brother were not at home I was dispatched, with one of the men, to bring home my father – or was it my brother? I am not too clear on this. My sister, Susi, who must still have been at home at that time was, I believe, sent to bring home the other absent member of the family. I am, as I just said, a little confused still about the exact sequence of events here.

When we were all home, we were told by the intruders to pack one suitcase of whatever necessities we would surely need. Since it was Friday my mother naturally took with Shabbat candles and the chalot she had baked the previous day. We were all taken to an assembly hall as I mentioned above. Try as I might, I can't remember exactly where my grandfather and grandmother were, but I remember that they were later in Poland with us – not necessarily in Krakow. I have since been reminded that my grandfather was apparently not on the list for deportation but decided to remain with us, and so came to Poland with us. I even have a vague recollection of my grandfather being taken out of hospital at that time. (This last may be two separate recollections having become intertwined). I imagine my grandmother must have been with us all the time.

There, in that hall, we saw hundreds of our fellow-Jews, all as bewildered and apprehensive as were we, milling around in utter confusion. We were not left in doubt for too long and soon were taken to the central railway station, ordered onto a multi-carriage train which, when full, started our journey toward where... what...?

At least, we – the Kessler family – did not have to worry about a fair number of our uncles, aunts and cousins, who had escaped the clutches of the Nazis. As I mentioned already family Zimetbaum had left Germany, first for Italy in 1935 (Onkel Herman) followed by Tante Fanny and their two sons, Ralph and Jesse, in 1936 who got to the United States via Cuba. Chaim had managed to reach the shores of Palestine already in 1933. Regina and David, Ewa and Meir (?) and all the children of both families, Marie and Zudik, and the Kernkraut sons – all the above escaped the Nazis' net.

On the other hand, I mentioned uncle Yisrael's, his wife's and daughters' fate, earlier, and as far as I am aware neither Naftali, his wife and two daughters, nor Efraim, his wife and four children survived the Holocaust. This meant that two of the Berggruen sisters (one of whom was my mother), together with their husbands, and four of the Kessler brothers (including my father), together with their wives, as well as nine first degree cousins, at least, were murdered by the Nazis during the holocaust, as were also two grandparents – one Kessler and one Berggruen. In addition, a not inconsiderable number of other fairly close family relations also lost their lives in the holocaust. *MAY THEIR SOULS ALL REST IN PEACE.*

This leaves us, apart from my brother, two sisters and me, with family David and Regina Kessler; family Meier and Eva Scheiner; and Zudik and Marie Gleitman. Chaim, of course also survived, thank G-D (see above). Some of the Sonnenblick branch of the family also managed to reach Palestine.

Regina and David had already managed to escape to Italy in 1937, leaving their three children in my parent's care. The three children, Alla, Bezalel and Harry, stayed with us for approximately eight months before joining their parents in Italy early in 1938. Tante Eva and her family and the Gleitmans were still in Leipzig when the deportations to Poland took place. They somehow escaped the net at the end of October 1938 but had to find shelter somewhere safer than their own homes. On our deportation on the 28th of October – about which I am about to write - our flat had been sealed. They, therefore, considered it wise to move into that flat, at no 4, Berliner Strasse, until they could escape from Germany. They all crowded into that flat till after Kristallnacht, when they finally succeeded in escaping to Italy, I know not how.

Regina and David were now in Milan, Italy, awaiting either certificates to settle in Palestine legally or be fortunate to join an aliyah 'B' – illegal immigrant – ship organized by the Jewish Agency. My parents sent my brother to Milan, sometime in the early part of 1938, well before the deportations, to take various precious (valuable) items to our family there for their needs in Palestine. I have been made aware only recently that our parents had already given to Regina and David, on their leaving Leipzig for Italy in 1937, a sum of 2000 Lira (we often wondered if these may have been pounds sterling) which were to serve as payment to the proper authority for certificates for our parents or to purchase property there, to enable them to enter Palestine legally.

They also gave my brother a letter to their brother and sister asking them to take with them to Palestine their own nieces and nephews – i.e. my brother, two sisters and myself. For whatever reason, and they must have had a compelling reason which was and is unknown to us, they felt unable to accede to this request. My brother returned to Leipzig, while those in Italy eventually boarded the aliyah 'B' (illegal immigrant) ship *Jerusalem* and sailed for Palestine early in 1939, I think. The 'illegal immigrants' were put ashore on the Ashkelon beach and became, eventually, full-fledged residents.

To continue with our story about the deportation and our doings in Poland.

So, here we are Family Selma (Sima Yochvet) + Abraham Hirsch Kessler, together with Oma Bluma Berta Kessler and Opa Yehuda Leib Berggruen , having been taken from the assembly point at the Gymnasium of the Carlibach High school to the Hauptbahnhof of Leipzig, the Central Railway Station. We were herded onto this multi-carriage train, with hundreds, maybe thousands of fellow Jews – on a Friday afternoon, travelling to where? No one knew, as yet. Altogether four such packed trains were dispatched from Leipzig that day. But I repeat the question, to where?

As the day wore on, there was much confused chatter: the men trying to foresee what the future held; the women trying to keep the children occupied, amused, entertained, while getting ready for Shabbat. *Yes! On the train!*

And so, it was!

As the day came to an end, many of the women who had had the foresight, as had my mother, took out the candles and lit them to welcome the Shabbat. In many of the carriages the men formed *minyanim* – a quorum of at least ten males aged 13 and over – and the Sabbath Eve *Maariv* (evening prayer) was recited, much of it sung. Even wine for *kiddush* was found, the consecration sung and the wine drunk. The challot were then brought out, and shared, the blessing said and, as if at our table at home, even *zemirot*, (the Shabbat liturgy) were sung. What our guards – jailors really – thought we did not know, nor care. So the journey continued, hour after dreary and frightening hour.

Eventually, the train stopped, sometime around midnight, I think. Here we were ordered to leave the train and we began our march toward what we eventually learned was an unmanned crossing into Poland, near Beuthen. Our train was sent to one of the smaller and less frequented

67

destinations. The major deportation brought some thousands of Polish Jews to the border between Germany and Poland at the little town of Zbaszyn. Here the Polish border guards would not allow the Jews to enter. The Germans, on their side, fired their rifles into the air to keep them in No-Man's-Land for a considerable time. I suppose that from that point of view, we were lucky.

The column of Jews was long. The menfolk, at least those who were able to, continued carrying their suitcases which many had been told to bring with what each considered the most precious and valuable items from their homes. On either side of the column, every few paces, were SS and other Nazi troops hurrying us on, many with huge dogs – German Shepherds – often with whips and truncheons, which were not for show only and were used frequently. At the end of the column was a lorry, or several lorries, I don't really know, which collected all the suitcases dropped by the 'marchers' who were unable to carry such heavy burdens for such a long time.

We marched for hours in total darkness until we realized that the SS guards were no longer accompanying us. We now took stock of our surroundings. Those at the head of the column saw some light in the distance and we all made for that, arriving there while it was still dark. Fortunately, some early riser in the village – a farmer, no doubt - roused the local priest of the place who very kindly opened up the Church hall into which we all crowded. I think that some of the women of that village organized hot drinks and we stayed in that hall until morning when local officials arrived. These set up tables and interviewed each family, who were then sent on their way, to where they preferred to go.

We, that is my parents, chose to make our first stop the small town of Zawiercie where Efraim, one of my father's brothers, lived. Grandmother came with us but grandfather preferred to find family in Nowe Sacz from where he had come to Germany. We were given permits, train tickets, and directions and went on our way – mother, father and his mother, brother, two sisters, I and our one suitcase which my father had carried all this time and not abandoned.

On arrival in Zawiercie, we had to walk about a half a kilometre or more along one side of the track, cross to the other side of the track, and retrace our steps all the way and more to the street in which my uncle lived. At the crossing were two policemen who said a cordial good morning, I think. Why is this important for me? The occurrence immediately following will explain. We continued to walk towards the street where my uncle lived. There, walking towards us, were three Polish soldiers. As they approached, they started to pretend that they were drunk - perhaps they really were - I would not be surprised.Here we were, already exhausted and my father carrying a fairly heavy suitcase. The soldiers, as they came level with us, started to weave about; one lurched into my father. They all stopped and started to swear at us.

"Zyd! go to Palestine!"

If only we could have.

This was followed by further cursing. One of them punched my father in the face which not only made him drop the suitcase but knocked him to the ground. They then laughed and walked on as if nothing had happened. All the while the policemen at the railway crossing were witnesses to this incident but did not react in any way, although they were only some dozens of meters away. Their only reaction was to smile at the soldiers indulgently. This is an incident carved into my memory which I cannot forget – it was, of course, nothing compared to later events. But I suppose it was a small indication of the shape of things to come. It also taught me that Anti-Semitism was not confined to Germany and Germans, not by a long way.

My uncle Efraim and aunt Tiebel and their four children – Shmuel, Moshe, Gitl, Boris - made room for us in their not particularly large home, and made us feel most welcome, as far as I remember. However, my parents decided not to prolong our stay and three or four weeks later we moved, via Katowice, to Krakow. Here I was to spend some 9-10 months.

I have few memories of what we did here. One or two incidences are still with me. I can't recall the area or street where we lived. From correspondence of the time I know that one street was Krakusa, another was called Krakowska, and there may have been one or two other places also. I do not, of course, remember what the accommodation was like, except that I think it must have been rather crowded. We had no visible means of support and must have relied on selling off some of the items my father had 'lugged' in the suitcase mentioned earlier, and on the local Jewish welfare organization which, naturally, had many calls on its resources particularly at that time.

One of my nephews appears to have found in one of the letters which were being exchanged by my parents with those parts of the family who had reached Palestine that at one stage my mother had to either pawn or sell her gold wedding ring in order to be able to buy food for her children. On another occasion our aunt Regina appears to have sent 500 zloty to help us. Life was not easy at that time.

Since my parents had apparently either sent or given my brother cheques in fairly considerable amounts to take to our family in Italy in the first half of 1938, before they sailed for Palestine, it was hoped and expected that some attempt would be made by them to either obtain certificates for us or that they would purchase some property or land in my parents' name which would have entitled my parents to receive the necessary permits to reside in Palestine. I am persuaded that members of our family already in Palestine surely made attempts to enable us to reach the Holy Land. However, it is, of course, a well-known fact that at that uncertain time particularly the filing systems of our public institutions were not always what they should have been. Certainly, no trace has so far been found of any application formally made in Palestine (Israel now) to the Zionist Organization and/or the Jewish Agency for the issue of the appropriate certificates for my parents' entry into Palestine.

At Chanukah, the community in Krakow held a big celebration, including on-stage performances by some of the children. Having been considered – by me, at least - an expert performer on the harmonica, I was promptly enlisted as one of the performers (quite rightly so, I may say modestly). And with the addition of another 'mouth organist', who happened to be an old, well, a young school mate. If my memory again has not deserted me, she was a rather pretty girl. We entertained the huge audience with several select pieces, to tremendous applause, I recall.

Krakow 1939

There are a few other items from this period which stick in my mind:

I think we did not have proper school lessons. Rather we went, daily, to a kind of hostel/club and 'did' various things. I was reminded the other day by someone who was also there at that time that we, the boys, played football almost daily and that I was considered a very good footballer. On other occasions, I remember going to green parts of the city near our 'home' with my two sisters. I think we also enjoyed our first ever *Droshky* ride.

I may also boast that in the short time – a total of ten months - that I resided in Poland I managed to acquire a fairly fluent knowledge of spoken Polish. I must however in all honesty confess that on leaving Poland, not having anyone with whom to converse in that language, I also swiftly forgot it all!

Woh! Hold on - where is my brother while all of this was going on? I should have mentioned earlier that while still in Zawierci, indeed immediately on arrival there, my father sent telegrams all over the place in order to obtain permission for Zalel to return to Leipzig to collect his belongings and join his group in Italy for his journey to what was then Palestine. As I already mentioned one of his *hachshara* periods was a course in carpentry. Indeed, he had made by himself a large wooden case which later served as a wardrobe for his clothes. It contained all his belongings already when he, together with us all, was deported to Poland.

In fact, all documentation for joining his youth group in Trieste for their journey to Palestine was prepared and awaiting him in Berlin. My father had obtained permission for Zal, to return to Germany; actually, the permit was valid for a direct journey to Berlin only to pick up his certificate - allowing him to enter and settle in Palestine - and leave, Germany of course.

According to my brother the route of the train to Berlin was via Leipzig and Zal, who had not read the authorization from the Germans, simply alighted in Leipzig automatically. Here he found families Scheiner and Gleitman hiding out in our flat in Berliner Strasse. He may also have realized that his certificate awaited him in Berlin. He left his belongings, went to Berlin, collected his official documents and left for Trieste. All this happened within one week (eight days, actually) of our deportation.

Having left his belongings in Leipzig our uncle Zudik took it upon himself to pack and send them on to Palestine. Zalel, continued his journey through to Trieste, Italy where his group, and boat awaited him. Then onwards to Palestine, where he first went to Mikveh Israel. Only when he reached Palestine, did he read all the various documents in his possession and realized that the Nazis, when granting him permission to return to Germany for two days to pick up his documents limited the permission to a direct journey to Berlin and out again. He thus broke the rules unwittingly by alighting in Leipzig. However, all's well that ends well!

Since he himself wrote his memoirs I need not elaborate on his 'doings' further, except to add that he subsequently joined the religious Hapoel Hamizrachi kibbutz Tirath Zvi in the Beit Shaan valley. He then moved, I believe, to another kibbutz with his *garin* (group), to kibbutz Alumim, for more training and wound up eventually in kibbutz Sa'ad in the south of the country, not far from Gaza.

Eventually he decided he wanted to study at the University. He enrolled at the Hebrew University in Jerusalem, lived in a rented room, I think, and worked at what I know not, to support himself while obtaining his

Bachelor then Master and finally his Ph.D (Doctor's) degree. He taught and researched at the Bar - Ilan University and is now a Professor Emeritus in Agronomy. Furthermore, he became a researcher at the Volcani Institute as well as at the Faculty of Agriculture of the Hebrew University, which was situated in Rehovot, his home-town.

I may add, and this is not just 'by the way', that while working at the Experimental Laboratory in Rehovot he met his laboratory assistant, Chava, in 1951. They fell in love and married in 1954. Since I believe, I mention some of these incidents elsewhere I will not elaborate further at this stage.

My sister Susi, on the other hand, is, sadly, no longer with us and cannot tell her own story. She died more than ten years ago and I would like to include just a little about her. Shortly after Dorle and I left for England with the Kindertransport (see below), Susi, went to Bialystok on hachshara with her Youth aliyah group. When the Germans invaded Poland the Russians, in pursuance of the Ribbentrop-Molotov accords, invaded helpless Poland from the other side to occupy 'their' half - eastern Poland, including Bialystok.

Susi and her group somehow reached Vilna early in 1940 and continued their hachshara there until they left for Kovno where, apparently, they completed all the required documentation for their onward journey, which at that point was Moscow. Here they were accommodated in a fairly decent hotel where they stayed for a week or two after which they travelled by train to Odessa from where they took a ship to Istanbul in Turkey. It was now already 1941 and here, I believe, she was fortunate to meet one of our Sonnenblick relatives, David Sonnenblick and his family, who were in Turkey at the time before they also reached Palestine. On Susi's arrival in Turkey – in a very much bedraggled and half-starved way, I was told – she was naturally very pleased to meet family again. The family, I am told, fed her and gave her fresh clothes, since she had been unable to bring anything from whence she had come. She then went on her way with her group, winding up in the agricultural school of Kfar HaNoar Hadati, a Youth aliyah settlement not far from Haifa. Susi must have been not yet 16 years old when she reached Palestine. She stayed at that school till the end of the 1942/3 school year when she was just some three months short of her 18th birthday.

On leaving Kfar HaNoar she came to Tel Aviv where she was taken in by our aunt Regina and uncle David and became, more or less, part of their family. At Kfar HaNoar she had become romantically involved with a young man who no doubt has his own involved history, since he too originated in Germany (a small town near Frankfurt, I believe). Manfred (or Meir as he became when he began using his Hebrew name), also left the youth village at that time in mid-1943 and joined a kibbutz. He tells me that he left after two days, in order to join Susi. My aunt and uncle took him in also. Here they both lived until they married in November 1945. I could tell all this in much greater detail and continue their saga but this is my story; so enough. I will only add that the wedding was arranged by and held at my aunt and uncle Regina's and David's home. Since I was in the army at that time, I could not make the attempt even to reach Palestine and join in the wedding celebrations.

Having settled things for my brother, and my sister Susi, my parents tried desperately to obtain **certificates to go to Palestine. In order to cover all eventualities, they registered also for** *Aliyah Bet.* This was what the British considered illegal immigration whilst the Yishuv (the then resident Jewish community) called it "extra-legal" because of all the impossible restrictions at that time. The British held the League of Nations mandate for Palestine and had severely restricted entry permits into Israel in spite of their undertaking to the League to establish a Jewish Homeland at the time when they were granted the Mandate over Palestine – hence the so-called illegal immigration.

Kindertransport

My parents then made superhuman efforts to find a solution for my 10-year-old sister, Dorle, and for me. They managed to have us accepted for the *Kindertransport* to England which, from Poland at least, was organized, largely, to the best of my knowledge, by the Polish Jewish Refugee Committee. By that time the British Authorities had been persuaded to issue 10,000 entry permits for children from the danger zones in Europe to come to Britain, provided the necessary sponsors in Britain were available. We were lucky to be accepted – my 'little' sister and I.

The central assembly point for the limited number of children from Poland was the small town of Otwock, not far from Warsaw. My father took us to Warsaw – first me only because my sister's acceptance had been delayed for some reason. He brought her a week or two later. I am not sure if we were met in Warsaw by someone from the Refugee Committee or whether our father took us all the way to Otwock, probably the latter. I do recall, most distinctly, that there were large posters all over the station in Warsaw, as well as constant loudspeaker announcements, about general mobilization. I must confess that, young as we were, both my sister aged 10, and I, all of 12 years old, were very frightened.

However, this was not the dominant emotion which was rather the feeling of distress about the imminent parting with our parents for an indefinite and unknown time. I cannot imagine, even now, the emotions flooding our parents at the thought of having to send away their two young ones, not being able to visualize the immediate future. However, they kept reassuring us that they would soon be in Palestine and would have us join them as soon as possible. I believe both my little sister and I clung to this hope – perhaps we wanted it to be so, and believed it would be so, such was the confidence we always had in our parents.

In Otwock we met many children – we were about a hundred, I believe – some were known to us, many not, but as children usually do, we quickly found common ground. I recall a rather amusing occurrence - to me, at least, although not to at least one other, the victim, involved in the incident. One of the boys dropped his watch and something went wrong inside. He was, naturally, very upset. Before he could find or take it to a watch repairer another boy said to him "let me see – I am sure I can repair it". When asked to explain, he told the gathered crowd that his uncle, here in Poland where the boy had spent the last 10 months after his own deportation from Germany, had a watch repair business. His uncle took him to his business almost daily and started to teach him "the business". In addition, he had made for his nephew a complete set of watchmaker tools – in miniature – which the boy promptly produced and displayed for all to see. Imagine the "oohs" and "ahs" of admiration and wonder.

The boy with the broken watch, relieved that he would have his precious possession back almost immediately, handed the watch to our young 'genius' for his immediate attention. With all of us forming a circle around the couple – watch owner and watch repairer – the 'genius' went to work. He opened the back of the watch, carefully took out each little part – spring, wheels, casing, everything. He then fiddled about a bit. I could not see what he did and I believe none of the boys could. He then tried to put back the pieces he had taken out. One, two, three – this in the right place, others maybe not. In other words, it was easy to dismantle the time-piece, but to put it back together was an entirely different story.

He managed to gather everything together, not necessarily in their correct places, picked all up in both hands, handed the pieces to the owner with the words, and I quote: "There is something wrong with your watch. You had better take it to a watchmaker."

We all first gasped, then roared with laughter, except the watch owner, of course. That no murder was committed that day was only the result of us all physically restraining the injured party – although we all sympathized with him.

Soon after this incident we were told that our four weeks waiting was about to end. For Dorle, the time in Otwock was less then three weeks, my father having brought her to join me a week after he had taken me to the assembly point. We were almost on our way, together with the few adults who were our *madrichim* (guides) and who accompanied us on the train from Otwock, via Warsaw, to Gdynia, and actually accompanied us all the way to England.

It was now nearing the end of August 1939. The *SS Warszawa*, Poland's largest passenger liner – or so I was told – awaited us in Gdynia. I think we, about seventy of us now still in Otwock, were all anxious to get on with it and face the adventure awaiting us. Having said good bye to our parents – to our mother still in Krakow and to our father in Otwock – we now began to actually feel the separation, I think my little sister more than I. I think back now and reach the conclusion that I must have been a rather thoughtless and shallow boy. Or was this a way of protecting myself from this almost heartbreaking episode in our life? What my parents felt I can only guess at now that I'm so much older and having myself become a parent.

78

Kindertransport group in Otwock

I think all of us; Benno, Herbert, Jack (Booby) Reich and his sister Helene, and really all these almost seventy children on the boat with us choked back the tears for as long as we could. I will only add here that three of the 70 children had to be left in Otwock because no sponsor's certificates were received for them in time. I am pleased, however, to be able to record that my friend Herbert who still lives in London and whom I mentioned above told me a while ago that by the merest chance he met the three who had fortunately survived the holocaust. How they recognized one another after all these years only the Almighty knows!

England here we come

We boarded the *SS Warshawa* on August the 25[t],1939 and set sail on the same day. That was exactly one week before Hitler and his hordes invaded Poland . We soon settled in, and were on our way to our new life. On leaving the port we crowded the railings to get a last glimpse of the land where we had left our parents. Apart from the adventure awaiting us was this feeling of confusion – when would we be reunited with our loved ones, especially when would we see our parents again?

As the ship came around, preparing to leave the harbour, we all saw a huge German battleship, already standing at the ready, outside the Polish port. This, we were told, was the battleship *Konigsberg*, its huge guns already trained on little Poland whose army consisted mainly of cavalry, in addition to the poorly armed infantry. I don't know if they, the Poles, had tanks or something of an Air Force. Recorded history of the time informs us that the Germans just rolled over everything, bombed unprotected cities into oblivion and just gave free reign to their natural barbarism. Not for nothing did the Romans refer to the Germanic tribes as "The Barbarians".

But enough of this for now at least. We will, no doubt, return to this again, later in this tale. So, we boarded our vessel of escape, as it turned out, and began our adventure to a new life. We spent four days on the high seas traversing the Baltic Sea, the North Sea, and the Straits of Dover. We skirted Malmo, Rostock, Copenhagen, and Goteborg, Amsterdam and other ports on the route, not being close enough to see any of them. We sailed through the Skagerrak, survived the Kattegat and sailed through the North Sea as far as the English Channel. At last we arrived in England. The seas had been extremely rough and we were all too sea-sick to notice what went on around us. Most, if not all of us, vomited again and again. Every time the ship heaved, so did we.

However, all *good* (and less good) things come to an end and so did our ordeal! Upon arrival, we were rewarded with a wonderful sight that we witnessed as our ship sailed up the Thames Estuary. We watched the raising of the arms of Tower Bridge before coming to anchor just a short distance before the bridge. I don't recall the name of the wharf where we wound-up, but it gave us an excellent view of the iconic Tower of London.

81

We were all surprised, naturally, more by the opening and raising of the bridge than the imposing sight of the Tower of London – which was, of course, a sight never before seen by any of us. I am inclined to believe that none of us had ever heard the history of the tower. We were most impressed and could hardly take our eyes off the bridge and the tower as we slowly descended the gangplank to the dock. We each carried the small suitcase or other container with all we owned in this world. After being ushered onto buses we drove off to our first destination in England: The Jewish Shelter.

The *Jewish Shelter* was a haven in London's East End. This place had been the first stop of many Jewish immigrants, searching for a better life, who found their first shelter in England for a century or more when arriving from Russia, Poland and other European countries where pogroms and Jew-baiting and persecution was rife and where life for many had just become unbearable.

This is my Entry Permit to Great Britain with the Kindertransport on August 29, 1939 – just 3 days before Hitler's Nazi hordes crashed into Poland.

4/002   9786

This document of identity is issued with the approval of His Majesty's Government in the United Kingdom to young persons to be admitted to the United Kingdom for educational purposes under the care of the Inter-Aid Committee for children.

THIS DOCUMENT REQUIRES NO VISA.

11104

PERSONAL PARTICULARS.

Name KESSLER, Bernard

Sex Male   Date of Birth 13-7-27.

Place LEIPZIG.

Full Names and Address of Parents
KESSLER, Abraham Hirsz & Sima
Jochwed
Rekawka 4,
KRAKOW/Poland.

The East End of London was the area where most Jews had concentrated when first arriving in London. Many, perhaps even most, have since moved to other parts of London and indeed to other cities in Britain and the world. But here, in the Shelter, under the management of the able and really kind Mr Gedalia, we were fed and made comfortable.

That same day, and for two days following, one child after another disappeared, having been collected by the families who had sponsored them with the authorities in Britain. Other families came to choose one of the refugee children and take them to their homes. In such a way my sister, Dorle, was taken and put on a train to Nottingham to be met, eventually, by a family there. But that is her tale. I don't want to encroach. She has just started writing her own memoirs.

I must just add that she was put on the train to Nottingham alone while her 12 year-old brother was left in the Shelter, two very young children in a strange land. A 10-year old child, newly arrived in a strange country, not speaking a word of English. She was, however, expected to be met at the station of her destination. Owing to a 'misunderstanding' she was not met, she told me, and this will most probably appear in the memoirs she herself is writing, that she arrived at the station in Nottingham. Everyone alighted and the station emptied. Not finding anyone she made her way to the waiting room – which was already dark – sat down and cried. A policeman appeared, saw this little girl of ten and asked her what the matter was. He spoke to her in English which she could not understand; through her tears she spoke to him in German which, of course, he could not understand.

Outside the station was a car where a priest was collecting his family. They, fortunately, had with them a German maid. The policeman asked them to help with this little refugee girl. After a few questions the priest offered to take her to his home until things were sorted out. Coming from a religious Jewish home Dorle was not too happy about this but eventually agreed to go with them, including the policeman, I believe. From the priest's house they telephoned, again and again, to the people who were to be Dorle's Jewish foster parents.

Eventually everything was sorted out. But it was a harrowing experience for such a young girl and, no doubt, left its mark on her. What I am particularly unable to comprehend even now is why, in heaven's name, was it necessary to part two young children such as we were – bearing in mind the circumstances which brought us to England - instead of finding one home for both of us. As I already said this is her history and I will not encroach on it further except where it interleaves with mine.

Similarly, my brother Zalel's story is his and my sister Susi's is hers. Sadly she, Susi, is no longer with us and will not be able to write about her life. However I have written a paragraph or so above highlighting some of the events in her life and I am sure my remaining sibling (we are now in the month of May, 2018, and we have since also lost my brother, Bezalel) will no doubt include passages relating to our deceased sister in their own biographical reminiscences. Bezalel, I know, did write his memoirs of which I have a copy.

So, we are left at the Jewish Shelter some 2-3 days before the outbreak of World War II. I don't recall how many of us remained, but at this point we were attached to the appropriate classes of the Jews Free School whose children were all being evacuated to the countryside. This evacuation process of 1,500,000 children from the larger cities in Britain was code-named by the British authorities "Operation Pied Piper". It was done to keep the children out of harm's way in the face of the imminently expected onslaught of the mighty German war machine.

Our destination was the peaceful and pastoral country town of Ely, principal town of the Isle of Ely of Hereward the Wake fame and the memory of the Norman invasion of England in the year 1066 by William the Conqueror. It was a lovely little town near Cambridge and was the seat of a most beautiful cathedral, of which a little more later in this tale.

On arrival we were dispersed (billeted) among the local population most of whom, until our arrival, had never met a Jew or knew that we were people just like they. This did not prevent their most generous display of kindness, of taking us all, particularly the refugee children, to their hearts. Together with another refugee boy, Benno, who I think had been with us in Otwock and had come to England a little before us, I was taken in by Mr. & Mrs Crowley, a couple who had no children of their own, I believe, but who owned a confectionery shop. Anyway, here we were, in this house of non-Jews, bewitched, bothered, and very much bewildered. I believe we arrived there on Friday, September 1st – the same day that the might of the Nazi onslaught on Poland began.

Although I was not aware of it at the time, Neville Chamberlain, the British Prime Minister, together with the then Prime Minister of France, Eduard Daladier, sent an ultimatum to Hitler demanding the immediate withdrawal of all German forces from Poland. They should of course have done this earlier in the year when Hitler annexed Czechoslovakia, or perhaps even at the time of the 'Anschluss' of Austria in 1938, instead of waving the paper to the crowd and exclaiming "Peace in our time" on his return from a meeting with Hitler after that event. Many are of the opinion that the war might have been avoided had the ultimatum been given before the Austrian Anschluss and thus even avoided the Holocaust,

Hitler, as could have been expected, ignored the ultimatum and his Blitzkrieg, the first in history, steamrollered on. For me this meant sitting down to lunch on Sunday September the 3rd, with my non-Jewish foster parents and hearing Neville Chamberlain, the Prime Minister of the United Kingdom – what, in fact, still was The British Empire - announce that since 48 hours had elapsed following the German invasion of Poland and Hitler's ignoring of the Anglo-French demand for their withdrawal, a state of war now existed with Germany.

During this lunch I had my first, direct, encounter with *treifa* (non-kosher) meat. Our very kind land-lady cut up the meat into thin slices to make eating easier for me. As I said already, I knew no English and could not explain. So, I pronged a piece onto the fork, lifted the fork to my mouth, but as the fork neared my lips I was overcome by a strong feeling of nausea and had to rush out to the back yard and actually vomited.

At that exact time, we heard the first sirens – the up and down wailing which were termed Air Raid Warnings – of the war. I have a vague memory of an explosion some distance away. We were told later that since there was an airfield not far away this was the Nazis' first attempt to bomb Britain into submission.

85

Coming back to the lunch table I could not explain to my very concerned hostess that I was not actually ill. My English language was, of course, still non-existent. Fortunately, my fellow refugee child, Benno, who was more than three years older than I, was able to explain, in very broken English and by gesturing with his hands, that I was a vegetarian, and my adherence to this form of diet. To this day, incidentally, I maintain a strictly kosher home. After this episode our hostess – nay foster-mother – made sure I received only vegetarian food.

EVACUATED BOYS AND THEIR ELY BENEFACTRESS.

[Starr & Rignall

they arrived in Ely in September, 1939, Mrs. Knowles, wife of the Vicar of Ely, has taken a he welfare of boys of the Jews' Free School. In this recent picture of them, she is seated he group. The Headmaster (Dr. E. Bernste and c r members of the staff are also

Our Hostel in Ely

The Jewish organizations in London were meanwhile busy trying to find a solution to the problem of the refugee children, many of whom were orthodox and kosher eating. Somehow the Pastor of Ely Church, which was opposite Ely Cathedral, The Reverent Hinton Knowles, and particularly his wife, heard of our predicament. Together with the active

86

participation of Dr. Enoch Bernstein, Headmaster of the Jews' Free School, the Reverend and Mrs. Knowles found a building which was put at the disposal of the School for all the refugee children. This building became to all intents and purposes not only our hostel but rather our home and our school, during our sojourn in Ely.

A rabbi, or Reverend, became our live-in housemaster, together with his family – including two sons and a daughter, his wife being the 'House-Mother'. His name Mr. Kon, or possibly Spiro – I am not sure to this day. We referred to him as "Rabbi" although I was never sure that he had *semicha*, the formal confirmation of this rabbinical status.

My recollection of those far off days is somewhat hazy and may appear rather confused. I recall receiving pocket money in the princely amount of 3 or 4 pence – I don't remember if that was per month or week. I fancy it was the former. This was in the pre-decimal days when there were 12 *old* pence to a shilling and 20 shillings to the pound. However, some time later, when I was appointed to fulfil certain duties, my pocket money was increased to a whole shilling. This had to serve for everything a child needed or wanted: sweets, liquorish, cinema occasionally and, above all, stamps to write to my parents and to my siblings. This means not just stamps to Nottingham where my little sister was, but also international stamps to my parents in Poland and to Palestine where I had a brother and sister, as well as other relatives.

In mentioning going to the cinema I must confess my delinquent tendencies. We discovered a way of sneaking in from the back, through which patrons generally left after the show. This was left open frequently and we used this opportunity every chance which presented itself, no matter what category the film was. As to the stamps, I blush in embarrassment to relate that my little sister found it necessary to send me stamps or international money orders (I don't remember exactly what they were called) to enable me to write to her as well as to the rest of the family. I had not, of course, asked her to do this but she felt it necessary to do so. I tried later to compensate her and hope I succeeded in some measure. But that is for a little later in this story. We must progress with some of my recollections – limited as they are.

The refugee boys resident in the hostel in our Succah in Ely

Chanukah 1939 was soon upon us and celebrated in the appropriate manner, although this again was my first Chanuccah away from my family – thinking about this now makes me realize that the origin of this festival too was an attempt to destroy us, thwarted fortunately by the Hasmoneans led by Judah the Macabee.

Purim 1940 followed. I don't recall if we dressed up as was the tradition for Jewish children on that festival. But here too was another attempt to destroy us. We seem to encounter a 'Haman" (the villain of the Purim story) in every generation. Thankfully they are unsuccessful.

Pesach 1940 – my first Pesach away from home and family – was a particularly saddening occasion. Add to the separation from our families what it says in the *haggadah* service on *seder* night: *'bechol dor vador omdim aleinu lechaloteinu'* which loosely translated says "in every generation are those who rise up to destroy us."

Shavuot 1940 – I recall strange feelings which cannot really be described here. All these festivals - without our parents for the first time; it was not easy to get accustomed to the new circumstances in our lives. Then, still without my family, on Friday, the 13th of July 1940 I became 13 years old – the equivalent Hebrew date was Tammuz, 13th

88

5687 which that year fell on the same day. According to Jewish tradition I became *Bar-Mitzvah*, responsible for my own actions. In other words, I became a man, obligated in my own right to fulfil all the mitzvot (commandments). Until that time this yoke was borne by my father.

Our rabbi looked up the charts and found that the portion of the Torah on the Shabbat following my 13th birthday according to the Hebrew calendar was parshat *Balak*. It was customary for the Bar-Mitzvah boy to be called to the reading of the Torah on the first such occasion following reaching that date. How I worked and slaved to learn the whole *sidra (parsha)*, which I would climax with an outstanding *maftir* and *haftora*. Imagine my consternation when it was discovered about a week before the great occasion that my Bar Mitzva portion was in fact *Pinchas*, one week later.

I was, however, determined to recite at least the maftir (the last section) and haftora (the additional reading) and made superhuman efforts, staying up late at night, in order to learn it and recite it on the day. However, I was more ambitious. I wanted, on that ever so important day of my life, to recite from the *Sefer Torah* as much of my *sidra/parsha* as I could memorize. I redoubled my efforts to learn as much as possible, practicing each section by section from the last towards the beginning. I did not succeed to complete all the *parsha* but was able to read, if I really remember and this is not wishful thinking after the event, more than half, the latter part, of the Sidra/parsha – and very well did I acquit myself too.

My major regret was not the lack of presents on the occasion but rather the absence of my family, especially my parents, and friends. Even my little sister Dorle was unable to join me. I assume we did have some sort of a celebration but nothing of note which sticks in my mind.

And so, life continued. By that time, I had naturally acquired a good knowledge of the language of the land in which I lived, and it struck me, suddenly, that I ought to write my personal memoirs. I took one of my empty exercise books, drew a line halfway down, wrote on the top half in English –"My Story" by Bernhardt Kessler, and the same in German on the bottom half, "Meine Geschichte" by Bernhardt Kessler.

89

I filled the first page in both English and German. Well, you guessed correctly: there it ended – my fascinating autobiography.

So now, many years later, under pressure from various members of my family, I am finally putting on paper the personal history of Bernard Kessler – at least as much of it as I remember - this time in English only. If I can gather enough strength and inspiration to translate it into Hebrew or maybe have it translated by one of my children I may yet do so. I now regret not having persevered at the time when I still had, fresh in my mind, my life up to the time we reached England and which, at my age, is no longer remembered.

Our school went to considerable lengths to find ways to divert our thoughts from our personal situation, alone in a strange country, among strangers, in wartime conditions, worrying about our families – parents, siblings, aunts, uncles, cousins and so on. My recollection of that time is that letters, or indeed any notifications about the life of other members of the family, were extremely scarce. While my parents were still in the ghetto in Krakow, they wrote fairly regularly – it's a pity that I saved so few of the letters – letters addressed to both my sister, Dorle, and to me. I imagine I usually sent them on to Dorle – not that I remember this distinctly.

From my family in Palestine, letters were also fairly sporadic – maybe because I was such a desultory correspondent myself. As to friends from my schooldays in Leipzig – strangely there simply were very few with me in Ely, as far as I remember. This was compensated for by other friends with whom I came from Otwock and those I made in the hostel in Ely. I do wish I knew what happened to all my schoolfellows from Leipzig. Some must surely have reached England, the USA, Israel and/or other parts of the world.

The main school's effort, therefore, was to find suitable and numerous distractions to occupy our minds. We were introduced to pottery, with all the proper equipment, including a kiln, proper tools, turntables, etc. We were initiated into making tiles, pots, vases and other items. They were then put into the kiln, and when ready and cooled we painted them in many ways, glazed them and again had them put in the kiln to complete our 'artistic' endeavours. When not occupied with pottery we were doing basketry – that is, learning to weave and fashion baskets of various kinds, shapes and sizes. We were taught drawing and painting – I was never very good at that.

When it came to sports, I was more in my element. At some stage I became the reserve goalkeeper for our team – and I was pretty good; but the actual goalie, Lustig, was better, I admit it. When I eventually joined the team, my main position was forward inside left, where I was very good – even if I say so myself. The football team at that time was set up as follows: goalie, two backs (defenders), then three midfield players (called half-backs) and five forwards – outside right; inside right; centre forward; inside left (me); outside left. We played against other schools and did not do too badly, even against the best of them.

Once a year we held Sports Day, where we competed against one another. This included high jump (at which I was good), long jump (at which I was not) and running. I was not particularly good at sprinting, but I did rather well as a middle-distance runner, especially the one mile. I can't recall if we had the discus or javelin. We did have boxing and I was paired with a tallish, lanky boy called Lesley Weinreb. Obviously, I had hoped to win the bout, but no, quite early in our match – in Round One to be precise - he landed a punch on my nose, which brought tears to my eyes. and so ended my boxing career.

One more incident I must mention, describing the growing maturity of this young male. On the day of our evacuation from London when at Liverpool Street station boarding the train with our gas mask slung over our shoulders, we saw that a large group of school-uniformed girls also got on the train. These were the girls of the Central Girls Secondary (or High) School, as I believe it was called, who were also bound for Ely and the neighbourhood. At that time, they held no particular interest for me – I was only 12 years old and rather slow and shy – but in the fullness of time one does grow both physically and emotionally. My friends and I made a habit of sitting on the wall at the back of the garden of our house in Ely at the time that the girls went home from their school and ogled and ogled and ogled. What strange feelings went through us I can only imagine now – we were, after all growing boys and they were growing girls – and hormones are hormones. There was naturally no actual contact – they were usually chaperoned – but we could dream, couldn't we? This, too, helped to distract us from our actual situation.

91

Our school arranged other distractions under the guise of civics lesson. In addition to a spate of civics lectures on a variety of subjects, we were taken to the local Police Station where the workings of the police were explained to us - the same with the Fire Service, Hospital Service and Town Hall. We were invited to visit the very beautiful Ely cathedral and had the Vicar himself show us around and explain everything. This was a most interesting and enlightening lesson in both English history and Gothic architecture - bringing us back to the Norman conquest and the implacable resistance to William the Conqueror's invasion of England by Hereward the Wake.

Talking of Ely cathedral reminds me that not only was the cathedral itself both beautiful and interesting, but it had in front of it a very large and beautiful expanse of green lawn. This is the place where a friend taught me to ride a bicycle – not important, but nice to remember. Every time I fell down – and I did so often in the beginning – I fell onto soft grass rather than asphalt. Lucky me!

What may still be worth mentioning is the extensive interest in music at our school (and hostel). First let me tell you, dear reader, that we had a Pierrot Troupe under the able guidance of our music and gymnastics master (what an interesting combination) Mr. H. H. Josephs. I regret to this day that I was not a member of this troupe. He organized performances in Ely and on tours to the villages surrounding Ely with the greatest success. The area as a whole was named the Fenland because in the relative distant past it consisted of swamps surrounding 'terra firma', hence the Isle of Ely. The swamps had been drained and the area given over to farms and orchards – particularly tasty apples called Cox's Orange Pippin - as well as to very pretty villages all around.

Mr. Joseph was also the initiator, organizer, producer, director, musical director and piano accompanist of operettas, principally of Gilbert and Sullivan – such as: The Pirates of Penzance, HMS Pinafore, The Mikado and others - performed by pupils of the school, myself included. In addition, he composed the music to the libretto written by another JFS teacher, Mr S. M. Rich, called *The Pirates Lair* which we - again yours truly included - performed a number of times with great success. Some of the melodies, and words, still linger fondly in my memory.

The sponsor of one of the boys, a wealthy man it would seem, wanted his 'charge' to enter for the matriculation examination and paid for extra tuition to prepare the boy for that examination. Apparently, he was persuaded that it would be more appropriate to support, at the same time, several other boys as well, since the school was not in a position to allocate a teacher for special lessons to one boy only. He agreed and left the choice of the other boys to our class teacher, Mr. Bernard Cousins. I suppose I was not among the worst of the pupils since I was one of the fortunate choices of our teacher and entered the special stream – 10 children – which benefited from additional lessons towards the examination for the much - coveted Certificate of Education. He paired us, two by two, and we worked together like that at a much faster pace than the rest of the class. We also had additional classes to make up what we lacked till then, since the examinations were approaching fairly rapidly.

Talking about our teacher, Mr. Cousins, affords me the opportunity to add a little praise about this wonderful man. It was always possible to come to him with any special, individual problem any of us may have had, and we had many as can be imagined. More than that, he took it upon himself to take us, in small groups, to visit nearby Cambridge. His aim, at least in part I am sure, was to show us the place we might strive to reach and thus encourage us to study harder.

His main purpose however was, I believe, to distract us and make us forget our personal sorrows for a little while, at least, by taking us boating (I think it was called punting, with one long pole, not with oars) on the river Cam. Before that we usually toured some of the renowned colleges, to let us see where we might land up – if we were sufficiently diligent and intelligent of course. After the boating he took us to 'high tea', with cakes and biscuits and very thin watercress sandwiches, before returning to Ely. I must stress that to the best of my knowledge these outings were all conducted at his own personal expense. As I said, he was a wonderful man.

I had, by now, reached the age of 14+ and this seemed to present a problem for those who were supporting me financially. Now, there's the rub...

The year was already 1942 and I was more than halfway to my 15th birthday. The Committee which paid for my upkeep decided that rather than continuing my education it was time I learned a trade by which I might earn my livelihood. So, they took me from the hostel in Ely, never mind that I was studying for the Certificate of Education, brought me to London when I was almost 15 years - minus 6 to 8 weeks – that is still 14 years old – and helped me find accommodation and work. In fact, I was handed over – so to speak – to the care of the Jewish Board of Guardians (the title says it all). Here I met my 'supervisor, advisor may be a better description - Mr. Gee – who was a very kind and helpful person, I realize on reflection. Let me explain the process. Mr. Gee found me a room with a Jewish family to whom I paid one – pound sterling a week from my very meagre wages for rent and 'keep' – i.e. meals which I hope, think and believe were kosher. I imagine the 'Committee' must have supplemented the payment.

I was then again brought to see Mr. Gee, since The Jewish Board of Guardians was the leading organization doling out help, support and guidance for needy and poor Jews. Here I was offered various opportunities concerning available work at that time, received recommendations and was advised where to go.

The first offer was to a Bristle & Brush maker's workshop. This did not appeal to me at all and I declined graciously, I hope. The other choice with which I was presented was to be apprenticed to a Cabinet-maker – not an ordinary carpenter, you understand, but a creator of quality furniture. Learning to make such quality furniture sounded quite appealing, after all, my brother had been on a carpentry *hachshara* in Germany some years before. So off I went early the following morning to my new assignment. The boss, or maybe the foreman, received me graciously, seated me on a stool, presented me with a longish plank of wood and some sheets of sandpaper, and showed me how to sandpaper the wood correctly – you had to 'study' the grain and work with it – not against it. The plank I was working on was not small, and there was plenty of sandpaper, so I spent the whole day on this project.

Need I explain that by the time I went to my new home my right arm – and my left, for that matter – ached rather a lot. Still, to learn an interesting trade required sacrifice, patience and perseverance. I was prepared for that. I quite looked forward to my next lesson in this fascinating trade. Although much was happening to me in a short time, I slept rather well. I was, naturally, very tired – but I don't recall if or what I dreamed that night. I got up early the next morning, devoured my breakfast, and trotted off eagerly to work. Entering the workshop, I put on my apron and asked for my next task. Imagine my consternation on being given the same plank of wood and told to continue sandpapering it. I had no choice but to comply. This went on for the whole week at the end of which I had had enough of cabinetmaking. I told them I would not return the following week – so much for patience and persevering.

I realize now, having experienced a little more of life that perhaps I should have demonstrated a little more staying power, or *sitzfleisch* as we called it. My decision to cease my attempt to become a cabinetmaker necessitated my return to the Board of Guardians to ask them to find me other gainful employment. The only other occupation offered me was with a firm of handbag makers. So, I trotted off to that establishment and here they really began to teach me the trade, from the word Go! I worked at that place till early 1945. Having enlisted in October of 1944 I was finally called to the colours, as it was termed, early in 1945 – but more of that later.

I now turn to a description of my new home and family – the Kaye family – and my life at that time. The Kaye family was an average Jewish working class/lower-middle class family consisting of husband (working), wife (housewife), one (or was it two) sons and one daughter (Phyllis). I don't much remember the sons but the daughter was younger than I (although not much) and, therefore, still in school. They were very kind people and shared their home and life with me trying to make me part of the family so I would feel more at home. After work, we ate the evening meal together and then socialized – that is, talked, played cards or monopoly, sometimes went to the cinema together.

I went on my first 'date' with the daughter, who by that time was around 14 years old and quite pretty. She decided to be on the safe side with such a Romeo as I, or so she imagined me to be, and brought along her friend as chaperone. Thus, I was on a date, my first ever, with two girls at the same time, having one arm round the shoulder of one and the other round the shoulder of the other. This was an experiment which I never repeated. My room was not big but quite pleasant, and I did not share it with anyone. This was already a new experience, much to my liking. However, I yearned for familiar young faces, of friends with a similar background.

I soon found other children who had been in Ely, most of whom had joined one of the Jewish clubs or Youth Movements. I found friends who had joined the Zionist Youth Movement – Habonim. Since I came from a Zionist-oriented family, I quite naturally joined this group also. They were not religiously oriented, but they were not anti-religious either. We usually met once a week, at least, and learned about the movement, about Palestine, about the return to our ancient homeland, and about the kibbutzim with which our movement was affiliated. We learned about the pride of returning to the land as farmers – which some of my friends eventually found attractive and practiced.

My workplace also made demands on my time and effort – as a result of the demands of the war. When still in Ely there were, of course, not infrequent Air Raid warnings. I had mentioned earlier that at least one airfield was in the vicinity and was regularly targeted by the Luftwaffe. This kind of disturbance, if I may so describe it, was much more frequent, even regular – may I say nightly – in London. First, German bomber planes in fairly large numbers, although nothing like the 1000 bomber raids launched on German cities later by the allies. Then came their dive-bombers. One heard the whistle and screech as the planes dived towards their targets, a rather spine-chilling sound, raining down on us not only explosives but also incendiary bombs, which caused many widespread fires.

Eventually, I think it was in 1944, we were also treated to Hitler's first secret weapon. The V1 and V2 rockets, Werner von Braun's invention, 'rained' down on us. He, Hitler, was not yet in a position – thank the Almighty – to threaten us with nuclear weapons on which the Germans, as well as the allies, were working. The V1 and V2 rockets caused much damage and were especially terrifying since they could not be heard approaching as the large bombers and lighter dive bombers could. One could not anticipate when the rocket's engine would stop and the rocket sweep down on you. This was so swift that there was hardly time to take shelter. To help cope with this curse, people working in factories were enlisted for night duty to minimize the damage caused by this scourge. I too volunteered to help and was on duty every other night, more or less, on the roof of the building where I worked. We had buckets, some filled with water, some with sand, and a kind of paddle with which to beat out any flames resulting from a falling incendiary bomb.

I am glad to say that none fell on my building – at least not when I was on duty. I could see, over the rooftops, the havoc caused by Goering's Luftwaffe's daily onslaught on London – burning and destroyed houses, buildings reduced to rubble in many areas of the city. I don't need to mention the obvious dead and injured of which there were many – too many. In retrospect I can only admire the fortitude of the average Londoner, from every stratum of society, including the royal family, and all our determination not to surrender to despair and abandon this capital city to the barbarians. I can even give myself a pat on the back – for I, too, felt like that.

Although I heard only rarely from my siblings, Zal and Susi, who were both in Palestine, I heard even more rarely from my parents who had been left in Poland, first the Ghetto in Krakow, then the camps – first Plaszow, then, as far as we know, Auschwitz - at least my mother. We have less information about the fate of my father – not the where, nor the when or how.

My *little* sister, Dorle, and I maintained contact. As we had not seen each other since being so thoughtlessly parted on our first arrival in London, we both had a longing to see each other again. So, when I was 16 years old, in the summer of 1943, and she 14, I brought her to London for a week's holiday. I was able to lodge her at the Jewish hostel which all the youth movements used for their meetings and other social activities. I still remember the address: 72, Cazenove Road, N16, I think. My memory not being what it was, I don't remember all we did during that week. However, among other things, I showed her the sights of London, including Regents Park, Hyde Park, St. James' Park, Trafalgar Square, Whitehall, the Houses of Parliament, the Thames river, Buckingham Palace, London Zoo, Madame Tussauds. Was it here that we looked at our misshapen bodies in the Hall of Mirrors: all was contorted in so many amusing ways – really very hilarious.

97

I don't remember if we went to Greenwich, but we did go to see a ballet. I think it was at the Opera House in Covent Garden, but I can't remember which ballet. It could have been Swan Lake, Giselle, Sleeping Beauty or The Nutcracker Suit – maybe even La Fille Mal Garde. It didn't really matter. Whichever it was, we must have enjoyed it tremendously. As to the selection listed above, they are all ballets that I have seen at one time or another – if not with Dorle, then at some other time with Marion, my wife and/or our children, Simone, David and Naomi. Dorle, may remember more and remind me later: she always had a much better memory than I. If she does, she may include it in her memoirs. I just remember it was so good to see her and be with her, for even such a brief interlude.

The Jewish Brigade

Jews served in the armies of all the allies – Britain, France, America, Russia and all other representative units, like the Dutch, Belgians, Polish, and Czechs. From Palestine too several thousand volunteers served with the Allies, as part of regular British Army units. This was despite the British White Paper of 1939 which limited entry permits to Palestine to Jews – including those trying to escape from the Nazis. Some died by drowning, while making the attempt to reach Palestine, when they were stopped by British warships. Others died at the hands of the Nazis on being turned back to whence they came, because they had nowhere else to go. But neither this, nor the fact that Jews from Europe were giving their loyal service in the war against the Nazis, could persuade the British Colonial Authorities to relent.

In Palestine itself the Jewish Agency which was the representative body of the *Yishuv* – the Jewish community settled in Palestine – had been urging the British Authorities to allow the special units recruited in Palestine to serve, and fight, under their own flag and emblem. The Palestine Regiment, as it was called, consisting of three battalions of Jewish Palestinian infantry and support units, was eager and willing to serve the British war effort despite the severe restrictions on the number of Jewish newcomers to the country.

The Authorities had so far refused on the grounds that the Arab residents of Palestine would object, be hurt, etc and thus might influence the Arab countries in the area against the war effort. After all, Field Marshall Rommel and his Africa Corps were rampaging across Africa, while the Mufti of Jerusalem lived extremely well in Berlin under Adolf Hitler's protection. David Ben-Gurion, Chairman of the Jewish Agency, summed it up in these words: "We will fight the White Paper as if there is no war, and fight the war as if there is no White Paper."

However, in 1944, Winston Churchill, an ardent Zionist – withstanding the political pressure from his own Foreign and Commonwealth Office – finally acceded to the request. He explained his decision by stating that the people who had suffered most, and were still suffering most, at the hands of the Nazi slaughterers had a moral right to fight their most brutal enemy under their own flag and emblem.

Thus, the Jewish Brigade was born, named in translation into English: the Jewish Fighting Force. It was an independent unit of the British army, fighting under its own flag. The unit was to be a Brigade Group – hence the name the Jewish Brigade –comprising some 5000+ men, based on the three battalions of the Palestine regiment, supplemented by artillery, transport, engineering and other supporting units. Soldiers serving already in units of the British army were permitted to apply for transfer to the Brigade and the Jewish Agency office in Britain was allowed to recruit volunteers for that unit. Altogether over 300 soldiers serving in the Brigade came from Britain and, I am proud to say, yours truly among them.

I registered with the Jewish Agency in the autumn of 1944, a month or so after my 17th birthday, but was only inducted into the army on March 1[st,] 1945. This was still nearly 4½ months before my 18th birthday. My friends and I underwent basic training of 5 - 6 weeks, as I recall. We were then granted 12 days embarkation leave, even before our advanced battalion training, and were put aboard a troopship on our way to Italy and what remained of the war. I don't remember at which port or the name of the ship. I tend to think we boarded the vessel somewhere on the west coast of Scotland – why else was the journey to Italy so long.

Boy was I young! Imagine the feeling full of joy and anticipation at the prospect of at last "having a go" at those brutal Nazis. I am not sure, now, in retrospect, that I am not somewhat glad, perhaps lucky, to have been spared the field of battle. Who knows now what the outcome for me personally may have been? Still, even now I would feel a satisfaction if I had had the opportunity to "have a go" at our mortal enemy.

The author in the Jewish Brigade

Anyway, here we are on this huge troopship carrying 2000 troops of various units sailing through the English Channel and the Bay of Biscay. The sea was not quiet, to put it mildly – the Bay of Biscay was well known to sailors for its turbulence – and it was not only the boat which was heaving. Even just thinking about it now makes me feel somewhat queasy. If my memory does not betray me completely, we were on that vessel a whole week. It took us past the Rock of Gibraltar where we were given several hours shore leave to enable us to visit the Rock. In our stroll, we saw both the ravens and the Barbary Apes. Legend has it that as long as these creatures remain resident on The Rock the British Empire will endure.

To our immense relief we found that the Mediterranean Sea was considerably calmer than the Atlantic Ocean and the Bay of Biscay. We provided our own entertainment; I expect to keep us busy and save us from boredom and thoughts of what lay ahead of us – primarily what was happening to our people, including our own families left behind in the Europe from which we had originally come. Then – I think it was a day before reaching our port of disembarkation in the very south of Italy - the Germans finally surrendered. The date was May 8th, 1945. Our joy was beyond description although for many of us – especially those destined for the Jewish Brigade – a feeling of frustration, mingled with the elation we all felt, because it prevented us from 'having a go' at the murderers ourselves.

Anyway, the senior officers on board decided on an extended celebration, inviting every unit to present some form of entertainment: songs, be they individual or group; recitations; sketches; and whatever one could think of. We too, of the Jewish Brigade, regaled a shipload of over 2000 troops with our Hebrew songs. I remember distinctly that we were received with tumultuous applause. At that time we, obviously, were still "personae grata".

Well the next day we landed, at the bottom of the Boot of Italy – possibly the port of Brindisi, or maybe Bari? I don't *think* it was Naples, but I am not really sure, it might have been. Nor do I remember whether we were in a camp there for a day or two, or if we boarded two-ton or three-ton lorries immediately for our onward journey up the whole length of the Boot of Italy to join our Brigade in the extreme north-east of the country. We passed through many towns and villages on our way northbound, too numerous to mention, but all picturesque and welcoming. The trip took several days, and we stopped overnight in several camps on the way, until we reached our destination – Tarvisio.

Here we were allocated to our designated units with which we started our more advanced battalion training. I was absorbed into company D of the First Battalion and still hold in my possession what I believe is the battle-battered battalion flag. Is it, or is it not? I guess I will never be 100% sure.

I don't really remember what additional training we received, but we were certainly included in the daily routine of duties. Not only were we allocated such chores as kitchen duty, cleaning the dining area, helping the cooks and washing up the dishes, but also more onerous tasks such as cleaning the latrines etc. We were also sent out on sentry duty, or guarding prisoners, initially with more experienced soldiers. Tarvisio was in the farthest north-eastern corner of Italy, bordering Austria and Yugoslavia. I never reached Yugoslavia, I don't know why, but I visited Austria quite frequently. Our short day-leave passes enabled us to visit Villach and Klagenfurt many times. A leave - pass of two or three days, enabled one to visit further afield like Vienna or Linz.

With my comrades in arms in the Jewish Brigade

A not inconsiderable number of my more veteran fellow 'Brigaders' went much, much further afield. Their mission: to locate survivors of the death and concentration camps and bring them to Italian assembly points for onward transportation to Palestine. This was, of course, illegal immigration in the eyes of the British Authorities, but we really had no choice because Britain, which was the mandatory power in the land, still refused to open the doors of Palestine to enable the pitiful remnant of the Holocaust to reach the haven they so desperately craved to reach. This may have been one of the considerations of the British Army High Command when we were ordered to move from Italy to the channel coast. Originally it was intended that we form part of the Allied Occupation Forces, holding down a specific area of Germany.

From the moment we crossed the German border, some of our soldiers – we had many who had lost both close and distant relatives – behaved as was to be expected, whenever they came across any German, on foot or on bicycles. Some 'raided' farms and 'appropriated' chickens and other farm animals – and caused mayhem in various ways and places. Our hatred for the whole German people was boundless – and who could blame us! The British Army High Command therefore came to the conclusion that it would be best to have the whole Brigade continue through Germany until we reached the western border of Europe.

The journey from Italy to the channel coast of Europe took us six days and nights, until we finally reached our destinations in France, Belgium and Holland. Our journey took us through town and country – including at least one of the liberated concentration camps - if I am not mistaken it was the Landsberg camp. Bear in mind that this was just a few months only after the end of the war which had finally brought about their liberation – their salvation! The approaches to the camp, as well as all the streets through it, were lined with the liberated survivors of our people who stood and cheered us with tear-stained faces, to see Jewish soldiers, speaking Hebrew, bearing the Jewish National flag, with blue/white/blue + gold *Magen David* embossed shoulder emblems on their uniform. It was, of course, not surprising that many of us in the Brigade were just as emotional.

Proudly holding the Jewish Brigade flag

On another occasion we passed through – or visited – Bergen-Belsen where the reception was equally emotional. As can be imagined, the camp administration always prepared lists of the survivors of each camp – this enabled us to search through the lists to see if any of our own loved ones, left behind in Europe throughout the war, survived. I was not fortunate enough to find any trace of my parents or other relatives. I may add that we also wrote to the various relief and search organizations with similar disappointing results.

Continuing our journey through Germany we eventually reached our re-assigned destination. My unit was stationed on Walcheren Island, much of which was under water – the Germans, before their retreat, had mined the whole area and then blown-up the dykes to make landings in Holland by the Allied invasion forces more difficult. Our task was to guard German soldiers and escort them from their camp each morning to find and lift up the mines (which were mainly under water) and return the German's to their camp in the evening. Their carpentry workshop was kept very busy making coffins for those blown up daily, usually two or three per day, I think. I don't consider myself a vicious or unfeeling person, even then, but I cannot confess to any sympathy for our charges – indeed, at the time we felt a sense of elation at the toll of those blown up. What we had first heard about, and more recently *seen* – our personal losses so fresh in our minds – made us completely insensitive to our prisoners' fate.

Our stay on Walcheren Island gave us the opportunity, during our regular short periods of leave, to visit Antwerp, Brussels, Ghent, Bruges, Lille, Tournai, Amsterdam and other interesting places in France, Belgium, Holland and West Germany. All this took place so many years ago that I can neither recall the adventures in each place nor, of those I do recall, where and when exactly they took place. What I do recall was that the Senior Jewish Chaplain to His Majesty's forces visited the Brigade H.Q. At that meeting a group of us, volunteers to the Brigade from Britain, were invited to be photographed with Rabbi Israel Brodie, as he then was, and who later became Chief Rabbi of the British Isles and the whole British Empire – later the British Commonwealth of Nations. Incidentally, Rabbi Bernard Casper, Senior Chaplain to the Brigade also appears in the picture. I can even recognize my friend Henry Stern in the picture who on his *aliya* (immigration) to Palestine joined and later became the internal secretary of Kibbutz Lavie, I believe.

I do remember my friend Freddy Katz (Kaye in later years), giving me my very first lesson in driving a car either in Ghent or Bruges. In fact, I'm almost sure it was Bruges – and what a beautiful city that was, and is still, I believe. At the time Freddy was an officer's driver, driving a jeep, although he was terribly short-sighted. My first (and only) lesson was on a really rainy day. The deluge was so severe that Freddy could hardly see a yard or two in front of him. He had taken the wheel again and with his face pressed almost to the front windshield put his foot on the accelerator. We were driving along the canal. Need I say more? How we did not wind up in the canal I can't imagine to this day. It was a very sobering experience.

I would like to add here that Freddy found, after the war, that his parents had managed to escape to Shanghai, or was it Cochin. They came to England and he and his sister, Judith, who had also reached the British shores before the start of hostilities in 1939, were happily

106

reunited – a whole family once more, one of the relatively few. Freddy and I kept in touch. My wife, Marion, after we married, and I attended his wedding (he married his boss' daughter). Much later he and his wife hosted us, Ilana and me, on a visit to London after I had immigrated to Israel following Marion's death and my remarriage some years later to Ilana. Our visit at that time coincided with his eldest daughter's wedding day- to which we were naturally invited.

One incident may be of interest. In one of the army camps in which we stayed I was seconded to our Regimental or Unit Police. Unlike the Military Police branch of the army which dealt with all criminal activity in the army as a regular police force the Regimental Police dealt with minor infringements within the regiment. My task in that unit was to be part of the guard detail at the gate of the camp. As I mentioned earlier our more experienced veteran soldiers went out to find and assemble holocaust survivors for eventual transfer to Palestine. They required clothes, food and above all transport, to clothe, feed and transport these survivors to assembly points prior to their boarding the ships which were to transport them to the Holy Land – illegally, according to the British authorities. Well, one night, when I was on guard duty, several three-ton lorries disappeared and had not returned the following morning when, on inspection, their absence was discovered. I must confess that I was completely unaware of this – guard duty was divided into hours-on and hours-off. But I was questioned very thoroughly by the Field Security Service. Fortunately, there was nothing I could tell them. I knew nothing, which was just as well. If I had known anything, they would surely have discovered it. I was never a convincing liar.

There were, no doubt, many other incidences which did not leave any lasting impressions, since I can't recall them at will. So., I will bring my Jewish Brigade remembrances to their conclusion, recording just one more memorable occurrence which took place in 1946, I believe.

I think the High Command of the Army felt our presence somewhat irksome, perhaps even inimical to the mandatory Palestine government, fearing that our activities would prejudice their relations with the Arab world. I believe the arch Anti-Semite, Ernest Bevin, then Britain's Foreign Sectary, brought a lot of pressure to bear, and the then Prime Minister of Britain, Clement Attlee, was not too well disposed to our cause either. It was a great pity that an ungrateful British electorate had voted out of office the great wartime Premier, Winston Churchill. So, it was decided to disband the Brigade and return those from the British Mandate of Palestine who were almost all of the unit to their homeland. The rest were re-allocated to British army units.

The Chief Rabbi of Palestine – Rabbi Herzog - inspecting the Jewish Brigade troops before their return to Palestine.

The whole Brigade had a big, big parade in Tournai, where Palestine's Chief Rabbi Herzog was the honoured guest. He inspected and addressed the more than 5000 Jewish soldiers on parade. I was proud to be one of those standing there.

I may reveal, here in this journal, and after the passage of time, what is it –71/2 years since then – that quite a number of my friends and fellow soldiers from the UK were braver and more adventurous than I. They attached themselves to the Palestinian returnees and went on *Aliya Bet*,

108

so to speak. The War of Israel's Independence was in the offing and they participated, using the experience they gained in the Brigade. In some cases, they became casualties, even fatal ones. This was in addition to the fatal casualties that the brigade suffered in battles in Italy against the Nazis and the thousands who fell in battle as part of the regular British and Allied forces. I salute them all here: *May Their Souls Rest in Peace.*

I was rather more timid, and was transferred to the home base of the Sussex Regiment. Well maybe not completely timid. When my friend Max and I discovered that the regiment to which we were attached was, at that very time, undergoing special training on how to search kibbutzim and homes for what the Mandatory Authorities referred to as "illegal weapons" we refused flatly to participate. Suddenly we became very brave. How can we be expected to act against the best interests of our own people, indeed our own families, especially after what we had all just witnessed in Europe?

That was our position when brought before our commanding officer. The Colonel was very understanding. He immediately arranged for Max and me to be transferred to the Royal Fusiliers who were on service in occupied Germany. On reflection, after the passage of time, we both realized that we might have been of greater service to our brethren and to the country on the threshold of its birth had we stayed with the Sussex regiment, gone with them to Palestine, and acted as some sort of undercover agents warning the locals of the places to be raided. But we were still children in many ways, ignorant and limited in wisdom – I was not yet 20 years old. Besides, it is easy at this time, so many years afterwards, to think we should have done this, or that, or the other…

And so, begins another episode in my time as a soldier.

I think our commanders, non-commissioned and commissioned, realized almost immediately that neither Max nor I were ideal soldiers. They did, however, discover that we both spoke German which, at that time, was a 'salable commodity' – in other words, a useful asset to the British Occupation Forces. So, our Commanding Officer got in touch with the unit of serving interpreters in Germany who were always in need of personnel who could act as interpreters at court trials, or even before that, at investigations of both war and civil criminals. We were seconded to the Interpreters Pool in Bielefeld from where we were allocated as required, sometimes to sit in on an investigation, sometimes to interpret at trials. I can't honestly say that any of the cases we attended were of particular interest or importance – nothing special sticks in the mind. All the major events were no doubt taken care of by professionally trained interpreters.

The author after being transferred to the Royal Fusiliers

After a while, I was sent to Berlin to a holding camp on the border between the British and Russian sector. This was the time that German prisoners-of-war were being returned to Germany from camps in the Soviet Union. We had to receive them and interrogate them before sending them home to their families. There was little to do in the evenings, so we sat around and talked, argued and discussed what was going on around us. As I mentioned earlier, I was still rather young and 'wet behind the ears'. I had not yet learned what there was to learn about Communism, and particularly about Comrade Stalin. All I knew at the time was that the Russians had stopped the might of the German army outside Moscow, beaten the Nazis at Stalingrad, capturing what remained of the Sixth German Army including their commander, General Friedrich Paulus, liberated most of the concentration and death camps and entered Berlin victorious.

I do know better – much better – now. But at the time, arguing with some of my fellow soldiers who were not so enthusiastic about the Soviets, I was full of praise for the Russians. I think it amused me also to act a little as the devil's advocate. Our commander at that lonely outpost – surrounded by the Russians in whose zone this camp was situated – was not amused by my arguments when he heard of them. I was brought before him and he was fuming, bordering on bucolic. He gave me a lecture on what is proper for a British soldier, and promptly had me returned to the Interpreters Pool in Bielefeld.

They, too, did not know what to do with me, so I was sent back to my regiment, the Royal Fusiliers. At that time, before my transfer from Bielefeld back to the regiment, I had enough time still to go to the opera where I heard Bizet's Carmen sung in German… *in German - can you imagine?*

Anyway, my posting took me to Eindhoven in Holland where I found a number of my former 'Brigaders' and several other friends – Max, of course, Freddy and others. Our principal recreation here was to go to a particular dance hall, with girls we had met of course, and enjoy leisurely evenings. We particularly used to enjoy dancing the tango, not as professionals might have done, but with zest and full of enthusiasm.

Some time, while still abroad, I fell ill and had to be hospitalized in an army hospital. I don't remember exactly where or when. The doctors there discovered that I suffered from Quinsy, a not very pleasant swelling inside one side of the throat which made breathing rather difficult. As I recovered from this on the right side it promptly developed on the left. So, I was obliged to spend more time in hospital, but eventually I recovered and returned to my Unit.

And so, we whiled away the time until we were sent back to 'Blighty' (a 'pet' name for Britain) to be discharged. During our 'stay' abroad – Holland, Belgium and Germany – we were, of course, granted Home leave. It is a very important part of my history since it deals with my first encounter with the girl who was to become my wife and mother of my three biological children. (All will become clear as we continue with this auto-biographical tale).

Marion

Marion at work for the Jewish National Fund (London, U.K. office)

And so, I find myself on home leave, in London. It was August,1946, I had no way of knowing which of my friends – from school, hostel, youth movement, army (Brigade or otherwise) – may be in London at this time also. What to do, in the 19 days allotted to me at that time?

As I was wandering about alone on the streets in the West-End – the entertainment centre of London – I suddenly bumped into a friend from the hostel in Ely. He was another one who was on the same *Kindertransport* and was also a comrade from the Jewish Brigade. His name was Herbert Haberberg and the charming girl on his arm to whom he introduced to me, was his fiancée, Millie. After a brief chat, we went to a café for a coffee and during the conversation they – surely it was Millie – asked why I was walking about alone on my leave. Didn't I have a girl with whom to spend time on leave?

On learning that I was completely unattached, she offered to introduce me to her best friend, Marion, who had been instrumental in Millie and Herbert getting together. Marion had, apparently, 'just *become available*'. I had wondered often what '*just become available*' really meant. However, since she was indeed available, a meeting was arranged on the spot and we met the same day or the next – I don't recall exactly when. I do recall most clearly that I was 'smitten' from the word go.

She was small – it is better described as petit – being 5'2" to my 5'7/8" – dark brown hair, dark brown eyes, with a flex of sparkling green now and then (or so I would like to recall), well proportioned, with a good figure. Her nature, and temperament, was such that all used to describe her as 5'2" of dynamite.

Well - we met; and the same afternoon, I think, we went to a musical show: *Annie Get Your Gun*, which was one of the hit shows in London's West-End at the time. Since we could not purchase tickets for the evening performance – the house was packed – we decided on a matinee show that afternoon. The storyline was about Annie Oakley, a legendary figure of the Wild West in the USA. *How we enjoyed that show!* I believe it definitely was a combination of the leave, the show and particularly the company. In fact, we met every day after that and went to a matinee performance of another hit musical running at that time in London – *Oklahoma* – about young love in the cornfields of the US which, of course, we also enjoyed very much.

Another show we saw during my leave at that time, possibly even the first one to which we went, was called *Bless the Bride*. It featured one of Marion's favourite performers, the French troubadour Georges Guetary. I recall coming away from the show singing one of the main songs: "This is our lovely day, this is the day I shall remember the day I am dying…" I really felt that way.

We went to the parks of London – Regents Park, St James's Park, Hyde Park, Green Park and others, rowed on the lake, visited Box Hill, which was one of the beauty spots a little out of London, visited restaurants ; even a night club – which, if I can recall, was named Veraswamy or similar - at which another customer who must have been a little 'tipsy' stopped us while we were dancing to raise his glass to toast us and said – aloud – "What A lovely Couple You Make". We felt really good.

So, my leave drew to a close. We promised to write to each other – and so we did. I now had some good reason to anxiously await the end of my army service and return to London. I must confess our correspondence soon turned very passionate – at least mine did. I'm sure so did hers. Furthermore, the exchange of letters became frequent, almost daily, I think. I am sure I had another Home leave before my army discharge and again we enjoyed the time together: the theatre; ballet, opera, concerts (including The Albert Hall Promenade Concerts), Brighton for a day outing, etc. Of course, not all at once. This leave was in July, 1947 during which we celebrated my 20th birthday, again 19 days, by which time our romance had blossomed to a definite status of permanency and we already started to plan our future – or at least to consider what we hoped – indeed planned to do.

I was then posted back to the UK in December of 1947, was granted what was referred to as demobilization leave, and at the beginning of February,1948 was discharged from military service which took final effect at the end of March – I was a free man again.

And so, my three-year army service ended. I was now all of 20 years old, and completely responsible for my own life and action. I also now had a fiancée, having become engaged to Marion, and we were planning our wedding as soon as possible.

However, first I had to find lodgings and work in order to support myself. A number of my friends had already been discharged from the army. Benno Katz, who had known Marion before and who was my partner with the family in Ely before we went to the hostel; my good friend Max Jotkowitz, whose father ran a Kosher catering business from his house which Max had joined; Freddy Kaye (who was still Katz at that time) and a number of others from my Brigade and other army days, as well as former hostel and Kindertransport friends and ex-youth movement acquaintances. I found lodgings soon enough, for a time in Bethune Road and eventually Max's sister, Eva, who had married meanwhile and who now owned her own house in the same district, offered me a room which I gladly accepted.

As to employment – Freddy and I were accepted by a firm making plastic shoulder dust covers for women's coats and costumes. These we tried to sell to the buyers in London's big Department Stores, with a singular lack of success. Our approach line – "I represent Pabas Ltd" – had very little, if any, effect on any of the buyers we approached. Apparently, neither of us were cut out to be salesmen. After several months of this 'torture' we both felt we could no longer bear the humiliation of our lack of success and decided to go each his own way, businesswise at least. As it says in the Bible: "Abraham said to his nephew Lot – if you turn to the left, I'll turn to the right; and vice – versa." Freddy found work with a Jewish firm in NW London, a very Jewish populated area, canning something or other (I don't recall what exactly). What is of greater import is that he met the Boss's daughter, fell in love and was loved in return, married her and settled down to a happy married life, eventually fathering two girls and a boy.

I, on the other hand, was considering my next steps. This was 1948, and in the British Mandate of Palestine there was an on-going war between the Yishuv and Arab irregular troops. The Jewish Agency was recruiting volunteers to go to Palestine, later to Israel after May 15th, to fight in special units called *MaHaL* – these were the first letters in Hebrew for "Volunteers from Outside Israel."

The United Nations had just passed a resolution for a Partition Plan for Palestine on November 29th, 1947 – dividing the country into an Arab and a Jewish State.

117

Just after the UN voted to partition what was then called Palestine.

I considered joining, but then there was Marion. Our relations had blossomed from the letter writing days when I was still in the army to a full -blown romance and we were planning our future together – marriage, children, and all that went with it. But when? Marion intended to come with me to Palestine/Israel. Her parents, although supporting the idea of the remnants of the 'pleita' – survivors of the Holocaust – being absorbed in Palestine/Israel, were not keen for their daughter, their first born, to go into what certainly was danger in uncharted waters – especially with this penniless, jobless, tradeless, professionless and – in their eyes – *prospectless* foreigner.

I couldn't really blame them. On consideration, and in consultation with friends who themselves were registered to join *MaHaL*, our friends persuaded us that, since we intended to marry even before going to Israel, we should give ourselves a chance to be together for a few months. If we went immediately, we would, on arrival, be separated to different units and duties. Our friends' arguments won us over – we did not want, after all, to be separated immediately at that time – and so we decided to postpone our journey to Israel. This meant, of course, that I would have to find a job, at least temporarily.

Marion already worked in a Zionist Organization – she was secretary and PA to the Public Relations director of the Jewish National Fund. I would not be going to Israel immediately so that I, too, wanted to work within a Zionist framework. Since it was the Jewish Agency which did the recruiting for not just *olim* (immigrants) but also for volunteers to participate in the war, it was recommended to me to seek employment with that organization. Meanwhile, after my disastrous attempt at salesmanship with the firm Pabas, and until I could find employment within the Zionist Organization, I had returned to the firm for which I worked before joining the army – making handbags and leather goods. Here I stayed for some time, in order to support myself until Marion and I married and started on our life's journey together.

We had planned to be married and stay a few months in England, as persuaded by our friends, before leaving for Israel. The alternatives were to stay a few months first, then marry and go to Israel immediately after that or stay a few months and then go to Israel and marry *there*. Opting for the first of the options, we had originally planned our wedding for July/August 1948 – indeed we had made all the arrangements for sometime, in August. Strangely I don't remember the exact date. I think it was the 10th, a little after I turned 21 years in July.

None of our plans suited her parents in the least. Their reasons were perfectly clear, and from their point of view absolutely reasonable. (1) As I said earlier, I was a penniless foreigner without visible means of support and completely untrained for any kind of work except making handbags. (2) It was my intention to take their daughter far away to a war-stricken land, with an unknown future. Who could know if we would live or die and if we came through all the dangers how would I, the man who had to support their 'little girl', be able to maintain a normal household?

But since Marion was still only 20 years old at that time, her parents' permission was still required for a us to be able to get married. This became a major stumbling block in our plans, since Marion would not attain her 21st birthday until October 5th, and as I said above, her parents, were not happy about their eldest daughter's intentions. I say, eldest, because Marion had a sister, Sylvia, several years younger than Marion.

At some stage of our 'negotiations' with her parents, they signed the necessary consent form in a fit of anger. The synagogue ceremony and the rabbi were duly booked, and our friends were invited. I had no family in England at that time except my younger sister Dorle. The rest of my family all lived in Israel already and international travel and hotel accommodation was not cheap in those days. Nor is it today.

But we still hoped for her parents' *approval* and not merely their consent. They reluctantly agreed to give us their blessing if we agreed to postpone our departure for Israel for some months at least, to allow them to make arrangements for what they considered a suitable marriage ceremony and proper celebration. They promised to arrange our wedding in December 1948 or in January 1949. I did not want to be the cause of a complete breakdown in my future bride's relationship with her parents, so I reluctantly agreed. We both wanted to avoid the risk of a major rupture in the family. But it took all my powers of persuasion to make Marion agree also because she understood her parents, and their motives, far better than I – as you will see below. In the end, we were both young and very naïve and did not realize that Marion's parents had plans and hopes of their own.

So, on August 10th, the day we were to have married, I had to stand on the steps of the synagogue and turn away all our invited guests with a very lame explanation and in much embarrassment. True enough, as soon as we had cancelled our wedding plans Marion's parents reneged on their promises. When they sat down with Marion and me, to plan the wedding that was supposed to be a maximum of five to six months ahead, their first remarks showed us the true intent of their plans.

"It's impossible to arrange a wedding at such short notice," for the whole family. And the family was quite large – sisters and brothers, aunts and uncles, cousins of all shades and varieties, friends – far and wide, above all business colleagues and others. Then there was booking the synagogue, a suitably impressive hall which would have to be booked well in advance, the menu for the meal, ordering a wedding gown, music, and photographer. They would need a minimum of *18 months to 2 years* to arrange all that.

By that stage both Marion and I had had enough – no - *more* than enough. All we wanted was a simple wedding. Since we were unable to persuade them, and they us, we arrived at the inevitable impasse. And so, we told them bluntly that we would re-arrange our own wedding in October, after Marion reached her 21st birthday on the 5th of that month. We added that we hoped they would come to our wedding, stand by their daughter's side and would give us both their blessing and wish us well.

By that time, Marion was not living at home anymore. I don't recall if she was thrown out because she refused to submit to her parents' demands or left herself because it simply became intolerable for her to remain at home. I am persuaded that it must have been the latter because I even remember having to let her have my suitcase so she could pack some of her clothes. I considered not mentioning what happened to the suitcase but decided I would after all 'tell the tale'. She arrived at her parents' home, her home for over 20 years – at that time young women simply did not leave their parents home and protection until their wedding day – and started to pack her few belongings. This so infuriated her mother that she 'snatched' the suitcase from Marion, emptied what was packed already, threw the case on the floor and jumped on it several times. The case had to be thrown away.

However, we found another way to bring away the most essential items – after all, even ordinary carrier bags can serve the purpose. And so, she left her home. We moved into our rented home already some days before our wedding. Our flat, which was on the first floor, contained a bedroom, lounge, kitchen, bathroom and toilet. This was our first and very happy home.

As we were living there together some days before our formal wedding, I remember that for some of our friends it was something of a problem for my bride to arrive at the synagogue together with the groom from the flat we already occupied. As in almost all matters, a solution can always be found. My sister, Dorle, had a very good school friend, Rita Cohen, who lived with her family in Clapton, not far from our flat and even closer to the venue of our wedding ceremony. This family Cohen – Asher, his wife Hanna, and their children, Rita, Shaul, Leslie (Leizer) and Russy (Ruthy) – had more or less adopted Dorle, my sister, who lived at that time in the Girls Hostel in Cazenove Road. So, family Cohen added my bride and me to their 'collection'. They were very orthodox but did not impose their strong religious feelings on others. I

121

am forever in their debt for their warm kindnesses to us at that very difficult time in our lives.

Anyway, Mrs. Cohen, Hanna, asked Marion to come and stay with her the night before the wedding. It was not fitting, she said, for the bridegroom to see the bride on THE DAY until the actual wedding ceremony when both stood under the *chupa* (the wedding canopy). She and her family would be the bride's chaperones. They would bring her to the ceremony and stand with her in the synagogue. And so, it was.

Meanwhile, one or the other of Marion's aunts and/or uncles had been busy and, it seems, were able to persuade her parents that established facts are established facts and they, together with various aunts, uncles and cousins must attend the ceremony. I must thank the family Cohen also, because they too made every effort not only to assuage our anger and sadness but also to contact Marion's parents to add their own efforts to those of aunts and uncles, all of whom managed to make them realize what a loss this break in the family would mean to them also.

Not only that, but Marion's parents even arranged – at very, very short notice – for a reception of sorts in their home (which was not very large). Since there was very little room in their home, most of the people present were relatives. Marion and I felt obligated to attend – even if only very briefly.

However, we could not stay long since Max and his father had gone to a great deal of trouble to arrange the wedding *se'uda* (feast) in their own home and we, together with our own invited guests, repaired to their home after a brief traditional Jewish toast of "L'Chaim" at the parental home. It was all very, very sad and put a blight on our festivities. Our wedding was celebrated in two homes – family in one place, friends in another. *And it could all have been avoided.* The memory of that particular time does not cause me to feel particularly calm. The divided celebration made it, in some ways, a somewhat bitter-sweet day.

Marion and me on our wedding day

After the initial get together at my new in-laws flat and our actual wedding feast at my friend's house, Marion and I, tired but elated, went home to the flat we had rented some days earlier to truly start our married life.

All this happened at the end of October 1948. So here we were, two 21-year-olds, setting out to conquer the world. No money, no experience in anything, no support from anyone except our own determination to 'make it'.

I had returned to the trade I had learned before joining the Jewish Brigade, making handbags and briefcases and I was earning what might be termed reasonable wages. Those, together with Marion's salary, served to maintain us in our years of married life. But we never considered buying a permanent home in England because we did not want to feel the 'burden' of permanency in London. On reflection, many years later, I realize that this was definitely a wrong decision: an owned flat or house can always be sold, and the funds used for the intended immigration.

We did however have a brief 'honeymoon' – including one day in Brighton.

At this stage, I would like to relate an incident which occurred at the time. As I mentioned before, Marion worked for the Jewish National fund which had its offices in Southampton Row, just round the corner from the Zionist Federation and the Jewish Agency. Halfway between the two offices was Bloomsbury Square, a lovely bit of greenery with trees, grass and benches to sit on. There were grassy public squares like this all over London, particularly in the West-End.

We, Marion and I, had gotten into the habit of meeting in the square and having our sandwich lunch there together. One day, when I had arrived early and sat on one of the benches waiting for Marion, an elderly man, whom I had noticed walking by on other days, came and sat down next to me. People who know me are fully aware that I am not much of a talker (more so now than I used to be, but still not a talker). The old man, with his long white beard, started to ask me who I was, what I was doing there, etc. What can I say: within no time he had my whole history – almost since birth. He then related to my recent marriage – he must have seen Marion with me on other occasions when he passed through the square.

He then, very gently, gave me a few lessons from the Talmud about marriage, and how to contribute to its success. "Kiss your wife when you leave for work. Kiss her again on your return home. Compliment her on her attire, whatever she is wearing – take special note and mention it if she buys a new dress. Show appreciation for her cooking and tell her how tasty her food is and talk with her about your day as well as her day. Finally, if for whatever reason you nevertheless quarrel on occasion, as couples do, never let the sun go down on your anger – never go to bed angry. If you do this," he concluded, "you and your bride can weather any storm which may come your way."

Marion in the park

He then left, before Marion's arrival. I did not see him in that square again, and began to wonder if I had dreamed or imagined it all. But no; because sometime later when we had moved to live in the West-End of London I had occasion to go to the West-End Synagogue in Dean Street and found that he was the Rabbi Emeritus of that synagogue. I was very

125

happy to see him. Needless to say, I never forgot what he taught me. I have tried so to live my married life and hope I have succeeded in both my marriages. More of that later.

We had not yet decided when we would go on aliyah and so our lives ran on – November, December, 1948, January, February and so on, till August, 1949. Since we had not yet fixed a definite date for our aliyah I felt, as I explained earlier, that I wanted to work for the Zionist cause.

I was told that there might be work available at the Zionist Federation or the Jewish Agency. I applied for employment and was very pleased to be accepted. So, I left my trade and went to work for the Jewish Agency at its historic location at 77 Great Russell Street, just across from the British Museum. This was the address where David Ben-Gurion visited when in the United Kingdom, where Chaim Weizmann spent time, where Max Nordau and a long list of other Zionist leaders and dignitaries either had their offices, when in the UK, or met for their many and important, meetings. As a matter of fact, Max Nordau had a very comfortable black leather armchair in his office which I inherited when I was finally accepted to work for the aliyah department of the Jewish Agency. The chair was in my allocated office; and there it stayed during my period of service for the 'Agency'. One might suppose that his spirit had something of an influence on me.

I had thought, nay, intended that my work for aliyah in Britain would be of short duration. We expected, as our friends had pressed us to do, to remain in London for six to nine months before fulfilling our plans to go on *aliyah* (emigration to Israel).

But as the saying goes: "Man proposes, G-D disposes."

Man proposes, G-D disposes

Marion's father had suffered for years with heart problems. As the time of our intended *aliyah* drew nearer, his health did not improve. So, we decided to extend our stay in London. I felt, however, that I wanted at least to be more closely connected with the immense efforts of the Yishuv, until we realized our ambitions and implemented our aliyah. Marion was already working for a Zionist organization.

Not that we wavered in our loyalties or intention to make Israel our home, but one thing and another kept coming up to postpone our plans. First it was Marion's father's health. In addition to his heart problems, it was found later that he also suffered from stomach cancer. He always refused to 'go under the knife' as he termed it. He, eventually, succumbed to his illnesses and died in 1964.

I must say here that our relations with Marion's family did improve somewhat after our marriage, but never became really warm. Nevertheless I think they realized that they had to accept what was now an established fact: their daughter and I were husband and wife, and we all tried to make the best of it.

Harry, Marion's father, was what was known as a Master Tailor. This meant professionally he was several 'steps' higher than an ordinary tailor. The nearest comparison I can make is that between a cabinetmaker and a carpenter. He was in fact a genius in his trade. If only he had been a businessman as well he could, and would, have made a big fortune. He earned quite well, but money flowed through his fingers like a waterfall. He reasoned that money was there to be spent. As it was, although he owned his own workshop and had his own employees he always had to work for 'Manufacturers' – they were the ones who obtained the contracts and commissioned the work from master tailors. Therefore they, naturally, also made the big profits.

My father-in-law tried, on numerous occasions to lure me into coming to 'learn the trade' in his workshop. I always declined, but did not reject his offers to teach me some specialties (secrets) of his trade. I was not even bad at it, so much so that in due course, after our children were born, I managed to cut the cloth for some skirts (complete circles) and dresses for my own daughters and on at least two occasions cut the materials for my wife's evening dresses. I cut, she sowed. We were very pleased with ourselves and indeed with the result, as one can imagine. Both times the results were quite lovely strapless evening gowns which Marion wore for weddings that we attended and other formal evening occasions. She looked lovely. In my dinner jacket and black bow tie I think I did not disgrace her.

I am trying to get it clear in my mind why it took so long for us to realize our ambition to come on aliyah.

Well, first it was the persuasive arguments of our friends, especially the point assuring us that the armed struggle that Israel's neighbours were waging against the *yishuv* would carry on for a very long time, and we would still be able to participate in the struggle. How young and innocent we were! The struggle, in fact, is still continuing, but on many different levels and in many different forms.

Marion's father's health problems initially (and his decease years later), her mother's stroke and subsequent weaknesses, her sister's psychiatric ailments and eventual hospitalization – all these played their part, as did an illness that befell Marion later, leading to an operation. To be frank I must add also my own apprehension about Israel's Health Services. I had, for a long time suffered from shortness of breath and was unsure as to the cause. I realize now that this was really another excuse that I talked myself into and should not have been a factor bearing any weight on this matter – but, I fear, it did influence me.

Then the birth of our children also 'held us up', if I may put it that way. My work in the Jewish Agency, Aliyah Department and Marion's work with the Jewish National Fund provided us with a sufficiently reasonable excuse for our tardiness in the matter of our aliyah.

And so. it was that six months turned into a year, a year into two years, then three and so on. By the time I came finally to realize my aspiration to go on aliyah, 25 years had gone by and my beloved Marion was no longer among the living. I did, however fulfil my pledge to her and to our three children and at least had her 'remains' re-interred in Jerusalem's *Har Hamenuchot* cemetery.

But let us return to the point in this tale before I started, briefly, to ruminate.

I started my job with the Jewish Agency's Aliyah Department in August/September 1949. First I was the filing clerk, then I was given various tasks dealing with the arrangements to be made for our aliyah applicants: to arrange medical examinations with the Israel Embassy approved doctors which had to be scheduled; visas had to be obtained from the Israeli Consulate; household-forwarding agents had to be found, checked, and if approved, recommended. Also, travel arrangements made, first by ship from Marseilles, then by Air (El Al only, of course). The destination in Israel also had to be arranged. Immigrants were registered for Intensive Hebrew language courses *(ulpanim)*, both on kibbutzim and in town and temporary hostels booked. Housing, where possible, was obtained. Travel was either individual or in groups. In the case of the latter, while travel was still by boat, was always with an experienced 'group leader', of which I, occasionally, was one, at least until Marseilles, the port of departure.

The Aliyah Department consisted of the director, Mona Woislawski, her secretary (English only), and yours truly – 'chief cook and bottlewasher' (in other words: maid, nay, man of all work).

Within a year or so, our Jerusalem head office wisely decided that in order to encourage and advise potential *Olim* (immigrants) it was essential that a qualified resident of Israel, familiar with life in Israel, should come to advise those interested (that person was called in Hebrew a *shaliach* – emissary). Our first shaliach stayed with us for a year. He was followed by a *shaliach* who was already a senior official in the Aliyah Department in Jerusalem, a close and trusted person of the department head at that time, Shlomo Zalman Shragai (who himself was a former mayor of Jerusalem and one of the leaders of the religious Mizrachi party).

This *shaliach*, Naftali Bar Giora, very quickly, acquired the reigns of our office and decided to have me appointed Secretary of the Department in England (not exactly Secretary of State but a major advance in my position and in the Jewish Agency hierarchy) One of the changes for the better that this involved was that we acquired a dedicated filing clerk and added a Hebrew secretary to our staff. My main task was to take care of the administration – including the acquisition of all necessary materials and equipment – and assume responsibility for all the staff, with the exception of the director (Miss

Woislawski) and the *shaliach* (Naftalie Bar Giora). The office at that time consisted of, apart from the two already mentioned, secretary/administrator (yours truly), two secretaries – one Hebrew and one English, and of course the filing clerk.

It soon became apparent that to cover the whole country we would need to open branch offices in Manchester and Glasgow. This is what we did – each branch office consisted of one *shaliach* and one secretary. My administrative responsibility embraced all three offices, and this included the occasional visit to one or another of the provincial offices. The length that each *shaliach* served was usually two years, and it became part of my job to accustom each new *shaliach* to the work involved. In other words, teach him or her the ropes. I had, of course, to attend all sorts of meetings and, on occasion, report to the various committees, both verbally and in writing, about the work of my department.

The responsibilities increased by leaps and bounds which caused the department head in Jerusalem to upgrade my position – I was appointed Executive Director, in charge of all our local staff which had grown to five or six – sometimes even more - in London and two more in the provinces. Furthermore, additional *shlichim* were seconded to our London office who acted as roving emissaries. Towards the end of this journal I relate to most of the shlichim who joined us in the U.K. over the years

Before returning to my bride and our personal, private affairs I would like here to record the names of not all but some of the senior *shlichim* – who were the directors of the office in charge of interviewing and advising potential *olim* about life in Israel. All local matters and technical arrangements, including bookings to and in Israel, were left to me – hence Naftalie's instruction to me that if I corresponded with any office in Israel it must be in Hebrew. So I did. My time in the Jewish Brigade stood me in good stead here.

Now as to some of the senior *shlichim* following Naftalie. First there was She'ar Yashuv ("Shubi") Olsvanger – son of the well-known Yiddish author and humorist, Immanuel Olsvanger. Shubi later became director of the *Mo'adon LaOleh* (the Immigrants Club) in Jerusalem. Other notable names were *Moshe Shamir* – author of many books, some taught in Israel's schools, who also served for a time in Israel's Knesset; *Daniel Bar-Eli* , a former senior Jerusalem Police Officer; *Yitzchak Meir* – former head of the Youth Aliyah village *Yemin Orde* (which bore the name of Orde Wingate, a central figure in an important slice of *Yishuv* history) who later joined our Ministry of Foreign Affairs and served as Israel's Consul-General in Canada, then as Ambassador to Switzerland and – either before or after – in Belgium. Others included lawyers, journalists, bankers, business- men and others, including several ladies.

Enough! Enough! Let's get back to our story.

Our normal life has started. Get up in the morning, have breakfast, go to work, return home, etc, etc, etc. All fairly routine. Marion worked the usual office hours. In addition to those, it was part of her job to attend many evening fund-raising dinners and other gatherings, take notes of the many speeches made at these events and write-up a review and/or a report of the occasion, including the highlights of the speeches. The speakers on these festive dinners were sometimes local luminaries, sometimes important visitors from Israel such as – at least on one occasion – Golda Meir, at that time Israel's Foreign Minister. At the gathering addressed by Golda Meir, a number of members of an ultra-Orthodox organization stationed themselves strategically in various parts of the hall and proceeded to heckle, shouting "What about more religion in Israel?" and such-like. People in the audience got very angry and wanted to throw out those who were disrupting. But Golda told them to leave the hecklers alone and then told the hecklers themselves: "Come on aliyah in large numbers. Then you can do democratically what you consider right!"

Since the dessert at these functions, to many of which I accompanied Marion, invariably consisted of 'petit fours', marzipan - based delights, we always swooped enough of them into Marion's small evening handbag to take home to the children (later when we had them). They did like them. We did this also at weddings to which we were invited – such as when our friend Freddy Katz (Kaye) married his Gertrude.

132

My hours at work were somewhat more erratic – in fact, I worked very long hours, including most Sundays, which was not a usual work- day in England but which was more convenient for many of our clients who came to inquire about possibilities for their aliyah. Our evening work also was prolonged for similar reasons – to allow enquirers to call on us after the usual hours of work. We did not let this interfere with our lives. We went to the cinema, to the theatre, the ballet, the opera, a concert now and then, met friends, went dancing and occasionally allowed ourselves to go to a nightclub. Because we settled into a routine –and owing to Marion's parents' poor health – it was relatively easy to find reasons, if reasons were needed (and for us they were), to stay in England for another year and then another. When, to our great sorrow, our landlady died, the house which had been our first marital home was sold and we had to find other accommodation.

First my friend Max's sister, Eva, had a spare room in her house. We again moved in, temporarily, but soon found it inconvenient for one reason and another. Marion's father had a workshop on the fringes of London's West End and also lived nearby – a stone's throw from University College Hospital. The workshop consisted of two very, very large rooms plus a toilet and closet. He offered us one of the rooms as a temporary measure, until we found our feet. He cleared out one of the rooms for us, leaving one very large room only for the workshop where he and the two, three, sometimes four people worked.

Since everything for Marion and me was of a very temporary nature – we thought all the time that we would move to Israel within weeks or months – at the most, we accepted his kind offer. No doubt he had also, though not exclusively, underlying motives. Anyway, we moved in. The place was also convenient for both our places of work. My father-in-law took this opportunity to teach me some of the tricks of his trade, of which Marion and I were able to make some use later, as I mentioned earlier.

This was a period – 1947/8/9, 1950 – when we all tried to stabilize our relationships. It was also the time that the British Government began to relax the travel restrictions and foreign exchange regulations which were still in force, the aftermath of World War II. The first relaxation of the currency regulations which had been imposed during WWII occurred already in 1947/8 I think and Marion's family holidayed in Europe at that time. I have this recorded in the numerous letters Marion and I exchanged while she was away – daily, sometimes twice a day, some even while I was still a soldier in Germany before my demobilization in February of 1948.

My father-in-law, Harry, decided to take his family for a well- deserved holiday to France and Italy – after we were married already. He invited Marion and me to join them and since we could not afford such an extravagance, he offered to pay for the whole holiday. It was probably an attempt to make up for what still rankled concerning the wedding arrangements. I was a little proud and wanted to decline, but his offer was so genuine that he would have felt insulted at a refusal. Also, Marion would have been deprived of a very necessary break and remembering our three -day honeymoon, (of which one day was spent in Brighton, because we could not afford more) I, too, wanted to compensate Marion. So, we agreed and 'joined the party'.

The first part of our holiday was at one of the major hotels on the promenade in Nice – I think it was called the Negresco. For me, and for Marion also I believe, the place was a dream. When we came down to breakfast after the first night, we found that unlike most modern hotels this was not a buffet breakfast. You entered the breakfast room, sat down at your reserved table, had a waiter approach and gave your order. I was the only kosher eater in the family. They all happily ordered what they ordered (we won't go into details, I don't think) but the waiter was somewhat dumbfounded when nothing he offered would do for me. In the end we settled on the only dish available for me – an omelette.

Thereafter, morning after morning, the waiter came to take everyone's order and when my turn came he didn't ask what I wanted, he just said "pour monsieur? Un omelette?" This is one of the outstanding incidents of my first holiday to Nice that I remember. But I remember also that on the whole we all enjoyed our stay there, what with visits to the casino in Monte Carlo, the beach at Juan le Pins, which was very near to Nice. This is where we met my old friend Freddie who, having failed in his attempt in Ghent (or was it Bruges?) to teach me to drive a Jeep now tried to teach me to swim!

Alas, here too he had to admit defeat. He made me lay on my stomach, propping me up in the water with both his hands; but the moment he removed his hands I plunged, head- first, feeling as if all the oceans in the world were trying to get on top of me. "Thus endeth my swimming lesson," and I never tried again.

On this occasion we continued to Italy by train. On arriving at the border town of Ventimiglia, around midnight, we found the Station, including the bar and restaurant, closed down for the night. Fortunately, the bartender was still around, just getting ready to go home. He had pity on the weary travellers, opened the bar – which had the biggest collection of bottled drinks I had ever seen before or since, made us good Italian coffee, added some pastries and/or sandwiches, to tide us over till our train left the following morning.

We then moved to Italy, to Lake Como to be precise. This may have been a year or two later – who can remember exactly? A lovely area in the north of Italy, not too far from Milan, everyone agrees, especially the lakeside town of Stresa which had been recommended to us as one of the major attractions for tourists. We had chosen a very good hotel but now I don't remember the name. During the first night we were 'under attack' from the local mosquitoes, a specially tough breed it would seem. If this was not enough, we had to battle against a number of bees and/or wasps the next morning. As bad luck would have it one

135

of these flying creatures took a liking to my Marion – no doubt her blood was sweeter than the average person's. She, on the other hand, preferred to like them at a distance. The one mentioned decided nevertheless to have a taste.

The unfortunate result was that we discovered that Marion was allergic to the creature. The bite began to swell, and Marion developed a temperature and felt really ill. The local doctor could not deal with the problem (or perhaps we had no confidence in him, which is a more likely explanation) and we were therefore forced to cut short our holiday and return to England. Thankfully Marion recovered after the proper treatment, soon after our return to England. I now have a very strong feeling that the Italian doctor could easily have coped.

Since that particular holiday included a few days stay in Milan before we went to Stresa, the holiday was not really wasted. In fact, we enjoyed our visit in Milan very much. The famous Duomo (Cathedral) was very beautiful (still is, I know, having visited Milan again many years later, under different circumstances) and I remember we were all

136

so tired on that day that we sat down on the steps of that cathedral. I'm sure that I have a photo of that day somewhere. The Opera House (the world renowned La Scala), was also beautiful. We also visited the Victor Emanuel Galleria and many other sights. Milan was not Rome, of course, but it had and has much to offer.

The next four to five years, we made successful efforts to find the financial means to visit one or another place in Europe. One year it was Switzerland (Lausanne, Vevey and Montreux). The next time it was Lucerne with Mount Pilatus (according to tradition named after Pontius Pilate) and Burgenstock on the Vierwaldstaettersee. Mount Rigi was also in the vicinity within easy reach and on to Interlaken from where the Jungfrau could be clearly seen and admired. But we did not climb it. I think we also included, on this or on another occasion, Locarno which was situated on the Northern end of Lake Maggiore, at the Swiss end of the Lake. On that occasion we did not take a boat trip into Italy – we saved this for another time.

We tried whenever possible to include at least three places on each visit on the continent. Then it was the turn of the Lowlands and Paris, of course. Holland and Belgium - which included Amsterdam, Brussels and Antwerp, among other cities. In all the places we visited during all our vacations the Jewish quarter, Museums and Galleries were first on our lists – and the cities themselves, of course. Germany was never on our itinerary – for obvious reasons.

We also travelled around in Britain. In the beginning of the 1950's, or maybe at the end of the 1940's, my father-in-law Harry, decided to teach me to drive his Vauxhall car. You may remember that I had failed in my earlier attempt with Freddy in his jeep. On this occasion, however, I encountered no problem and passed the driving test the first time.

Being now the proud possessor of a driving license, and Harry being very generous always, Marion and I borrowed the car for various tours in England. We travelled to Stratford-on-Avon for a Shakespeare play, visiting several cities on route, including Warwick. The Earl of that city was termed the "Kingmaker" during the "War of the Roses". That was the time when Yorkshire and Lancashire warred for the crown of Britain in the middle ages. Other cities in the area proved interesting as well. Another time it was Oxford, or Cambridge, or the south coast of England. At least once we toured the south-west of England – this included the Wye valley, south Wales, Gloucestershire, Somerset, Hampshire and Devon. I don't recall driving down as far south-west as Cornwall with Marion and wonder why – although I did so many years later, on one of my England visits with Ilana – an unforgettable holiday. There must have been other journeys but they don't spring to mind at the moment.

However, the highlight of our travels at that time occurred in early 1951. We decided that although our aliyah was still delayed, we must at least *visit* Israel – mainly to re-establish contact with my family. After all, I had not seen my brother and older sister for thirteen years by then. I also wanted them to meet my wife (they had been unable to come to England for the wedding). Fares on the National Airlines were rather expensive, for us at least, but we found a small, recently established, charter company – and thereby hangs a tale, which I may as well record here.

Five ex-Royal Air Force servicemen, which included at least two pilots, got together, pooled their resources (which consisted mainly of their military discharge grants) obtained loans for any balance required and purchased two surplus airplanes. These they cannibalized and reassembled into one usable flying object – at least so we hoped. They had, of course, to obtain certificates of airworthiness before putting the plane to actual use, so we felt reasonably certain of arriving in one piece at our chosen destination. We booked our charter flight on this newly established airline – I wonder if ours was their first flight out? We always felt that the plane was held together with string and cellotape, maybe with a little spittle here and there into the bargain. But it flew and delivered us at our destination and returned us to London as planned.

This was our first venture into the air. It was all very exciting, but nerve racking too. The flight to Israel took *24 hours*, stopping three times on the way to refuel: first in Marseilles, then in Malta, and last in El Adem (in Libya) before going on to land in Israels' Lydda airport, as it was then called. It was by now nearly midnight (11.00 pm approx.) and we were lucky to find a taxi. Our destination was my sister Susi's home in Tel Aviv's Montefiori district. We arrived there around midnight – the taxi driver decided to wait to see if someone answered the door, in case we needed to be taken elsewhere. He was very thoughtful and considerate. I knocked on the door very gently, not wishing to arouse the whole neighbourhood. No response. I knocked a little louder – still nothing. For the third time – this time a really loud knock – and suddenly there was movement from behind the closed door.

A voice, in Hebrew, whispered through the door: "Who's there?" On identifying ourselves, the door was thrown open. By that time the whole household was awake – maybe even the whole neighbourhood – and one doesn't need an overdeveloped imagination to picture the scene.

Because the period of our visit to Israel was during what was termed *tzena* (austerity), we had brought with us various eatable items which were particularly in short supply, not wishing to eat up the family's ration. We promptly brought out coffee, sugar, various other items and the 'piece de resistance' – a whole salami and a whole large roasted chicken, which needed only to be warmed. They all decided that the occasion called for an immediate celebration. The table was laid, everything was brought out and we gorged ourselves there and then, in the middle of the night. What a welcome!!! I shall remember it as long as I live.

While on our visit in Tel Aviv at that time there were two minor incidents which may be interesting to record, since I still remember them.

One evening we were all strolling along the promenade eating ice cream (what else?) when a group of Tel Aviv's young persons coming in our direction – noisy and brash – bumped into me, knocking down my ice cream, and walking on. I was so stunned for a moment – no word of apology or acknowledgement or anything – I just stood for some seconds looking after them, mouth hanging open. Then, when I had gathered my wits, I yelled, *oy!* But my brother Bezalel turned to me and said if you wanted to react you should have done so immediately, not 20 seconds after they have passed already. I suppose he was right, but the memory of what happened to my father in Zawierczie, years earlier, still rankled with me so much – there was of course no real comparison, but…

139

The other incident was when Meir and Susi took us to see a film. It was so boring for us all and completely uninteresting. Marion and I suggested that we leave in the middle. But my brother-in-law, Meir, reacted with the words – "we paid for it so must endure it to the end." We did not argue with him – he, after all, was the one who had paid for the tickets!

I should also mention here that on our 1951 visit, Susi already had two children – Nurit, born in 1948 and Rami, born in 1951. They had a swing in the back yard on which three-year-old Nurit loved to play and while we were there, she 'employed' Marion continuously in pushing the swing. *"Od! Od! Od!"* ("More! More! More!) she would shout whenever Marion slackened in her attention to the small mite. I can't say that I remember any other details of our visit. We visited all our relatives, one by one and at the end of what we considered this brief reunion returned – 24 hours flying, three stops again – to our jobs in London.

Not long after our return to London, the weather in Tel Aviv turned, not necessarily cold but very rainy. Susi's and Meir's street, being in a valley (now the Ayalon multi-lane fast motorway through Tel Aviv), suffered what can only be described as a flood, drenching their home under a meter of water. They were obliged, of course, to move out and found temporary accommodation in Jaffa. Meir was at that time an officer in the standing army of Israel, in which he served for 25 years. From Jaffa they moved, with the help of the army, to their flat in the northern suburb of Tel Aviv called Ma'oz Aviv where we visited them some ten years later with our children.

In the summer of 1951, shortly after our visit to Israel, my brother came to England. I imagine it was not because he had to see me again, although it was good to be together again, if only for a short time. The reason for his visit was something to do with his scientific research. He was an agronomist and he came to conduct some consultations and maybe also solicit some financial support for his research, which had possible world-wide applications – especially for the very poor countries in Africa and Asia.

Be that as it may, he had to reach an address in the very centre of London. As I mentioned, I had recently learned to drive and was able to borrow my father-in-law Harry's car at will when he was not using it. So, I borrowed the car in order to take Bezalel to his appointment. It was a very rainy day and there was much traffic on the roads in central London. We got to Piccadilly Circus and I turned right to drive down Piccadilly. A little way down, just past the famous Ritz Hotel, at the beginning of Green Park, there was a bus stop where a bus was just picking up passengers. The rain was pelting down making for very difficult visibility. As I came level with the bus at the stop, the driver decided that that was the appropriate time to pull out from the stop. He was in a big bus and I was in a relatively 'little' car – so what did *he* care. So, I slammed my foot on the brake to avoid running straight into him. The road was extremely wet, causing the car to spin round and round several times, finally crashing into the rear of the bus.

Fortunately, no one was hurt, and the bus suffered no serious damage. The car, however, was not quite so lucky. Apart from damage all round to the body of the car one of the wheels actually buckled. I should have stopped there and then, but I was determined to deliver my brother on time for his meeting at the designated address which, fortunately, was nearby. And so, I did. Only then did I have the car taken for repairs. I am glad I don't recall Harry's reaction to the damage caused to his car, but I believe that apart from the shock he was happy to see us both unharmed and that no injury to persons resulted from this accident.

Let me turn briefly to my sister Dorle's activities at that time, although my memory is a little hazy. I know she was a very good student, having seen her school leaving report from her headmaster. She had joined a religious youth movement and, after working in several places (including house-cleaning in the hostel in London where she had found accommodation, the study of art photography, kindergarten teacher) she went on *hachshara* with her organization, Bnei Akiva, to several places, including Thaxted, Essex which was one of the agricultural training centres. This must have been from 1948 to 1950.

I was working in the aliyah department of the Jewish Agency at the time, and in 1950 I had the pleasure and privilege of arranging her aliyah, together with her *kvutza* (group). Their destination was the Beit Shaan Valley Kibbutz *Ein Hanatziv*. This was one of the kibbutzim belonging to the Hapoel Hamizrahi movement, the religious Torah V'Avoda organization. Dorle was not very happy on the kibbutz. The

141

kind of work was not what she was used to and the climate in that part of the country was, for her, too harsh and hot to bear. So, she decided to leave, but where to and what to do? After a period of work which failed to satisfy her, she wisely decided to enlist in the Air Force. Here, some time afterwards, she met Menahem, the young man who was to become her husband. I am not sure of this, but I think they married on January 1st, 1952. Dorle told me they moved around for several years in line with her husband's postings by the Air Force. He served in Israel's regular Defence Force and went where he was sent, rising from non-commissioned to commissioned officer in Israel's Air Force which he had joined very early in its development.

It is worth recording that the determination and devotion to duty of this young man was absolutely boundless as is witnessed by the way he came on aliyah. Menahem – aged fifteen years only – left his home in Alexandria, Egypt where he was born in 1931. His father had arranged for him to be accepted at the Amal Vocational Training School in Israel. He had golden hands and was an outstandingly brilliant student. He learned all about engines and mechanics and engineering. Eventually, he entered the Air Force and became one of the top, if not THE top maintenance technician of our Air Force. When the Air Force purchased, and later received new equipment, Menahem was sent to check it out.

It was because of these skills that he was sent on assignment to the US, France, Britain and other places. Indeed, on one occasion he was sent to Britain, while I and my family were living in London. This offered us the first opportunity to meet this new brother-in-law of mine. It was on this occasion that he took the opportunity to teach me 'Dynamic Tension' – a form of body exercise without the use of any sort of equipment. He also impressed me with his philosophical outlook on life. What impressed me most, I think, was his devotion to family – the immediate and the not so close. In fact, his conviction that the strength of a person rests first and foremost in his family was what I liked particularly.

Menahem's life was very demanding, both emotionally and physically, so much so that he suffered a fatal heart attack, when he was only forty years old, many years ago, bringing to a close a most distinguished service career. More importantly, a very happy marriage. How very sad that he died while on duty in the Air Force from a heart attack at such a young age leving a wife and two young children.

Dorle continues to live in that first house which they had built and cherished. I may add that the two children she had with Menahem are both married. Yocheved has one daughter called Roni. Yocheved herself obtained university degrees in both chemistry and psychology. She and her husband teach extra-curricular classes, preparing young students for college and university entrance examinations. They have even published textbooks to that purpose. (It may be of interest to note that Avi, her husband, is a musician by training having worked in this profession in the past both as violinist and a conductor. I think he also taught the violin).

Yochi's brother, Avi, has one daughter, Gavriella, named after my cousin Gavriel Zimetbaum who was murdered by the Nazis during the holocaust. I believe his name appears in one of post-WWII Nazi Hunter Beate Klarsfeld's lists of deportations from France. Avi received his degrees from Tel Aviv University. His subject included all aspects of the cinema: directing, scriptwriting, producing, filming and everything else that goes with the subject. He also worked in the field of cinematography, assisting Israeli film director, Dan Wolman. He also wrote scripts and taught the subject in schools. With great regret and much sorrow I am obliged here to add that Avi died of leukaemia a few years ago. At the time of his death, he was writing his doctoral dissertation, as a mature student, on the factors that drive human beings towards cultural and artistic endeavours.

By early 1955 our holiday jaunts abroad came to an abrupt end – at least for the time being – but certainly for the best of reasons. We had postponed having children, wanting to enjoy each other's company before turning our status as a couple into that of a family. But all good things come to an end and the time came for something even better. Having a family – having children – is another ball game altogether and Marion, now aged 27, finally became pregnant. Our first-born was a beautiful girl.

The start of our family

We were sitting around the Seder table – I was, as always, leading the formal service – it was April 1955 and this was the second Seder night, which was always celebrated in the Diaspora. Marion was expecting the baby to be born that day and to be sure she started having contractions. I rushed her to University College Hospital which was maybe five to ten minutes walk away.

I would like to insert here that it was the custom in all major teaching hospitals to have preparatory instructions to which both potential parents were invited. At our hospital we were shown all the equipment, introduced to the staff, including the doctors, nurses and midwives, and were told, with an uplift of the face towards the heavens, that HE was always on call in an emergency. We all naturally assumed that our instructress was referring to the Almighty – and only discovered later that she actually meant the Head of the Gynaecology and Obstetrics Department, whose office was situated on the top floor of the hospital.

One other fact was made clear to us – our hospital practiced what was then very much fashionable: Natural Childbirth. This was in accordance with the teachings of the Guru of childbirth at that time in Britain: Grantly Dick-Reed. To this day I don't know what "natural childbirth" is. I had always assumed that *all* childbirth was natural – apart from Caesarean deliveries.

Coming back to our rush to hospital with a very pregnant Marion, we had her examined in the proper department only to be sent away with the observation that "it's too early." So. home we went. It was getting late so we went to bed hoping to get a good night's sleep – who knew at this time when we would have a full night's sleep again, once the baby was born. But *noooooooh!* Our first-born decided to show us the shape of things to come.

Very early in the morning, only several short hours after going to sleep, we woke. The cause: a very wet bed. The waters had broken. We did not panic – I think! – but dressed quickly, took the suitcase, which had been packed and ready for more than a week, descended the two flights into the street and walked to the hospital at a leisurely pace: Marion couldn't walk too fast. I think we did it in just seven minutes.

On arrival Marion was taken straight to the delivery room; her contractions were coming fast and furious by then. I was dressed in some sort of doctor's gown, ushered into the delivery room to sit next to my wife, hold her hand and talk to her to keep her calm. *I* certainly wasn't! Marion pushed, and pushed and pushed. Then the head appeared, streaked with blood – from the birth canal, I am told now, but did not know it at the time – and I almost fainted at the sight. Well, wouldn't you?

The baby then came out in a rush, the time – 6.07 in the morning of April 8th, 1955, it was recorded – and here we were, parents, responsible for a little person. Our joy knew no bounds; nor did our apprehension, since we had no idea how to deal with this little 'mite. Which was the top? Which the bottom? I'm kidding, I think. But how do we feed her, wash her, change her diapers, and so on. I would like to insert here the fact that I became the acknowledged expert diaper washer at our child welfare centre at UCH (University College Hospital) whose methods were explained and diapers held up for all and sundry to see by Dr Charlotte Himsworth, our paediatrician, to show how white and clean the diaper can and should be. It must be pointed out that at that time – 1955, and well into the sixties – there were no disposable diapers. Instead such items were all of terry cotton or other similar material and had to be re-used again and again. All this had to be learned by us, as other parents had the world over, both before and after us.

I only mentioned our eldest, Simone, till now. Yet I refer to our children, in the plural. So, let me fill in this little, but important detail. As I already said, Simone was born in 1955 when both Marion and I were 27 years old. But because we had no intention of stopping at one, and feeling we were both getting older, we wanted more children as soon as possible. I have gone into some detail concerning Simone's birth, which was rather dramatic – or should that be *trau*matic? I cannot be equally verbose about the births of the other two, which, by comparison were relatively rather simple for me.

Our son David was next in line. He was born on 'the Ides of March', in Shakespeare's well- known phrase – that is March 15th, 1957. When it became David's turn to appear on the scene, I took Marion to the hospital. There the experts examined her, found that we were in the early stages and sent me to work promising to call me when the time approached for the actual birth. I did as I was bid and awaited the call from the hospital eagerly, intending to be present again at the birth. When the call came, I made my way back to the hospital. It was well into the morning and the traffic in central London was, as usual, quite heavy. My son was in too much of a hurry to await the arrival at the hospital of his father and when I finally *did* arrive, it was all over bar the shouting. This did not however diminish the joy and celebration of the event in any way.

By that stage we had learned all about washing diapers and considered ourselves experts. In this case, of course, we had a *Brit Mila* (circumcision) to cope with. But that was part of the routine in Jewish families and did not present any real problem.

Last in line, but certainly not in importance, came our beautiful Naomi. She was in even more of a hurry to greet her parents and siblings and face the world. I had, as usual gone to work early, leaving a very pregnant Marion at home with two children. On this occasion, if my memory serves me correctly, I was not even around to take Marion to hospital when the water broke. Just imagine, I am at work, a heavily pregnant Marion is at home with a three and a half year old daughter and a one and a half year old son when she has to rush to the hospital to give birth to our third child. (Naomi came to acquire the nickname "the Gnome" – although not for any physical reason. I think it started as No-mi then became Gnomey and finally evolved into the Gnome.)

I am not sure how we managed this birth really. Simone and David were too small to be left alone at home. Nor was it practical to drag them with her to the hospital. Marion would not call an ambulance so, I believe, either Harry (pa-in-law) or Anne (ma-in-law) or Sylvia (sis-in-law) or all three looked after the two children. Believe it or not, Marion walked to the hospital, on her own, and when I arrived it, the birth, was all over – again. And so, on October 12th, 1958, we had another beautiful girl. The Hebrew date coincided with our 10th wedding anniversary – what an anniversary present! We were overjoyed at this addition to our family.

Of course, I brought Simone and David to the hospital to meet their new sister. It was customary, in those far off days in England, for women, after giving birth, to be kept in hospital for 10 days. At the end of that time I took the pram – the Rolls Royce of prams at the time – and the two children to the hospital to collect my wife and baby number three. On the way back home we walked of course. We had all three on the one pram, one inside and the other two sat, one on either side. What a sight we must have made, trudging along there. The older two were absolutely enthralled by their newly born sister.

David and Naomi

Money was short. We were still living in our one room, next to my father-in-law's workshop and were waiting to obtain our public-housing flat. We still refused to do anything which might make us feel roots in England as our intended destination was still Israel. I recall again and again just how foolish I was. Marion would have accompanied me to Israel whenever I chose and I feel a sense of guilt to this day for

147

dallying so long. Eventually we moved into the public housing flat we had applied to receive. After the austerity we were used to, what luxury it was: three rooms of which two were bedrooms and one the lounge/living room, as well as a kitchen and a bathroom. The flat was not too far from my place of employment. (When the children got older, we were able to move to a larger flat, so that David – a boy – would not have to share a room with his sisters.)

Marion had left her job on the birth of our first child. She was determined to look after our brood on her own. Simone – this was our anglicized (or was it franchified) version of my mother's name – was not to be parcelled off to some 'keeper' so that Marion could go out to work again. Marion decided to stay home and be there for her, then for all three of our children.

We also lived a stone's throw from Regents Park. This is one of the most beautiful parks in England in which we spent many, many happy hours – almost daily, come rain come shine. In the summer months Marion would prepare a picnic lunch or supper. I would meet them all in the park after my work and we would enjoy family (quality) time – eat, talk, play – until it was time to return to our flat. Here, in this park, both Marion and the children met and made many friends. This park was considered by us our personal and private garden. Let me describe Simone's way of making friends. As we met someone new, she would go up to the person – age was not a factor – push them over (whenever she could) and ask: "What's your name, how old are you, and are you Jewish?"

Simone

When our offices moved from Great Russell Street, first to Tottenham
Court Road and then to Rex House in Lower Regent Street, some of our

lunchtime picnics with the children were held in St. James' Park which was just up the road from Rex House. Incidentally, this beautiful park stretched from Admiralty Arch and the Horse Guards parade ground all the way to Buckingham Palace, the London residence of the Royal family.

We now had three children and our lives settled into a routine. I worked fairly long hours. Marion stayed at home with the three children. Even when they started to go to school, she wanted to be home for them, in case she was needed.

By this time, after living in one room – large though it was – we were ensconced more or less comfortably, in our public housing flat. Our holiday breaks at that time consisted of one-day outings to the zoo, the seaside (Brighton principally), Box Hill and other beauty spots in the immediate vicinity of London. As the children grew older we became more adventurous and spent time at the sea-side in hotels, Jewish and Kosher of course, in Brighton, Bournemouth and other places.

The highlight at this time was our second visit to Israel after a ten- year interval. This was also our children's first visit to Israel. The year was 1961.

Simone was just short of six years old, David was just four and Naomi had reached the advanced age of two and a half. The trip this time was by boat. Our journey consisted of a train from London to Dover, the cross-channel ferry to Calais, a train to Marseilles, via Paris, and finally by ship to Israel. We had prepared everything for the journey – food for the children, a change of clothes for them, toys, even a potty. It was after all a very long journey. That particular accessory came in very useful at keeping our 8-seat cabin to ourselves. Even the most battle-hardened and adventurous traveller looking for an empty seat would almost certainly have been deterred by the sight of that potty!

Well, small children will be small children, and after they had spent the journey crawling around on the floor in the train, we arrived at Marseilles port very tired. Marion and I were exhausted and the children were both overtired and very, very dirty. We were not really in the mood to be greeted by a stewardess at the foot of the gangplank not with words of welcome, but with "My G-D, where have you been crawling around?" Well, maybe later, if and when she had children of her own she would learn to be a little more sensitive and understanding. Water under the Bridge now– let us forget it – but it made me very angry at the time.

We boarded the Zim liner *SS Theodor Herzl* and had a mostly enjoyable four-day cruise to Haifa. Why 'mostly', you ask? I'll tell you! Imagine a big liner and a very inquisitive four- year old boy. We had to keep our eyes open all the time. We must have looked the other way once and, whoops, where is David? No-one had seen him or shouted 'man overboard' – the ship's railings were fairly wide apart and we had already noticed his interest in watching the wash at the sides due to the movement of the vessel. The Purser of the ship organized a number of the crew members into a search party which went over the ship deck by deck; lower and lower, until we reached the engine room, and lo and behold, here was our young 'genius' having the ships 'workings' explained to him by the Chief Engineer. I ask you – four years old! Really! Anyway, all's well that ends well.

David

The cruise was memorable also for another reason. We had travelled 2nd class, because I could not afford better, and were in the same section as the many *olim* (immigrants), of whom there were quite a lot on board. Because of the number of passengers, and the limited space of the dining room, the meals were held in two sessions. We soon learned that those allocated the second session had the advantage. The staff were so pressed for time that we, in session one, were put through our meal in 'speedy Gonzales' style, to allow enough time for session two and then for the crew's meal. This, literally, caused the waiters on occasion to whip the plate from under your nose before you had completely finished eating. But it was all great fun, maybe not always at the time, but certainly upon reflection.

And so we reached our destination, the port of Haifa. As we neared the port, I recalled our first visit by plane, ten years earlier, and how we had craned our necks and looked out of the windows to catch a first glimpse of this our homeland, although it was pitch dark outside, and we saw only twinkling lights in the distance.

This time, it was so much more thrilling, this very slow approach, during daylight, first seeing a vague outline of landfall, hazy, but full of promise and expectations, then seeing the land more clearly. This was Haifa, with the Carmel range all around, not flat and undefined, but colourful, hilly, green and undulating. Eventually we could make out houses, trees, roads, vehicles and golden beaches. Then the pilot boat came to meet us and guide us into Haifa harbour. Finally, we reached the dock where we berthed. The hustle and bustle was all part of the thrill and excitement.

I had, of course, forgotten to mention that the trip was made possible by a grant of my own ticket from the Jewish Agency, while I paid for my family's tickets. I had really come on 'duty' so to speak, to be more familiar with current immigrant absorption methods, the better to be able to advise our potential immigrants. So, I looked forward to being met by an Aliyah Department representative who I expected would receive me on the dock after disembarkation.

I had also expected the disembarkation process to be rather lengthy. Imagine my surprise and pleasure to be called for on the ship's loudspeaker to meet the Jewish Agency representative who would assist my family and me to disembark first. Our surprise and pleasure, was compounded when we learned that the preferential treatment we enjoyed was actually due, in part at least, to my brother-in-law, Meir, using his influence as a Lt. Colonel in the Israel Defence Forces, who came aboard personally to help with our disembarkation. I must stress that, to my knowledge, Meir never on any other occasion used his status to obtain preferential treatment for anyone on a private matter. Our case, mentioned above, was an exception.

I am not too sure about the sequence of events here, so if I recite things not in their proper order, know that it is not of any importance where I stayed first and where next. During this all too brief interlude, we stayed with my sister Susi in Beer Sheva. Meir was stationed in the south at that time. Rami, who must have been nine or ten years old was already into aeroplanes. He constructed models which actually flew – and subsequently wound up, after his military service, working for Israel's Aircraft Industry. Where else !

We visited Dorle and Menahem in Ashkelon which was just on the point of expanding. A new building company (Afridar) had been granted authorization to develop and build a whole new neighbourhood on what were almost the dunes in the south of Ashkelon right by the sea. At the time we visited, Menahem was building an extension – with his own hands – to his two-roomed bungalow that they had purchased from Afridar. This was their family home where Dorle bore her two children – Yochevet (named after our mother) and Avi (short for Avraham, our father's name).

We also stayed with my brother Bezalel in Rehovot. He was working at that time at the Weizmann Institute as well as at the Volcani Institute and taught at the Bar Ilan University in Tel Aviv. His wife, Chava, whom he married in the early fifties, was a holocaust survivor – she had actually survived her incarceration in Auschwitz. She was my brother's lab assistant, when he worked and researched in the experimental laboratory in Rehovot. They fell in love and married. Chava was a divorcee, she had one son, Zvi, by her first marriage, whom my brother, on his marriage to the boy's mother, took into his home and although not adopting him formally treated him as his own. This boy eventually became a professor at Ben Gurion University in Beer Sheva and at the time of starting to write this memoire was Rector of that Institution. Not long after the marriage, Chava gave birth to another son, Romi, who, after his military service in the Israel Air Force – studied medicine and psychiatry and now practices in this profession. He has become an authority on Tourette syndrome.

154

On this vacation we also stayed with my cousin Zvi Kessler. In the two or three days we were with him, our daughter, Naomi, developed a very high temperature. On the recommendation of Zvi and his then wife Diana we called Dr. Vardi who at that time was the paediatrician in fashion – and Zvi was nothing if not fashionable. Forgetting that we were in Israel, where doctors don't make house calls, we asked him to come round, telling him that the young child's temperature had shot up to 103 or 104 Fahrenheit. He was not perturbed.

"Put on cold compresses and see how she is in the morning. If she is not better, if her temperature is not down in the morning, bring her to my surgery."

Marion and I were furious at what we thought was his indifference, but there was nothing we could do. Fortunately, the doctor turned out to be right. In the morning the temperature had evaporated, and all was well. Still, I think he should have come round just to be on the safe side.

As the visit was partially in connection with my work, I spent some hours at our head office in Jerusalem, visited branch offices in Tel Aviv and Haifa and visited some kibbutzim where our *ulpanim* (Hebrew language classes) were held. And so, our holiday came to an end. We returned to England, and to our usual routine.

Israel and the family

As mentioned earlier, Marion and I paid our first visit to Israel early in 1951, before we had children, and almost three years after the armistice between Israel and the various Arab armies was signed. The reader of these lines will recall that Israel was born in struggle. Israel's War of Independence started in 1947, before Britain relinquished its mandate in 1948, and came to its fragile end only in 1949 after the loss of many precious lives, the State having been declared on May 15th, 1948. Those who remember the history of the period need not be reminded that on the declaration of the establishment of the State of Israel, not only did the irregular Arab forces increase their attacks, but the Arab nations around sent in their regular armies. Egypt, Jordan, Syria, Lebanon and contingents from Iraq and Saudi Arabia all attempted to crush the newly established State of some 650,000 Jews. They did not succeed!

I may mention that after our first visit in 1951 and before our second visit ten years later, the young state of Israel was prevented by its neighbours from developing in peace. The Egyptians made problems about the Suez Canal. They moved troops into Sinai much closer to Israel's borders, deposed their monarch (King Farouk), overthrew Neguib (the original leader of the coup) and then Gamal Abdul Nasser, the new leader, looked for an opportunity to nationalize the Suez Canal and 'have a go' at us. However, we decided not to wait. In 1956, in response to terrorist raids from the Gaza Strip and intelligence concerning Nasser's plans, Israel swiftly moved its troops into Sinai in what came to be called "Operation Kadesh", stopping 10 kilometres short of the Suez Canal, as arranged in consultation with the British and French authorities.

Apart from numerous 'fedayeen' terrorist attacks on Israel between 1949 and 1956, this was Israel's second war. While all this was going on, the Aliyah offices throughout the world were going strong, bringing hundreds of thousands of immigrants from all over the world to the young country. Also from Arab countries, Asia, Africa and the Anglo-Saxon world – including Great Britain, my realm. We were kept very busy, although the numbers coming from Britain were small in comparison with places like Yemen, Iraq, Syria, Lebanon, India, Pakistan, Morocco, the Maghreb in general, etc. This vast movement of

157

people was to assuage the 'hunger' of Israel, generated by the closed gates policy which the British had imposed under the mandate and by the changed overall world situation after WWII. This small community, numbering some 650,000 souls, on the day of Israel's establishment, managed to accept and absorb more than a million newcomers in a matter of only several years.

As I said, we were all kept very, very busy; not only with aliyah arrangements (my part of the effort) but with fundraising (Marion's part of the work) to pay for all this. Transport had to be arranged, employment opportunities had to be created, schools provided for the children (and Hebrew classes for the adults), health services had to be expanded and houses built. Initially the newcomers largely lived in tented locations called *Ma'abarot*. A thriving nation had to be shaped. All this was *no* minor undertaking. We appear to have succeeded: Israel's population is now more than 8,000,000.

But I must now go back to family matters.

In 1963, Marion started having problems with her lower abdomen. Pain, some bleeding and general debility finally persuaded her to seek medical advice. Our family doctor referred us to the Outpatients Department of the hospital where the specialist who was called in diagnosed a large fibroid on one side of her womb. There was an outside chance that the fibroid alone could be surgically removed but it was the specialist's recommendation that, since we already had three children, it would be far safer to remove the uterus. After we discussed this from all angles, we accepted the specialist's opinion and the operation was performed – successfully, we were told. We were also told that it was found necessary, during the operation, to remove one of the fallopian tubes but, since there was no chance of an additional pregnancy, this should not have any real effect on Marion's life-style.

Ignoramus that I was I did not even enquire the reason why it became necessary to remove one of the tubes. Thinking back, in the light of what occurred 8-10 years later, I have much on which to reflect, although one cannot, of course, go back in time. So;,what is the use of speculating?

To help her recover, Marion was sent to convalesce for at least two weeks in Walton-on-the-Naze. We visited her there at least once, and corresponded by letter daily.

Shortly after that my father-in-law, Harry, succumbed to another heart attack which proved to be fatal. I don't remember the exact date, but it was near the time of President Kennedy's assassination in Dallas, Texas. The death certificate stated both 'infarct' and carcinoma of the abdomen. I think I have this right, because Harry always said he would not permit himself to be cut open.

This obviously placed another great burden on Marion, emotionally and practically, who felt it necessary to help her now aging mother. Her sister, Sylvia, was now 31 or 32 years old: there was a five years age difference between the sisters. Sylvia was unmarried and lived at home with her mother. Sylvia suffered from unrequited love. I think she never got over her first crush – love or infatuation, whatever it was – for one of my army friends who always treated her kindly. To the best of my knowledge he never encouraged her to think that she was more to him than Marion's kid sister.

Eventually she met someone else. I think this was an arranged match, what we call a *shidduch*. They became engaged and the wedding date was set. All the arrangements were made – synagogue, hall, caterers, photographer, flowers, music – all the trappings Marion and I had declined for our wedding. You remember my first cancelled wedding, with me standing on the synagogue steps, turning people away? Well, history *does* repeat itself, although not for the same reason. In this case it was not merely a postponement for practical reasons. Instead the groom simply changed his mind.

To this day I can't imagine why. Sylvia was an attractive and pleasant person. She would have made him a good wife. I can now confess that, personally, I did not think all that much of the intended groom. But, as I hinted, it was absolutely humiliating for Sylvia now to stand on the steps of the synagogue and turn away all the invited guests, while her parents and sister went about cancelling all the arrangements made. I, if I remember, stayed with Sylvia on the steps of the synagogue turning our invited guests away – again. This incident, for lack of a better word, was mind shattering for Sylvia, and played havoc with her emotions, as can well be imagined. It was, in my opinion, one of the main contributory causes to what happened to Sylvia later. That part already relates again to what happened later to Marion.

This was in 1965. You may recall that I mentioned earlier, my sister Dorle, her husband Menahem and their children Yochevet (Yochi) and Avi. As I mentioned, Menahem served in the Israeli Air Force, and on some of his work-related journeys on behalf of Israel's Air Force, he was accompanied by his family. Once, after spending 10 months in Fort Bliss, Texas, the whole family stayed with us in London for ten days on their return journey to Israel. We very much enjoyed their stay. We visited the parks, fed the squirrels, went to the zoo and on many other outings, the details of which have faded into almost forgotten memories.

Indeed, we had always been open to visitors, in the best Jewish tradition. Marion always invited new *shlichim* who were seconded to my department to come and dine with us on their first arrival in the UK in order to give them a feeling of welcome, so that they should not feel too strange in the place in which they suddenly found themselves. Naturally this meant their whole families – sometime it was just a wife and sometimes there were children also. On one occasion, in the early 1960s, when the newly arrived *shaliach* came to dine with us, everything went very smoothly until our son David's antics caused the *shaliach*'s tie to 'float' in his chicken soup. Not a major tragedy, but I wonder if he ever forgave our David. Still, we all lived on.

We also often invited people we met in the Central Synagogue to Shabbat lunch. On one occasion, in 1965, we brought home the Hollywood film actor, Cec Linder to feast with us. He had played Felix Leiter, James Bond's CIA contact, in the 1964 film *Goldfinger*. More recently, he had finished shooting a film called *The Good Shoe Maker and the Poor Fish Peddler* about the notorious Sacco and Vanzetti case in the United States in the nineteen twenties. Cec actually visited us several times. He was really charming; it was a pleasure to be his host.

Then, 1966 brought us new friends from the USA. The occasion was Rosh Hashana and the place was again the Central Synagogue. It started when I noticed someone who didn't have a *machzor* (prayer book) and so I offered to share mine. His name was Samuel Kassow and he was then a 19 year old Fulbright Scholar in London from the USA, having just obtained his BA degree at that tender age. His subject was History.

His is an interesting story. He was born in a Displaced Persons camp in Germany, I think – I'm a little vague about that now (advanced age, I

161

suspect). His mother, having undergone terrible times during WWII, became a partisan and fought the Nazis in the forests of Eastern Europe. After the war, while in that Displaced Persons Camp, she gave birth to Sam. I believe his father had been arrested by the Soviets and sent to what they referred to as a correction or re-education centre. When it became possible, she went to the US and settled there but I'm not sure if her husband too, Sam's father, reached the USA.

Marion and I invited Sam to our small council flat for the festive meal that traditionally follows the synagogue service. Since he had come to the service with a friend, female this time, another Fulbright Scholar called Helen Lipstadt, we naturally invited her also. The following week they were joined by the third member of their crowd – Bob Burka. All three became our good friends.

We have long ago lost track of Helen, who married and settled for some years in Paris with her husband. The other two are still friends with whom we are in touch, especially Sam, who visits us when he comes to Israel to do his research or attends a conference. He is now a Professor of History in Trinity College, Hartford, Connecticut, married with two daughters and one son. His specialty is Holocaust research. Bob Burka is a now a retired Washington lawyer. He, too, is married and also has three children. We are in touch with each other. As a matter of fact Ilana and I, during our visit to Washington a few years ago, visited Bob and his wife and enjoyed a few hours of their company.

The tense part of this period in my narrative, however, was the happenings in the Middle-East that were going on at the time. The Egyptian leader Gamal Abdel Nasser, having deposed King Farouk in his own country, having thrown out the British (and French) who had ruled Egypt for almost the whole of the 20th century till then, having ousted General Muhammad Naguib, the original, titular head of the ruling Junta which deposed the king, and having established the link with Syria – the United Arab Republic – now felt strong enough to 'have a go' at Israel and fulfil his 'wet' dream of destroying Israel.

In 1967, he began to amass troops on Israel's armistice borders, illegally closed the entrance to the Red Sea and started to mobilize his army and his allies for an all-out assault on Israel. Israel was not inclined to wait for his assault and, in a pre-emptive strike brilliantly executed by Israel's Air Force, destroyed almost all military airplanes of the prospective invaders – in one day.

This war, forced on Israel, took just a few days. It became known as the Six-Day War. At the threat of its outbreak, many young men and women volunteered to go to Israel – some to fight, if required, most to take over tasks which many of the reservists had to leave while doing their military service. An organization was established in a number of countries, including Britain, which registered and dispatched these young people to Israel. Marion left the seclusion of our home to volunteer for work with this organization, the *Volunteers Union*, and became the organizing secretary. This brought her back to the mainstream of Zionist work.

Later, when the Volunteers Union was no longer required, she started to work, once again, for another Zionist aliyah oriented office where she had already worked previously: PATWA – which stood for Professional and Technical Workers Aliyah. This second time round with this organization was now headed by Dr. Robbie Sable, the son of an earlier *shaliach* to that office. Robbie, incidentally, later became the legal adviser of Israel's Foreign Ministry. So now, Marion and I were, more or less, in the same 'business'.

The swift victory of Israel's Defence Forces brought a boost to Jewish communities throughout the world. In order to strengthen the bond between Israel and Diaspora Jewry prominent Israelis were sent all over to tell their brethren about our country and to encourage aliyah to our homeland. We, too, in Britain were honoured to receive eminent visitors who we hoped would help us in our work, both the fund-raising aspect and to encourage aliyah. Our particular emissaries included Rabbi Shlomo Goren and historian Mordechai (Morele) Bar-On.

The former was at that time completing five years as Chief Rabbi of Israel's Defence Forces; and would go on to become first Chief Rabbi of Tel Aviv and then serve as Ashkenazi Chief Rabbi of Israel from 1973 to 1983. He was, of course, a brilliant Talmudist whose habit it was to rise early every morning – 5 a.m. or earlier – in order to study at least one page or one chapter of the Talmud. It was my privilege to accompany him on some of his meetings which I always found most enlightening, at least those that I understood.

The other personality mentioned was Colonel Bar-On who had served as head of Moshe Dayan's bureau. He was the author of Yitzchak Rabin's address on Mount Scopus on the liberation and unification of Jerusalem following the Six-Day War. At the time I knew him, he was in the final stages of his service as Chief Education Officer of our Defense Forces, a post he filled from 1963 to 1968.

Around that time too, I had some internal medical problem – I don't remember exactly what it was, except that I was obliged to stay in hospital for five days. The problem was internal pain in the lower part of my body. The only way to discover the cause was to insert a tube, under a general anaesthetic. Thankfully nothing was found and whatever had caused the pain, in fact, disappeared. I guess I was lucky.

After my sojourn in hospital, one of our Jewish Agency/Israel Embassy doctors with whom we had become very friendly, offered to 'lend' us his home for a fortnight in 1967 to enable me to recuperate. His home was in Essex some 35 miles out of London, in a village named Stock. He took his wife and children on a holiday away from home in order to vacate it for us. We, our whole family, enjoyed the two weeks we spent in that quiet village very much.

The Six Day War that I mentioned above did not, however, bring peace to Israel. It was followed by the 'War of Attrition' which lasted from March 1969 till August 1970. In this war, Nasser tried to grind Israel down with occasional border incursions. That too failed.

In that same period, my niece Nurit, stayed with us on her visit to London at the end of 1969 or the beginning of 1970. We were always happy to see her, both on that occasion and later in the winter of 1972/3 when she visited with Alla's youngest, Yael. We could not accommodate them at that time because by then Marion's illness (see below) was in a more advanced stage and she was confined to her bed (more of that later).

As I said earlier Marion had not returned to full-time employment after the birth of Simone. She worked more than enough looking after her three children and our home. She had, of course, no sustained help from the extended family. Nor could we afford paid outside help. However, as mentioned above, she had started to work again for PATWA, another Zionist organization, on a part-time basis.

164

This led to our third visit to Israel, at the very end of 1970. One of Marion's purposes was also to learn more about the aliyah of professionals and what special obstacles these specialized potential immigrants would face.

By this time, I was Executive Director of the Aliyah Department in Great Britain, covering the head office in London and the offices in Manchester, and Glasgow and all the British Isles, including Northern Ireland, the Channel Islands and also the Republic of Ireland. In addition to aliyah from Britain, we also dealt with all technical arrangements, including visas and travel, for groups passing through London, i.e. from Australia and New Zealand. Furthermore, I was, by then, also the Children & Youth Aliyah representative for the British Isles.

On the visit, we came on the Zim liner the *SS Nili*. Again my own ticket was covered by my Jerusalem head office whilst I received partial help for the tickets for Marion and the children. While in Israel, on this visit, we were accommodated at various immigrant Absorption Centres, both so that we would have a place to stay while in Israel, and so that we would get a feel of what these initial temporary housing centres are like for the newcomer.

We arrived in Israel in late December 1970, and initially stayed with Susi and Meir, back in Maoz Aviv, a suburb of Tel Aviv. After a week in Tel Aviv we went to Jerusalem where the Jewish Agency had arranged accommodation for us in the immigrant Absorption Centre in a neighbourhood called Katamon. This was chosen to show us the less attractive of the centres which was located in one of the poorest areas of Jerusalem. Here we were allocated a three- room apartment, which had a kitchen for self-catering. It was evening and we were all very tired and promptly went to sleep.

Early next morning, while we were having breakfast in our kitchen, we heard repeated hooting of a car outside. At first we took no notice, but as the hooting continued we decided to try to find out what was going on. We went onto the balcony and looked out to the road. Lo-and-behold, standing next to his car, hooting away, was our friend Moshe Carmon who only recently had returned to Israel from his stint as a *shaliach* (emissary) in London. He insisted we descend to the car and asked us to bring swim wear and/or light clothes. Then he took us all on a day trip to *Ein Fashcha* (or *Einot Tzukim* in Hebrew) on the Dead Sea. Take note: the date was December 31st, 1970. The sun was blazing and it was hot, very hot – well over 90 degrees Fahrenheit, I should think. We enjoyed the day tremendously and could not thank our friend enough for taking the time and trouble to find out when and where we were and proving so helpful to us all.

On his return from his *shlichut,* Moshe not only returned to his occupation as a senior Customs and Excise official, but decided, in view of his imminent retirement from government employment to attend a handicraft course. This resulted in his fashioning a *chanukia* (candelabra for the festival of Chanukah) of special wood, one of his first successful efforts which he dedicated to Marion on her death in 1973 – the chanukia is still one of our treasured possessions and we use it yearly to light the candles for Chanukah.

After a few days in Jerusalem we travelled to Haifa, where we again stayed at an immigrant absorption centre. This one was basically a high-rise building, like a block of council flats in England, with separate family dwelling units but no kitchen. Instead, there was a communal dining room/café/restaurant.

My sister Dorle and her husband Menahem lived in Haifa at the time because Menahem was stationed in the north of Israel at the time. It was at their Haifa flat that we first met their very fierce dog Sa'ar. I recall that as we entered the apartment my brother-in-law warned us to move straight to the sofa and armchair, and not to wave our hands about. The fierce looking dog came to each in turn, sniffed, to satisfy his curiosity about these unexpected visitors to his charges, and only then could we 'breathe' and move, but not too suddenly. To be frank it was rather frightening at the time.

During this visit to Israel, as on the last, I had meetings with colleagues, learned about the current problems and possible solutions, and reported on the present situation in my area of activities. Youth Aliyah put a car and driver at our disposal and we visited a number of Youth Aliyah settlements to know better from close observation and many discussions what such places had to offer. They are, in fact, somewhat similar to Boarding Schools. I remember how we drove from place to place,

166

sometimes one or two places in one day, sometimes more, sometimes one village was just a few kilometres from the next, sometimes the distance was considerably greater. But short distance or long we were always five in the car. That is Marion and I, Simone aged almost 16 years old, David aged 14 and Naomi aged 12, and the driver, of course. Fortunately, the cars they provided were big.

We all loved to sing – Marion only didn't have a 'singing' voice – and we spent most of our car travelling time when not admiring the scenery around us singing, in harmony of course, all the Zionist songs we remembered. I think the driver enjoyed the entertainment also.

It goes without saying that we spent as much time as possible with our family. After Haifa we stayed with my brother Bezalel and his wife Chava, in Rehovot. I think our children took the opportunity to get to know their cousins. It was really good for the younger generation to get to know each other, especially as they are so close in age.

My most immediate impression of my visit, not only this visit but the earlier ones also, was how much and how quickly the scenery changes from one visit to the next. Trees grew where there were none the last time. New roads and houses were built at a phenomenal rate. Whole new areas were developed and completely new settlements sprang up all over the country.

To demonstrate how far this old-new little country has progressed in such a short time I go back to our first visit in 1951. Olim were coming in fast and furious. One had to provide work for them. Apart from houses, roads were being laid down. The newcomers to the country had to find work, to earn enough money to support themselves and their families. There was not enough money to do all that needed doing. In addition to houses and roads there was a crying need for hospitals and clinics, schools, welfare centres, and all the paraphernalia which a modern state required.

I recall one work crew on the road laid down an isle on one of Tel Aviv's major roads – a very busy road, with heaps of vehicular traffic – to enable the unsuspecting pedestrian to cross the road safely. Traffic lights cost a lot of money and were therefore not an option. Zebra crossing were, I believe, not in common use yet. Hence the isle was the obvious option. I can testify to the fact that during our three weeks stay in Tel Aviv the island put down in that road was lifted at least four times, if not more, and moved first 10 cm more to the left, then 7 cm to the right, then a few cm up, then down. I am convinced the purpose of the exercise was not the correct positioning of the isle but rather to keep these inexperienced road workers, presumably new immigrants, at work and provide their weekly pay packet. Rather thoughtful of the employer, don't you think? But I am a long way past 1951. Things have changed a lot – but we'll come to that in due course.

So, we come back to our 1971 visit to what we have always considered our homeland. Again we visited the family, nuclear and wider – including aunts and uncles, cousins, etc. Again we paid our respects to our respective headquarter offices, and visited sites of immigrant absorption, and just visited sites of interest and beauty – the old city of Jerusalem (this was now possible, following the Six-Day War), old Jaffa, the sea of Galilee, the Salt (Dead) Sea, Tel Aviv, Haifa, Masada, Herodion. We had a wonderful time. Marion was heroic, never mentioning her back pains throughout the visit.

Our return to London was uneventful. Our continued residence in London was again prolonged for one reason or another. In the past it had been the health problems of Marion's father. Then there were the births of the children, each in his or her turn. Now, her mother also was not in good health, having had one stroke and was likely to have another.

However, to be frank and honest, at least with myself – and now with you, dear reader of this memoire, if you have persevered and read this far – we just settled into a routine. It was comfortable. We saw no reason to hurry. Israel was still our goal. We were, after all, working for THE CAUSE. I certainly have mixed feelings about this. No matter what I tell myself, at least I gave my children's grandparents the opportunity to know their grandchildren.

It is just a great pity that Marion herself was not able finally to fulfil her dream. We are shortly coming to that chapter of my life. For a monumental change in all our lives was about to occur.

Tragedy

On our return, preparations began for the forthcoming Pesach festival. As I pointed out at the very beginning of this memoire I came from an orthodox family and although not strictly *frum*, as the Yiddish expression goes, we did keep a strictly kosher home – we still do – and went to the synagogue every Shabbat. So, preparation for Pesach was fairly thorough. The flat was cleaned thoroughly and food kosher for Pesach was ordered from Jolsons Deli. Cupboards were scrubbed and relined and as the Shabbat mood took over on Friday so the Pesach mood took possession of us at this time of the year.

Marion still had not mentioned any really serious back pain, although we had gone to our family doctor to consult him. As most family doctors, he told her that it was probably due to being on her feet too much, on having in the past carried our children too often. Simone was now almost 16, David had turned 14 and Naomi was just 12½, so I couldn't imagine what he meant. Anyway, the festival arrived.

On the morning of the first or second day 'Chag' (this latter is celebrated in the Diaspora) I returned from the synagogue to find that Marion was not at home because she had gone to the doctor with rather severe back pain. I rushed to the doctor and found that our usual doctor was on vacation and his locum – a little more alert and imaginative then our family doctor it would seem– had dispatched Marion immediately to the Emergency Room at our local hospital, University College Hospital.

I must confess that I was somewhat thrown into a panic. I rushed to the hospital and found Marion in the waiting section of the ER, having already seen the resident doctor who had summoned a specialist. This obviously did nothing to calm my nerves although Marion was quite composed. When Mr Bunton (consultant surgeons in England are addressed by the title Mr) examined her, he sent her for an x-ray which he then informed us showed a lesion on one of the ribs and that she would have to be admitted to hospital as soon as possible for further tests.

On the way home from hospital after making all the necessary arrangements, Marion said to me quietly: "cancer".

How she knew at once I can't imagine but later at home, she showed me the swelling under her armpit which had spread from the lump in her breast of which I had no knowledge. My understanding of this kind of medical problem was absolutely nil. It was really all new to me and very frightening. Arrangements for admittance to the hospital, in view of the specialist's written requirement, were swift. After various tests, it was soon established that the cancer was too large to allow for an operation, and the doctors decided to try to make smaller the growth by radio-therapy which may have made it possible for them then to attempt surgery – at least so they explained to me.

I am not convinced that that was a real possibility, but if they could encapsulate the growth maybe it could be contained. I had no idea at that point that the cancer had already metastasized. She was scheduled for a full course of radio-therapy treatment and remained in hospital for some six weeks at that time. The next two years were harrowing for us all, if I can so describe what we all went through – Marion most of all. She was treated now as an outpatient, coming in for regular checkups and treatment, only to be told at that stage what we may have suspected: that the cancer had indeed metastasized.

The doctors treating her were wonderful – and Marion herself was heroically brave. In the first six weeks she was under the care of Mohankumar Adiseishiah. During that time our friend Dr. Elliot Berry, who was then a resident registrar at UCH (University College Hospital), visited her every day and kept us informed. After that she came under the care of another Doctor, also Indian, called Srini Vasan, though still under the overall care of Dr Adiseishiah, with whom we became very friendly – having his family over to our home and visiting them. Dr. Vasan became her regular radiologist. All these doctors who attended her were top rate in their chosen specialty. I have nothing but the greatest admiration for them in their treatment of my wife as a patient and as a person.

Every time another place in her body where the cancer was found she went in for radio-therapy treatment. This happened every few months first, and then every few weeks, until eventually she was confined to a wheelchair. After wheeling her to hospital a number of times a nurse was eventually allocated. She came to our home daily, to give Marion the morphine injections she now needed to cope with the pain. At that time, since Marion was confined to bed, I had to learn not only to cope with bed pans but had to help Marion to turn to her side, then from side to side almost every 15 minutes – how I felt must be self-evident. How she felt is just unimaginable.

Then, at the beginning of February 1973, things had become so critical that Dr Vasan, who had visited Marion at home on several occasions, persuaded me, and her, that she could be better treated in hospital where she could be monitored constantly and treated accordingly. With great reluctance, we had her transferred to the hospital, but since then I ask myself frequently if that was the right decision. In the end I think it was, although had I known how hopeless and near to the end she was, I would not have consented.

Anyway, we stayed at the hospital for the rest of the day. As the evening wore on the doctor told us to go home and rest, assuring us that with the morphine treatment at such a level now she would not recognize us; and that when we returned in the morning she should be more alert, after having rested throughout the night as much as possible and may then be able to acknowledge us. How ignorant I was at the time and what a pity we went home; we were not there in the end – and we should have been, in order to take our leave properly. So, we went home and to bed – 'though I don't know if any of us slept much.

Towards morning, it was still dark outside, the telephone woke us. We had, no doubt, dozed off – exhaustion must surely have overtaken me. A member of the staff at the hospital told me that Marion had died. We were assured that in accordance with Jewish custom she was not left alone. But I am not too sure about that, and it still plagues me. In the morning, we dressed and went over to the hospital and were directed to where she rested. She appeared so peaceful – the pain she had suffered for two years or more was no longer evident on her face and our one consolation at that time was that at least her suffering was over. Her resting place at the hospital, now that I think back, was not what I would or should have expected. I can't really explain what I mean. I don't really know what I mean. Thinking of it now just makes me wonder.

Now I also started to ask myself if the removal of the one fallopian tube ten years earlier caused such an imbalance in Marion's body

171

metabolism and caused the development of the cancer. This is probably nonsense, as I've been told. Still, one can't but wonder. In any case, nothing can now be changed. Although we had struggled with this for more than two years, we were absolutely shattered. This woman, not yet 46 years old, had for years been the mainstay of our lives – in my case, 25, 26 even 27 years.

The friends we had made – friends from her youth, colleagues from her and my places of employment (and from my pre - Marion life), from our synagogue, school, Hebrew classes and others – rallied round to comfort us. They even collected sufficient funds to endow a scholarship at the Yemin Orde Youth Village in Israel. Facilities for the development of children had always been at the top of Marion's list of priorities. For example, she had been active with the local authority in our neighborhood in London to raise funds for an adventure playground for the local children. I may add, if I have not already mentioned it, that in her youth she had been an active member of the local Jewish youth club and appeared regularly in plays which their theatre group performed – often in a leading role. I dare say if I continue to reminisce about Marion many other items will come to mind but enough is enough – at least for now.

And so, this definitely brings to an end a very special period of my life. But before passing on to the next phase, I would like to write a little about Marion and my biological children – Simone, David, and Naomi. They all turned out to be 'Renaissance' personalities – their interests were extensive and widespread.

For example, Simone started to read, I think, well before she was five years old. She picked up whatever had writing on it – pamphlets, newspapers, books etc and just 'devoured' them. We did not put any restrictions on what she could and could not read and this trend is still with her.

David quite early on turned to writing, a habit he has turned to good use, and is still doing so. Naomi did both read and write – she too is still pursuing both trends. All three enjoyed what we term good literature – the classics and more modern. In fact, they still do. They all write, or wrote, poetry and/or song lyrics – one or the other also set some to music. All three enjoy classical music, chazanut, and what is often

172

termed popular music (is that the music of the masses – snobbishly so named?)

I mentioned Marion's aversion to sending the children to be taken care of by outsiders/ strangers. So, they did not attend kindergarten or other play groups. Only when they reached the age of compulsory education did they "leave home". The earliest effort was when Simone went to Barclay House, a Jewish school, for a little while before transferring to our local Primary school, Netley Street. Children normally attend primary school till age 11, when they transfer to what used to be called Secondary School, either Grammar School or "Secondary Modern". But when Simone reached the age of eight, the Headmistress called us in and told us that by the time she reached the age of nine, they would have nothing further to teach her, because her standard of scholarship was so far ahead of others at the school. They advised us to find her another, more suitable primary school with a higher standard.

At the time, the children in her school, as well as our neighbours' children, all conversed about what they had seen on television and other such items. Our children could not join in their conversations or games because we did not possess a TV – on principal I may add. We preferred them to read and such like and so they spoke of what they read, maybe of seeing a play or ballet or even hearing an opera. Their peers did not even understand what they were talking about, which made friendships difficult, if not impossible. This proved not only the case at school but also in our neighbourhood which basically was working class and largely non-Jewish. Perhaps we should have made more of an effort to find accommodation in a neighbourhood more suitable for our family. Once again, "water under the bridge" as the saying goes.

However, we decided then, on reflection, that we preferred all our children to be educated at a Jewish school and transferred all three children to Solomon Wolfson Primary school.

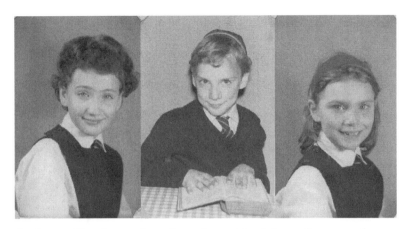

And regarding the matter of owning a television, after several years holding out against the children's pleas for a TV set, we finally succumbed, having been offered an old model of which the aunt of one of the girls in my office was anxious to dispose. The instrument was set up in our bedroom and the children were allowed to watch certain programs only for limited times. Enterprise and initiative are qualities to be encouraged, and our three children apparently possessed them in abundance. They certainly found various ways to watch prohibited programs. How? You may well ask. Marion had a three mirrored dressing table with a large centre mirror and longish adjustable mirrors on both sides (I believe that our eldest, Simone, still owns this item, which she has in her bedroom, and makes good use of it). When one of the smaller mirrors was angled in the proper way, you could see the reflected program on the TV from the hall just outside our bedroom.

Bedtime for our children was fairly early, 7 pm or 7.30 pm or so. If not too tired they were encouraged to read a little in bed before going to sleep. Marion and I, if we wanted to see an evening program on TV could only do so in the bedroom. The children would crawl on their bellies on the floor to the edge of the bedroom door, so that we would not see them (which we did, of course) having earlier angled the mirrors correctly for that purpose. They were thus able to watch the program. We did not make too much of a fuss and tended to ignore these antics, for a little while at least. Furthermore, if one of them, especially Simone, was at a particularly interesting part in a book she was reading

174

when 'lights out' was announced, she would huddle under her blanket reading her book by the light of a torch – until discovered.

Since it is a well- known pastime for children to paint or draw on the walls, we designated their room walls as permitted areas. These were soon filled with "moosies", as the children called their artistic wall – drawing efforts (frescos, if you will). I will refer to the moosies again a little later.

On reaching the age for them to transfer to secondary schools – 11 years old - both girls were awarded scholarships to the City of London School for Girls where both took advantage of an excellent education. Both did well, Simone winning the prize for classics in the equivalent here in Israel to class 10. Her second prize – The Balgrave Memorial Prize for Classics – was awarded her in her final class at that school. Naomi received good grades in her secondary school, even though she won no special prizes there. She did, however come away from her primary school, the Solomon Wolfson School, on her leaving that school for the City of London school, with the Hetty Domb Memorial prize, a prize very much treasured.

Let me also put into words the pleasure that Marion and I felt when our eldest responded to a challenge and participated in a competition including all schools in the British Isles. Israel's literature had become a world-wide affair. Children were invited to submit critical essays on a chosen book by an Israeli author. Simone chose to read and write about Amos Oz's book *My Michael*. An excellent essay by her gained her one of the ten prizes awarded – a trip to Israel. I believe she enjoyed every moment. I may also add that after the Six-Day war, she submitted a short poem to the Jewish Chronicle, and had it published, in memory of one of the paratroopers who lost his life in the successful military operation to liberate the Old City of Jerusalem in 1967.

David also attended the Solomon Wolfson primary school until age eleven when he entered the William Ellis Grammar School. Here, unfortunately, he encountered some anti-Semitism from a number of his classmates, perhaps even from some of his teachers. We therefore transferred him to the Hasmonean High School for Boys where, to his great luck, he found two teachers, both teaching him English, who encouraged him greatly, particularly with his writing. Even this did not compensate for the misery and unhappiness from which he suffered in that school also. He is, and always was, an individualist to the extent that he was not able to find his place in any regulated environment. That and his unhappiness there caused him simply to leave that environment when he was 15. I don't think his mother, nor I, really understood the depth of his problems at that time. There was very little his mother or I could do – perhaps we should have been more persistent, perhaps sought out more professional aid. At least, on reflection, we should have insisted that he went out to work, but about this time Marion became ill and we did not pressure him too much. So, David filled his time by writing.

Apart from school there were also religious Hebrew classes. These were held in the annex of our synagogue three times a week. These classes were attended by our three and a number of children from members of the congregation, including the Rabbi's three children and the Chazan's two children. The rabbi and his wife, Sylvia and Cyril Shine, were really charming. Their children, Ruth, Claire and Jeremy became good friends of our three children; Stewart and Mimi Hass, the children of the Chazan and his wife, Elaine and Shimon Hass, a little less so. The boy was a little older. The girl, our lot found somewhat troublesome, to put it mildly.

Since I have just mentioned Hebrew classes, I may as well insert here the information that in order to supplement our income, many years before that and for a good number of years, I became a Hebrew School teacher in one of the outlying suburbs of east London. I too taught three times a week: Sunday morning, Tuesday and Thursday afternoon. One particular incident stands out. One of my pupils, on reaching his Bar-Mitzva, stopped coming to class. I invited his father to see me. On meeting I asked what made his son stop. His father informed me that his son does not believe in all that religious stuff and only came till now because this orthodox congregation would not allow him to celebrate his Bar-Mitzva unless he first attended classes and took the appropriate examination. The father, apparently, did not believe in 'this stuff' either, at least so I had the impression, unfairly perhaps. But he wanted the boy to have his 'Day', perhaps to please the boy's grandparents or other relatives. Since the only synagogue in the area was this orthodox one, he had to go through the motions.

I encountered here the problem also of trying to give a reasonable answer to the obvious question asked by modern children in an age when science became more and more popular. How do I reconcile the biblical account of the creation with Charles Darwin's *Origin of the Species*. I had to explain to my 11/12 year olds that what we read in the bible as *one day* no doubt referred to one long period of development – made easier to understand for the more simple attitudes prevalent in those earlier eras. Well, such is life.

Speaking of Bar-Mitzva I would like to record another bizarre incident. We were regular, paid up members of the Central Synagogue in Great Portland Street, London for a good many years. When our son reached the age of thirteen, we naturally expected him to be called up to read his Bar-Mitzvah portion at our synagogue. It was the custom for both the father of the celebrant, and whoever taught him his portion (in which capacity I also stood), to stand by the boy, about to become a man, while he recites the parsha and haftorah, perhaps in order to assist/prompt when necessary. Our synagogue had a rule that the person standing with the celebrant must wear a Top Hat. I did not possess such an item. Nor would I borrow one for that single occasion. Imagine my chagrin when I was prevented from being up on the *bimah* with my son while he was reciting his portion and haftorah. One of the Honorary Officers of the synagogue stood in for me. But really – I ask you? Still, I must record that David acquitted himself very, very well. The synagogue provided a really nice Kiddush after the service was concluded. However, when all is said and done, I still would have preferred to stand by my son's side on that occasion.

Coming back to the children as a whole, one can imagine what the two years of Marion's illness meant to them. We relied on one another for so much. There was shopping, cleaning, cooking, etc. I cannot now separate who did what. All were helpful, some more and some even more. I just think and want to believe we all did what we could. I think, actually that Naomi was the cook, a good bit of the time. Even I did so at times. I am told, by those who know, that cleaning played only a minor part in our daily routine at that time. It was more tidying up really. Shopping and laundry were definitely shared. What is absolutely clear is that we were a five-pronged self-contained unit. Then, later, four-pronged with no outside help. (I feel I must insert, in all fairness,

177

that Marion's mother was, after all, elderly and herself not in the best of health). We did not invite, nor did we expect any help from anyone.

And now we come to Sylvia – poor, poor Sylvia. It would be only fair to modify the impression I must have given in what I wrote earlier about our relations with Marion's family. The coolness between us never extended to Marion's sister. Indeed, she was close to Marion – and to me also. She helped when she could, baby-sat not infrequently and was a sister and an aunt. When writing about Marion's and my wedding problems with her family, the reference was to her parents only. When I mentioned the incidence of the cancelled wedding, I mentioned what happened to Sylvia later when she was 'jilted' on her wedding day when her groom just did not appear for the ceremony and that, together with her earlier futile lover's crush – her unrequited love for one of our army friends – had devastating effects on her.

This was compounded when she was told about her sister's fatal illness. During that time, she particularly tried to help but, of course, to no avail. Her sister's illness appears to have been *the straw that broke the camel's back.* She started to have hallucinations of various kinds which did not really improve with treatment as time went on. She was diagnosed with schizophrenia. This situation did not, of course, contribute to an improvement in Marion's health either. It reached the stage that Sylvia, G-d Rest Her Soul – yes, she has since died – spent frequent episodes in a psychiatric hospital. It became an in-and-out situation, during which time we came on aliyah, and only David, on his return to live in London, maintained some sort of contact. Her mother too had by that time succumbed to another stroke which had proved fatal, not contributing to an improvement in Sylvia's recovery. There was, of course, nothing we could do.

On the way to a new life

What now that Marion has gone?

After the *shiva* (the seven - day morning period – according to Jewish tradition) we decided to go to Israel to be with our family. I suppose we, or at least I, craved for the comfort of my family. My relationship with Marion's family had never really flourished into any kind of intimate family contact, except perhaps with Sylvia, Marion's sister – as mentioned above.

The decision to go to Israel was not to my mother-in-law's liking, of course, but the break had to come sometime. We tried to think of our future and had reached our decision as a family. Now I was to learn that being so far apart for so many years from my biological family and growing up in a different cultural environment also did not allow easily for the normal family closeness to develop. This was probably my fault, if fault can be attributed, since I had imbibed the English reticence. Brother and sisters we were, but I cannot claim a really close relationship, except maybe with my younger sister who had also grown up in England. However, it was good to feel part of the family again. In all my married years to Marion she and our children were my family and I felt her loss more deeply than I can express.

The children and I spent a little over three weeks with my family in Israel during *Pesach* in 1973, then back to the grindstone. We trudged on while I started to make inquiries for our resettlement in Israel. The school year in England finished, the new school year started and we decided, in family conclave, by what I believe was a unanimous decision (I think even David was of our opinion at that time) to make the move at the end of the 1973/4 school year. This was also Simone's first year at London University. She was studying classics: Latin and ancient Greek language and literature.

We now started corresponding with our contacts in Israel in earnest: employment for me, university for Simone; school for Naomi, housing, pension arrangements from my present employment and a welter of other related matters. David at this stage presented no special problem – he would not go to school and what he would do would be looked into after our arrival in Israel.

179

After all these preliminary inquiries we felt another visit to Israel, in order to look into things on the spot, was appropriate. So off we went around Pesach time in 1974, for my fifth visit to Israel. I met many people, colleagues from work and others. I am sure we visited some schools in Jerusalem like Boyars, Gymnasia, Denmark, Next to University. We certainly talked to many people. Although nothing was arranged definitely at this time, we had established many contacts and were definitely on the right road.

Our aliyah was planned to take place in the summer of that year, after the current school year, and University year, came to an end in England. On reflection, it was not the best time for Naomi. She was now 15 years old, never the easiest time for a sensitive girl to make such drastic changes. It was not the loss of contact with her grandmother and aunt, or indeed the other relatives on her mother's side – that would be the problem, because the contact was not particularly strong to begin with. It would be the loss of regular contact with her school and friends that made the timing really difficult for her. However, I must point out and stress that she was at least as keen as the rest of us to make this move. For me it also meant that we four siblings would be near to each other again.

For Simone it was somewhat easier since the Classics Department at the Hebrew University agreed to accept her as a second - year student, and not oblige her to start from the beginning. Classical Studies was, of course, her subject. Already in her school she had won prizes in her Classics classes. She went on to obtain first her B.A. and then her M.A. in Classical Studies.

Naomi was enrolled in the prestigious school named 'Next to the University' – not only because of its location, which was naturally right next door to the Givat Ram campus of the Hebrew University, but also because many of the offspring of the senior and junior staff of the University attended that school. *(Note: the Givat Ram campus was one of four campuses of the Hebrew University – three in Jerusalem: Givat Ram; Mount Scopus and the Faculty of Medicine in Ein Karem, which formed part of Hadassah Hospital and included the Medical School as well as the Schools of Pharmacy and Dentistry. The fourth campus, housing the Faculty of Agriculture, was based in Rehovot.)*

So, while Simone studied for and obtained her B.A. and then an M.A. in Classical Studies at HU, Naomi joined the tenth grade at her chosen school, being at a great disadvantage because not having studied all the subjects her new classmates had absorbed from grade one. In tenth grade studies were angled for the *Bagrut* examinations – the Israeli equivalent examination to matriculation. This, of course, included much of Jewish and Israeli history as well as extensive portions of the *Tenach* – the Hebrew Bible. Some of this she had learned in England. But the emphasis, in mentioning it here, is on *'some of it' only*. Yet, although the education authorities made allowances for newcomers, permitting them to take some of the subjects in the exam in their native language, Naomi insisted wherever possible to take on the challenges in Hebrew – with few exceptions. In spite of the hardship she attained an average in this very important end-of-school examination of 8+.

Simone, having arrived in Israel at the 'advanced' age of 19, was excused from military service. This was a pity, on reflection, as I'm sure both she and the Defence Forces would have benefited from the experience! On the other hand, Naomi, on completing high school, was

181

conscripted into the Defence Forces most willingly. She applied and was accepted to a pre-army course in preparation for the role she was to play during her two years service. On being inducted into the army she was integrated into the Tank Corps where she served, at least part of the time on one of the bases near Jericho, on the way between Jerusalem and the Dead Sea. She was primarily concerned with the welfare of the soldiers in her base, as well as with their families, I believe. I suppose one could describe her as a military social worker.

I must digress and go back a little in time to the actual aliyah arrangements and the help my son David was to me at that time. As potential *olim* (immigrants) all four of us, had to go through the immigration process. For us this meant, principally, medical examinations, x-rays, injections, eye tests. We also had to invite at least three forwarding agencies to obtain estimates for the collection, packing and shipping of our goods – furniture, carpets, electrical appliances, books and records and clothes. In this matter, particularly, David was of real help. You see, both Simone and Naomi had to leave before us – in July of that year – in order to complete their enrolment at University and school respectively. Since David would not be attending either, he could stay and help me.

Talking about forwarding agents I may mention that at least one of them was fairly regularly the cheapest. He also had a good reputation for efficient work. In fact, this was the firm we chose to ship our goods. The director of this firm had over the years offered me various gifts, as was customary in business and I believe still is, in order to encourage me to recommend his firm to our olim. This I always refused to do and of course I refused to accept any of his gifts. However, during Marion's illness he sent her a big box of chocolates. I could not refuse to accept it – it would have been churlish to do so – it was, after all, a very generous gesture.

So David and I stayed behind another month during which I wound up all our affairs, including my office (I still continued to train my successor), return of the flat to the local authority, notification to the school of our departure (they had very generously written a suitable report for Naomi) and our travel arrangements.

Having established very good relations with the management of the London office of El Al during all the years of making travel arrangements for our olim, when my turn came, the management offered David and me seats in the first-class compartment, which we did not refuse. What a marvellous experience, and what a difference in the treatment of the passenger, including the food on board. My seat was next to the well-known film star and director Richard Attenborough. He was on his way to Israel where he was shooting his next film, *Rosebud*, in which he played an Englishman who had become a Muslim and a dangerous terrorist chief on the level of Yasser Arafat. Peter O'Toole played the British Government agent pitted against him. It was a very pleasant flight.

The date of our aliyah, for the record, was August 29th, 1974 – 35 years to the day of my landing in London as a Kindertransport refugee boy. The girls, having preceded us on July 29th, exactly one month earlier, were already ensconced in the Jerusalem Katamon Absorption centre and we, naturally, went to join them. We had chosen this Centre because it was within walking distance of Givat Mordechai where my sister Susi and her family lived. At the time I still did not travel by car on Shabbat so we could walk over to her on Shabbat. In this Absorption Centre we were allocated a three room flat which was perfectly adequate for the four of us at that time.

We now looked forward to our permanent housing and started to check out the several new areas in and around Jerusalem being built for this surge in immigration: Neve Yaacov, Ramot, Gilo and East Talpiot. This last one was also known as *Armon Hanatziv* or the 'governor's residence'. It had been the residence of the British High Commissioner for many years during the British Mandate and now served as the UN headquarters for the whole area. We opted for East Talpiot for several reasons. Firstly, we liked the area and the view from there toward the Dead Sea and Herodion. Secondly, it was the smallest and, therefore, the most intimate of the developing suburbs. Thirdly, above all, it was the nearest to the centre of Jerusalem: one could walk the six or seven kilometres to the city centre without any problem.

Now arose the question of the size of the flat, meaning really the number of rooms in the flat we were to be able to purchase, under the government-backed mortgage scheme, for our more permanent residence. Had Marion been alive and we a family of *five*, there would have been no question raised: we would have been allocated a *four* - room apartment: i.e. three bedrooms and a living room. Since we were only four, however, the regulations allowed for us to be allocated a three room flat only. However, as it is frequently stated (especially in Israel), regulations are one consideration, reality is another! And so, we argued that whereas the two girls would, of course, share a bedroom, I could not be expected to share a bedroom with my son. (The three rooms for four persons rule was based, in any case, on the assumption that four persons meant a married couple and two children.) My reasoning made sense, and was accepted by the powers that be. We were allocated a four room flat in East Talpiot into which we moved on the 15th January, 1975 which was the day our lift, with all our possessions, arrived.

Meanwhile, at the Absorption Centre, our flat was equipped with cupboards, table and four chairs, beds and bed linen, a cooker, gas ring and small refrigerator – perfectly adequate for the brief stay till the move to our permanent home. Incidentally, whereas we were not charged for our stay in the Absorption Centre, we were offered our permanent home on a rental basis – a very reasonable rent I may say, with the option to purchase, at what I can only again describe as a bargain price. This we eventually did, on being granted a mortgage by the Absorption Department of the Jewish Agency, and with additional help from the British Zionist Israel Office.

While staying at the Absorption Centre, we had become quite friendly with another family. They had arrived at the Centre about the same time we had. The father, Eli, was also a widower, a year younger than I, I thought, but in fact a year or two older than I, I was told recently. Eli was born in Israel, went to find his fortune in the US after completing his obligatory military service and got married in the US. His wife also had recently died and left him with four children, three girls and one boy.

Eli was actually a scion of an old Jerusalem family, dating back several generations. He had gone to the USA when he was about 22-24 years old I think – perhaps he wanted to forget his days in the *Lechi* organization as a youth. Unlike *Etzel* (the Irgun Tzvai Le'umi or 'National Military Organization') Lechi did not want to be incorporated into the recently founded Israel Defense Forces. Eli thought otherwise, joined the army for his stint, and only then went to try his luck in the USA. Coming on a visit to his homeland in 1957, he met Shoshana, the daughter of another old Jerusalem family, fell in love, married her and took her back with him to the USA. There they had their children and there they lived until June (?) 1974.

Why till then? Well, Shoshana, like Marion, died in 1973 and left Eli a widower with four children. And so, they came on aliyah to the Absorption Centre in June 1974, just a month before Simone and Naomi arrived there. The similarity of our situation was so uncanny that it became quite natural for us to become close friends. As I said earlier Naomi was a little short of 16 years old when we came to Israel. Ayala, Eli's eldest was 15. Talia, the next, was 14. Then came Nurit aged nine and last, but not least, Ami who was five at the time. The children played together when not in school or kindergarten, while Eli and I went about looking for work.

There was another widower at the Centre at the same time, Zacharia Kaye, a newcomer from Canada. He had three children: an older son aged 13 of whom we did not see much, and twins, boys aged nine. Although he, too, moved to East Talpiot, our friendship was somewhat looser. Eli and family moved to 'Block 112a and we were allocated a flat in Block 112b – the two entrances to the block. (Zach Kaye moved into block 113, a little way, perhaps 50-60 meters away from us. The local primary school and a small garden were situated in between).

So, it came about that both Eli and his family and we four Kesslers moved to our respective permanent home in Israel just a few months after our arrival. The flats were ready. Not so the streets. It was the height of winter and the street had not been paved yet. Instead of asphalt and pavements, we found deep mud everywhere. But who cared? At last we were home, and the roads and streets would soon be what they should be.

The lift had arrived very early in the morning, giving us enough time during the day to start unpacking the more urgently needed items first. The problem was that we didn't necessarily know where everything was, or which box contained what. So, we set to work to sort things out, moving things from room to room as we opened the boxes and gradually creating more space.

At least it was easy to identify the beds and mattresses, because they weren't in boxes. So, we moved just enough boxes to create room in each of the bedrooms and then set up the beds, so we had somewhere to sleep. Then we did the same with the cooker, setting it up in the kitchen so we could eat. We were glad there was a grocery shop close by (one of the things we had ensured in our choice of location), so we purchased essentials. We had been provided with a small table and chairs which served as kitchen furniture initially until we were all set up and could dispose of them. By early evening we were exhausted and decided to leave the rest of the unpacking and arranging till the next morning.

What a feeling! Our own home. And in Israel. What's more, in *Jerusalem*. We were all overwhelmed with emotion and were glad, I think, to retire to bed. Before retiring (and I must mention this as it was so unexpected), one of our new neighbours brought us bread and wine: a gift of welcome for us, the new arrivals. What a wonderful gesture. As to our neighbours, we were the best demonstration of the Hebrew expression, still relevant at the time, of "Kibbutz Galuyot" or the "Ingathering of The Exiles." The origin of the residents in our building alone was Romania, Chile, Morocco, USA, Russia, Britain, Ukraine, Bukhara, Uruguay, Canada, Poland, and France.

We had made friends with Rabbi Paul Lederman, who lived nearby and his wife, Shula and their family. More about him later. We had also made friends with Lionel and Natalie Rosenfeld. Lionel's father, whom I had known in England before our aliyah, was the chazan in one of London's Principal Synagogues. And there were many others whom I may mention, or not, in the course of these recollections.

Now to go on with my tale.

Having arrived in Israel as an immigrant I had not only to find permanent accommodation for my children and me, but to see to our sustenance, that is, find a suitable job. I turned first to my erstwhile employers and contacted the headquarters of the Aliyah Department of the Jewish Agency. They had promised me all and sundry the moment I indicated that, at last, I was ready and able, on my aliyah, to take up their regular offers of employment! Especially the regular offers of the then incumbent director-general of the department, General (Res) Uzi Narkiss, who had been the commander of the Jerusalem front in the Six-Day War and had re-united the city by capturing the Old City of Jerusalem. However, the offers I received from him and others in my old department were not what I expected and hoped for and I was therefore unable to accept their offers and so, regretfully, we parted company.

I was advised to apply to the Hebrew University for a position as head of the Reporting Section in their Public Relations Department. This I did and was invited for an interview with the Vice-President of the University, as well as with the director of the Public Relations Department. The former, Bernard Cherrick, an erstwhile Minister of Religion in Ireland, received me and after chatting for some minutes we were joined by Eliyahu Honig, the director of that department. Eliyahu was an *oleh* from Australia whose aliyah I had arranged when his group came through London on their way to a kibbutz many years before. (They were members of the Habonim youth movement.) He had, it would appear, left the kibbutz, studied at the Hebrew University and then went to work for that institution. Eliyahu pulled out some articles which had been written about me when leaving England for Israel, and some material I had written myself. He put it in front of Bernard Cherrick with the words "just the chap we were looking for." Rather complementary and very encouraging. The only things then left to discuss were my date of commencing work and the terms. This did not take long.

From left: David, Me, Judy (my secretary at HU), Tami (my Hebrew secretary at HU), Simone. At the back is Naomi.

We were now in the position as follows: Simone started University at the start of the academic year, some time towards the end of October. Naomi started school at the beginning of the school year – September 1st. I started to work at the Hebrew University on October 15th, 1974. It saddens me a little to recall that at that time David, then seventeen and a half, still had not found his feet (he will of course eventually, one expects) and I had no idea how he occupied his time. At the time, we were still in our temporary abode, looking forward to moving to our new flat. Much as the situation with David was on my mind I had much still to deal with and had to cope with a great deal of running around. I believe, thinking back, that after all the years working with and for olim, whilst in London, I only now began to appreciate what such an upheaval entailed for a family – not so much for an individual or couple, but certainly for a family.

I only wish I had devoted more time, much more time and thought to the David situation. While Simone, Nomi and I were all busy with our affairs, David was at home doing what? I'm not sure I understood the situation as I should have done. I am glad that he eventually found his

188

preferred occupation as an author. He has practiced this, in one way or another, since he was 13 years old, was it? Not always with roaring success – we are still hoping for a best seller. But he has had published so far, seven thrillers (four in hard cover and all seven in paperback) as well as one non-fiction book, in hard cover, which he co-authored with the subject of the book – not at all bad. All this limited success was achieved after David decided that he would do better in England, since he wrote in English, and all his contacts were there. However, I am very happy to say that he comes to Israel to be with us at least once, frequently twice a year – for Pesach and Succoth.

While David was doing 'his thing' – that is, the thing he loved and enjoyed doing, writing and sending out his literary efforts, so far with only limited success since his efforts have not yet yielded the best-seller we hope for and expect, at some stage while still in Israel he was persuaded to go out to work as well. This was principally Ilana's influence. I'll write about her later. The jobs he took were not particularly inspiring – he was, after all, not trained for anything – but they included the Youth Aliyah Research Centre. What his work entailed here is beyond me; I must ask him about this when next I see or speak with him. He then worked as a messenger. He worked for a firm copying architects drawing and for a firm printing and selling greeting cards with views of Israel. That was until he returned to London. Here too he worked while writing, until he found that it was essential, in his view, for him to concentrate on writing and 'pushing' his efforts.

Meanwhile Simone finished both her B.A. and M.A. degrees in classical studies at the Hebrew University with a great measure of success. While studying for her qualifications, she also worked part-time to help the family budget – well, at least, to make it unnecessary for me to give her an allowance. Her work at that time included writing reports in the Physics Department of the Hebrew University, at the institute researching anti-Semitism, and at the HU centre dealing with the psychometric entrance examination for prospective students. She also undertook babysitting to help her financially. On reflection, she felt that the only real use she could make of her studies in classics would be either to teach in school or wend her way up the University ladder towards becoming a lecturer and eventually a professor. Neither idea appealed to her particularly.

She had always been interested in Law, so she decided to take the four -
year course at the Hebrew University Faculty of Law and attain her law
degree. Like most students at that time, she worked for her living. Did I
mention above that my salary was not all that outstanding; but the fact
that I was employed by the HU relieved her, and me, of the necessity of
paying the fee for her studies. Since we lived in Jerusalem it also made
it possible for her to live at home while she studied. On graduating in
that subject, she applied to do her internship in law by clerking for a
half year for Judge Shoshana Netanyahu, of Israel's Supreme Court and
a further full year for one of the leading Jerusalem law firms, before
obtaining employment as a prosecutor in the Legal Department of
Jerusalem's area HQ of the Israel Police.

Naomi, as I wrote before, completed her High School, took a pre-army
course, and was inducted into the army and after her basic training
joined one of the Armoured Corps bases where she served, at the rank
of sergeant, as something in the nature of a Social Worker. She was
concerned with the welfare, including home circumstances, of the
soldiers. On conclusion of her two-year stint she too entered the
University, initially in the School of Social Work. I think she did not
enjoy her first year there. Anyway, she decided to change direction and
registered for the course in the Department of Communications. She,
too, worked for her living whilst studying for both her B.A. and M.A.

Let me add that, as mentioned in passing earlier, Naomi was just short
of 15 years when we came on aliyah, a difficult age for such a move.
Although she wanted this move as much as the rest of us, she
nevertheless felt the wrench with what she had known till then very
much. We decided therefore that a visit back to London would be
beneficial, and since one of her best school friends had persuaded her
parents to invite Naomi to spend her summer holiday with her
arrangements were easily and speedily completed. I think it was the
right decision.

All this took a number of years during which major changes occurred in
my life. As related already, my beloved wife, Marion, died early in
1973. We came to Israel in mid-1974. The children were growing up, as
children are wont to do. I worked long hours in my new position – I had
little to encourage me to run home for and much work to cope with –
we never did have enough staff to keep up-to date with the volume of

work which had to be completed. Simone, David and Naomi all had, after all, their own affairs to attend to. I suppose I must have felt lonely at times. I always was, and still am I am sure, a very reserved sort of person, not gregarious in the least. I was and still am not much of a talker. Small talk is not and never was part of my make-up. On rare occasion I went on what was, I suppose, a date. Female company was still a pleasant interlude since I was only in my late forties – not really old yet.

Apropos of nothing in particular except that it leads me into the next phase of my life let me here relate the following. Having obtained my driving license way back in 1952 in England, and since immigrants to Israel were awarded many custom and excise concessions, especially on import or purchase of a car, I took the opportunity afforded me and for the first time in my life became the owner of a car – an Italian Lancia Beta, no less. How proud I was of my new car. I might have hesitated about buying it. I was not really rich. I considered not only the cost of the car – one also had to consider the cost of upkeep. However, since my job description included a not inconsiderable amount of travel, I was awarded a car maintenance allowance as part of my salary. This enabled me to make the purchase with the minimum of a guilty twinge at this extravagance.

What Joy! What comfort! Before taking possession of the car I considered taking driving lessons again, because although I had, wisely I think, renewed my license in England every year, I had not driven a car in over 15 years. My father-in-law, Harry, had disposed of his car several years before he died. I had applied for and received my Israeli driving license by just showing my English license – renewing my license annually in England had paid off. A colleague at work recommended her brother who was a driving instructor and I invited him to help me refresh my driving experience.

The driving instructor told me, after three lessons that my 'refresher' course was over. I needed no more in order to go on the road in Israel. I think he compared me with the regular Israeli driver – favourably, I think. So, when the car importer informed me that my car had arrived and was ready to be collected, I trotted off to his showroom, full of confidence.

His place of business was right in the centre of town, in its busiest section. I entered the premises, completed the paper- work and suggested someone from the shop drive me home. This would enable me to practice a little in our quiet neighborhood. He looked at me as if I was completely crazy, shook his head, gave me the car keys, showed me to the car and said, "it's all yours".

One of the most frequently used expressions in Hebrew was, and still is "Ein Breira" – meaning there is no choice. Well, that was my situation now. So, having no choice, I opened the car door – no, I mean the 'tank' door, - it was such a strong car –, sat myself in the driver's seat and slowly, very gingerly, switched on the engine. I then released the handbrake, put my foot on the clutch, put the car into first gear (who thought of automatic car gears in 1975?) and slowly edged out of the cramped parking space of the importer.

Although a little apprehensive, I felt on top of the world. My route was from the centre of town to the University. I took a circuitous route deliberately, to give me more practice. I don't remember if it was in Emek Refaim or on Derech Beit Lechem that a bus which had been stationary, while picking up passengers, decided to move out from his parking spot into the road just as I came almost level with him. Remember what I related earlier when my brother visited me/us in London in 1951 – who said history does not repeat itself? But not necessarily with the same result, thank the Lord. I had to make a split-second decision to put my foot forcefully on the brake or find another solution. This time at least there was no rain.

With traffic coming from the opposite direction I did not have much room to manoeuvre. I opted to be bold. I thought – not really – my car would lengthen, or slim itself on demand and pass between the bus and the oncoming traffic. Well, we made it, but only with a scraping of the bus the whole length of my brand new pride and joy 'tank'. The car would not slim itself on demand after all. Fortunately I succeeded in arriving safely at the university, and having had my first accident on the day I took possession of my car, I now felt full of confidence, again, saying to myself "good that we have this out of the way – all should now be smooth sailing."

Driving to work and back now became a regular routine. Not only could I now avoid the bus journey to work on two separate crowded buses each way, but I was able to take Naomi to school every morning so she too could avoid this hardship. This routine went on for some time. Whenever Naomi had to be in school at 8.00 a.m. she travelled with me in our car.

Naomi and Me by the Lancia

I don't now recall if we ventured out of Jerusalem at that time. I expect we did visit my brother in Rehovot and my sister in Ashkelon and of course my sister in Jerusalem.

The next memorable event I must record here is still connected to the car which by now was no longer new – but then, neither was I. As it happened, I knew a number of people in what was Phase One of the East Talpiot new development. I mention Phase One because this was only the first part of this new Jerusalem neighbourhood which would eventually grow to a 20,000 souls Suburb – approximately.

We now had developed roads, a primary school, two synagogues (one Sephardi and one Ashkenazi) a community centre, and a bus service to town. Phase Two of the project was well under way. The growing population was very mixed: immigrants from all corners of the globe as

193

well as one building near ours housing families cleared from some of the slum areas of the city – yes, there were such in Jerusalem.

As in all new developments, there was much that needed to be done to turn the bricks and mortar into a living and breathing community. It was usual in all Jerusalem areas for locals to select, appoint, and/or elect a small group of interested citizens to push for the always necessary improvements of the existing conditions in the area. Some time after moving into our home, and in speaking to others in our area, we found that there was general dissatisfaction with the then existing local area committee. I decided to take a hand – having been urged to do so by friends and neighbours. I organized a meeting of residents in the area, representative of every building in the new area so far. At that meeting we established a new local council, comprising one representative from each building then lived in. This council elected the local committee – the equivalent of the governing cabinet – which would represent the residents vis-à-vis all official bodies of the city.

The first item of business was the election of the chairman of both the council and committee. It was proposed by all and sundry that since I organized the meeting in the first place, it would be appropriate for me to take on the task. Much against my better judgement I was persuaded to accept. So, I became what one of Julia's (Yael's) young classmates eventually termed "king of the neighbourhood." (I am soon getting to Julia and her mother). In this capacity I and the rest of the committee dealt with matters of transport, health, education, building, social welfare, leisure and a 'million' other subjects. We dealt not only with the municipal authority and all its relevant departments but also with government ministries and departments – the housing, transport, social services, religion, education, absorption, interior and other ministries.

We also were very much involved with the local Community Centre of which I also served as chairman of its managing body. Here, some of the outside personalities with whom I worked included Kalman Yaron, a senior researcher at the Martin Buber Institute for Adult Education and Lotte Salzberger, a senior member of the Paul Bearwald School of Social Work who later served as a Deputy Mayor of Jerusalem. Both were concerned with the social process of integrating this variety of residents flowing into this new Jerusalem suburb – this was a microcosm of the Ingathering of the Exiles (*kibbutz galuyot*, in Hebrew) from the four corners of the earth. Kalman was more concerned with adult education, Lotte more with social integration and welfare. Both worked with us through the Community Centre. I could wax eloquent and relate in detail the variety of newcomers from all parts of the globe as well as veteran Israelis who flocked to this Jerusalem suburb (the nearest to the city centre) but content myself with what is written till now. We now come to Julia – and her mother, of course.

Ilana (and Julia-Yael of course)

One morning in the very cold winter of the year 1976/7, I think, no, I'm sure, it was November 1976 and it was really very windy and cold, I was on my usual way to my car, to drive to my office at the Hebrew University. As I turned the corner from the car parking area I noticed, standing at the bus stop, this most attractive young woman. I had noticed her before, of course, both in the neighborhood and at the University – after all, I was only 49 years old and had been alone, that is without close female companionship, now almost four years. There she was, wrapped up for the winter, winter coat and knee-length boots, no hat, looking very cold. I had observed her on a number of occasions with a little 5/6 year - old, very pretty girl.

I never had any intention to 'start' a new relationship. My late wife was still very much on my mind. The young woman really was young, at that time she was still only 28 years old. Anyway, I assumed that she was also on her way to work at the University. I stopped the car and offered to take her to the University. At first, she hesitated, but since I must have appeared rather mild and innocent, she accepted the offer. We talked a little. I found that she lived only two buildings down the road from mine. It also appeared that she went home at the normal end of the working day. Until then I had usually worked long hours, but since my time was flexible, I suggested that she phone me when she was about to leave. If the time of her leaving coincided with my return to the neighbourhood, it would save her the two-bus 'shlep' and get her home to her daughter much earlier.

Quite naturally, and completely innocuously, the arrangement gradually became fairly regular. We got to the stage when Ilana, for that was her name, was prepared in the morning to come down to the parking area and wait by the car. Of course, we chatted. She had come on aliyah in June 1974, from Kiev, Ukraine, nearly two months before my girls and three months before David and I. I have already mentioned her daughter Julia (now Yael), but the family, at least those who came to Israel at that time, also consisted of Ilana's parents, sister and her father's mother whom I met eventually. Her father, Ilya, was a scientist, who was accepted at the Hebrew University as a full professor upon his arrival in Israel. His field was physical chemistry and he had an international reputation. Her mother, who had been an experienced children's' heart specialist in Kiev, found suitable employment as a physician.

The family also comprised Ilana's 17 – year old sister (a flaming redhead) who was accepted at the Hebrew University, where she specialized in her father's field. They were accompanied by their paternal grandmother, aged 88 at the time of her aliya. She had been a dentist in her younger days. I may insert here that my conversations with that old lady were always conducted in simple Hebrew which she taught herself by reading the "immigrant paper in easy Hebrew" and listening to the special broadcasts for newcomers, a dictionary in her hand.

On their arrival in Israel, the family went first to the Mevasseret Zion Absorption Centre just outside Jerusalem. This was considered the five-star, deluxe absorption centre. Here they would find accommodation and an *ulpan* (intensive Hebrew language study centre). They had Absorption Department personnel on the premises, so to speak. This included the academic employment unit whose task it was to place academics in gainful employment. At her first interview, soon after her arrival she did not open her mouth. She knew no Hebrew and the official knew no Russian. Two months later, having attended the Hebrew lessons made available at her Absorption Centre, on her second interview, the official was dumbfounded to note the strides she had made, conversing relatively freely with the new olah in Hebrew.

"Now," she told Ilana, "I can send you for interviews."

Among the places to which she sent her, was the Bezalel Academy of Arts and Design. They had a vacancy for the position of director of their Library. Although Ilana's degree was in that field, she did not like the subject. She had only studied it because of the few choices available in Kiev at that time, as I wrote above. Accordingly, she turned down the offer.

The official then told her of a vacancy in the National and Hebrew University Library – not as librarian but rather in their Restoration & Conservation Laboratory. When she came for her interview in late autumn, at the end of 1974, she was one of three applicants. The lady in charge of the Laboratory, Esther Alkalai, was originally from Bulgaria. She had already attained a world-wide reputation as a restorer and conservator of ancient documents and manuscripts, including papyrus, parchment and paper. She sat the three ladies down, tore pages from a telephone directory, and put them to work on these. I can't really describe what they were supposed to do, but it included variations in batches of 29 here, 30 there 40 or 50 on something else.

At the end of the week, she sent two away. She looked at Ilana, and at the sweater she was wearing (it was, after all, winter and very cold) and asked where she had obtained it. Ilana told her she had knitted it herself. Esther than asked her to show her hands.

"You'll do," she said. "Besides," she told her, "you have a little girl to support."

Ilana reminded me that the first time she met one of my children was when she met Naomi and me at the car and I pointed out to her that she, Ilana, would have to sit in the back – that the front seat was reserved for Naomi. I think she was taken aback somewhat, but I believe we overcame that hurdle and she doesn't hold a grudge – at least, I hope not.

The reader of this journal will have understood that this relationship turned into a much more permanent, indeed more personal relationship. The next hurdle to cross was my meeting with Ilana's little girl. I am persuaded that our first and subsequent meetings turned out successfully. Ilana invited me for coffee and cake, and I met Julia, aged six. I felt we took to one another at once. After I arrived at the flat, I sat down in one of the armchairs. Julia sat down opposite me and for a little while stared at me from under her eyebrows. She then jumped onto my lap and I was absolutely conquered. Ilana told me the next day that Julia told her mother "marry him – he likes, (or was it loves?) me very much."

Having been invited to her home to meet her little daughter to be evaluated by the little one, we now had the answer to this. The next phase was for Ilana to meet my other two children, as well as Naomi again, on our home ground. If I'm not mistaken this took the form of a meal in our home. I think it went rather well; at least I like to think so. My *brood* were very understanding, I think. I believe they took a liking to Ilana at once. In any event, they encouraged me – I don't think this was wishful thinking on my part – and our relationship developed. We must have 'gone out' to various events such as the cinema, or a concert – I can't remember.

I do remember, quite distinctly, that I took her to the Rimonim Hotel in Zfat (Safed, to you who don't understand the Hebrew name of the city) for her birthday, in mid-May 1977. By that time, we had known one

199

another for all of six months. The hotel was top class but our visits to some of the artist studios were less successful. I had always suffered from feelings of claustrophobia, not in closed places, rather in crowded places. This must have spoiled it somewhat for Ilana, although she did not remark on it nor show any feelings of being upset by the limit this put, on part of our visit (except maybe concern for my health and welfare). Nowadays of course she makes fun of it, which points to the result of our relationship since that time.

Our relationship flowered but I was not yet into the obvious eventual outcome of such a relationship. We had however become an item, to all intents and purposes. In November of that year – a whole year after our meeting – we decided to make another leap forward in our relationship. My next- door neighbour, Boris, had a two-room flat in which he lived on a rental basis, as we had done before we were offered an opportunity to purchase the four-room flat in which we lived. Naturally the terms offered being so very favourable, we accepted. Boris did not or could not. Anyway, Ilana lived in a replica of that flat, together with her daughter, also on a rental basis, only two entrances away. We approached Boris and suggested we might 'swap' flats (his for hers) which was also held on rental. He agreed, and with the consent of the housing authority the 'swap' was affected officially.

And so, on November 17th, 1977, exactly one year to the day we met, Ilana and Julia moved in with me. This was after I had finally proposed marriage to her. Simone and Naomi were thrilled to have a flat of their own. Each now had a room to herself, albeit in a separate flat next door to ours. David kept his room. Julia took over what had been my room and Ilana joined me in the large bedroom that had previously been shared by the girls. I tend to think that the girls – Simone and Naomi, perhaps David also, considered that if I was deeply involved with this woman, I would have no head to interfere in their lives. Therefore, as far as they were concerned, this was a completely satisfactory arrangement.

It is definitely worth mentioning that our little Julia had a lot of initiative. The morning after she and her mother moved in to our flat, she marched into the headmistress' study at school and announced to her, for the record – the school record, that is: "My name is no longer Rotmistrovski; I am now Julia Kessler!"

200

To all our great amazement Malka, the headmistress, did not flinch for a moment, and accepted the announcement as fact. "Kol hakavod Malka!" She so registered the child in the school records. (Bravo Malka.)

I must confess that I had hesitated about this marriage proposal because of the vast age difference. Ilana was only 29 years old while I was 50 by then. Another consideration was that if the union did not work out, how this might affect Julia, to have and lose another father. She must have thought herself abandoned once already when her biological father would not come with them to Israel from Russia. And then, what about my own children? How would they take to this more permanent change in all our status? What did I feel about Marion – wasn't this some kind of betrayal of my first marriage? What is more, what if 'chas vechalile' (heaven forbid) something also happened to Ilana? I did not think I could bear it again). Or maybe I just had cold feet or was afraid to give up my freedom. But what freedom, actually?

Fortunately, Ilana made it perfectly clear – as she usually does, to this day. It was not good for her, or for her daughter, or indeed for me and/or my own children to go on as we were. A decision had to be reached. This happened in the parking lot outside the Hebrew University & National Library where Ilana worked. She then got out of the car and started to walk towards the entrance of the building. I stared after her and could not bear the thought of losing her. I called her back to the car and proposed to her formally. Well, 'chevre', THE DIE WAS CAST. No going back on it now. What remained was only to set the date, and we decided on February seventh. I have not regretted the decision (this is me, in the guise of the reticent English gentleman). It was the natural thing to do. After that the move to our home took place quite naturally.

I would like to digress for a brief flashback and relate an event that I recall of Sylvester night. We don't really call this goyishe (non-Jewish) evening by that name. We refer to it properly as New Years Eve of the civil year 1976/7. Although not connected to anything Jewish the evening had become a matter of celebration for those not into the exclusive celebration of Jewish traditional festivals. It was, after all, considered by them as a universal holiday, especially by Russians, or rather ex-Russians in Israel who had not much to celebrate whilst living in the Soviet Union.

Ilana had invited a goodly number of her ex-Russian friends to celebrate the New Year of 1977 with her. We had known each other by then maybe a month, certainly no more than two, and she felt it appropriate that I meet her friends and join in their celebration. This wasn't really my 'thing' but it was nice to meet her friends. I remember they arranged a long table (from where I do not know) there must have been some twenty people round that table or more, all speaking Russian except when one or another turned to me. I watched Ilana and her immediate neighbour at the table (whose name was Lonia) consume a full bottle of vodka between them. I don't know about Lonia, but Ilana appeared to me absolutely sober at the end. Was she? I wonder! Anyway, everyone had a good time; the evening was a roaring success.

Now to put aside the brief interlude and return to the marriage proposal and the plans that followed. Ilana had been married in Kiev, by civil marriage. Since her husband was not prepared to leave with them, she had to divorce him to enable her to leave the Soviet Union with Julia, who was only four years old at the time. Ilana, on the other hand, was not prepared to stay in Kiev, especially as her parents and sister and one of her grandmothers were asking for permission to leave the Soviet Union. Her father, then the director of one of the major research institutes in Kiev, was followed by the KGB everywhere he went, although he was not technically a "Prisoner of Zion."

Eventually they were all given permission to leave and they came to Israel on June 4th, 1974. In order to marry here, Ilana was asked to provide documents of her marital status. She presented her marriage certificate and her divorce certificate, both civil documents, not religious. She also presented the required proof that she was, in fact, Jewish. The rabbinate, which was and still is the appropriate authority issuing marriage licenses, gave her a document stating that she was eligible to marry anyone except a Cohen (priest), presumably because of her divorce in Kiev.

We considered this decision strange, as both her marriage and her divorce were civil contracts and we thought they were not valid in Jewish law. If they were recognized, precluding her from marrying a Cohen, then maybe she should have been asked to undergo the *'Get'* (religious Jewish divorce) procedure before permission was granted. As it stood, her certificate, rather her document allowing her to marry, read she was 'free' to marry, not that she was single and/or divorced. I, on the other hand was asked only for proof that I was not a Cohen – having shown my valid *ketuba* (religious marriage document) and the formal death certificate of my first wife.

Now the question arose concerning the rabbi who would perform the ceremony. I already mentioned Paul Lederman. He was an orthodox rabbi who had come to live in Israel from The United States. Both Ilana and I had become friends with him and his wife Shula, another descendant of a veteran Jerusalem family. The official at the rabbinate insisted we have the official local area rabbi perform the ceremony, saying it was the policy of the rabbinate for that individual to officiate at such events. They conceded that our choice could participate, if we so wished.

Well, the local principal rabbi was a very nice man and we liked him. However, we would not allow anyone to dictate to us about who would officiate at our wedding. They had, of course no knowledge of the fact that Ilana was living with me already. So, I told them that if that is their condition then they are forcing me to either go to Cyprus for a civil ceremony or have Ilana live with me 'in sin', so to speak. The official, no doubt thinking of the child as well, immediately understood our point of view and issued the necessary certificate there and then enabling us to decide who would officiate at our wedding.

We had the marriage ceremony on the penthouse balcony of Ilana's parents, under the open sky. It was not easy for them. For Marion's parents in London, years earlier, I was a penniless foreigner. Now for Ilana's parents, especially for her father, I was a relatively old man marrying their young, attractive daughter, who would become the father of their granddaughter. Ilana's parents were, after all, only one year older than I. But the ceremony went off without a hitch. Rabbi Paul Lederman officiated, and we were very pleased that Lionel Rosenfeld had accepted our invitation to serve as chazan for the occasion. Lionel's father, whom I mentioned earlier, was a chazan in one of London's major synagogues. Lionel too, although a chartered accountant by profession, had a lovely voice and eventually became a chazan in one of London's major synagogues in the centre of town, first part time for the High Holidays and later more permanently.

The four kids at the wedding

After the religious part of the ceremony was completed, we had the celebratory 'nosh' that was mainly prepared by Ilana herself. There was no hall, no caterer, no photographer, no organized music and no real dancing. But the occasion was a very joyous one, although I wish now we had more photographic evidence of the occasion than the very few personal photos we do have. And I can't even find *them* most of the time. Those who participated included our families, some of Ilana's colleagues I think, and friends, as well as other friends from the neighbourhood and elsewhere. We were surprised, and very pleased to welcome a very good friend of Ilana's from Kiev, who now lived in Nahariya, and who had come all the way from that northern city to celebrate our wedding with us.

When we finished celebrating in her parents' penthouse, Ilana, the ever-welcoming hostess, invited those who were not yet sated with our company to come over to our nearby flat, less than a five -minute walk away, to continue to celebrate this joyous event. Although the details may be a little blurred (I am, after all in my 92nd year now) it remains for me, nevertheless, an unforgettable occasion. I had been married before to a lovely brunette, with deep brown eyes, for 25 years. It had been a true, deep love affair, which terminated only with her death in 1973. Now, five years later, I was embarking on another true love affair with another lovely lady, this time a blonde with great big beautiful deep blue eyes – a love which has lasted for more than 40+ years. May it so continue!!!

How lucky can a man be, to be so blessed twice in a lifetime? Many don't get to be so fortunate even once. I must be careful not to wax poetic. This is meant to be a practical description of my life to date. I may let you, the reader, into a little secret. The marriage, especially the earlier years, was not without its problems for both of us, but when you have deep and abiding love, and mutual respect, especially mutual respect, coupled with the determination to make it work, it usually does succeed. *I also had the words etched into my memory from what the old rabbi told me in Bloomsbury Square in London so many years before.*

All I can say now is: *Kol Hakavod*, Ilana – these words are meant just for you – thank you for all these years (I hope we shall have many more).

Our wedding celebrations were, of course, not yet over. Whereas my bride's friends at work were few and some could therefore attend our wedding at home, the number of senior and junior colleagues at my place of employment was considerably larger. I refer not only to my own department, but to many in other departments in the University's Administration building as well as in the various faculties. There would have been too many to accommodate in the limited space available in my parents-in-law's penthouse. So, we arranged for an hour or two break in my office and invited my boss, colleagues and friends in the Administration building, as well as friends from Ilana's laboratory and from some of the faculties to join us in our office.

I like to think that a good time was had by all. Again, Ilana had done the cooking and baking herself for the occasion. I still don't know why I did not arrange for a caterer for the occasion.

Since I am on the subject of Ilana, let me record some more information on this central subject in my life now. I may repeat here some of the things I have already mentioned. As I mentioned already Ilana, aged 26, had come to Israel from the Soviet Union (Kiev, in the Ukraine, to be exact) in June 1974 together with her parents, four year - old daughter, 17 year - old sister and her father's 88 years old mother.

Her mother was a children's heart specialist, She worked first at the Bikur Holim hospital in her own specialty, then for Kupat Holim as a paediatrician and finally, before retiring, at a special home for the handicapped known as the Swedish Village. She is now retired a good many years and still lives in Armon Hanatziv near us. (Regretfully she has meanwhile died and is buried in Jerusalem.)

Her father, a professor of physical chemistry, had been the director of a major Research Institute in Kiev, and was given a professorship in that subject at the Hebrew University where he taught post-graduate and doctoral students, as well as conducting research in his field. I am not too sure exactly what his research entailed. I would probably not have understood if he had tried to explain it to me.

But I did understand what he invented here in Jerusalem – and that he and his family were cheated out of the financial benefits of the invention. I'll try to describe the invention. It was, in fact, a special kind of small engine. The engine was incorporated in the workings of an

207

ordinary bicycle, at first When cycling normally, and especially downhill, the engine would accumulate power which made the uphill ride much easier. I think that was it, simply explained. When that worked properly the engine was tried on invalid wheelchairs – here, too, it worked well. There was much profit to be made by a businessman. Since he was a scientist and not a businessman, need I say more? (I won't go into details about the people whom he invited to work with him).

Sad to relate, but he died after going to Hadassah hospital for a routine check-up. He had had his first heart attack when he was in his mid-thirties (still in Kiev) and had been in the care of a cardiologist since then having regular, routine check-ups. On this particular occasion the doctors there were not satisfied with his condition and hospitalized him on the spot for further tests. They stopped all his regular medication prescribed by his erstwhile cardiologist while they undertook a new set of tests. His condition worsened and the family asked to bring in his former cardiologist, a request which was perfectly reasonable. However, the hospital refused this request saying they have their own specialists. Unfortunately, his condition worsened, and the medical team was unable to save him. He died on the 25th of November 1989.

Ilana's grandmother was naturally retired. She had been a dentist in Kiev years before coming to Israel. As I said earlier, she was 88 years old at the time of her aliyah from Kiev. The language of this land was not the easiest to learn, especially at such an advanced age. The lady, however, was determined not to miss what went on around her and sat daily by the radio and learned, and learned, and learned. For my part, I do not speak Russian. So, by the time I met her, several years after her arrival in Israel, our language of communication was Hebrew, with a little bit of Yiddish thrown in, here and there. She walked daily, in fact twice daily, for anything between half an hour and a full hour. She did this almost till the day she died, two months short of 100 years old.

Ilana's sister, Irena, who is her junior by nine years, became a B.Sc. student, in chemistry. I think her Masters' degree was already in physics or physical chemistry. She then obtained her doctorate, I believe from the Fritz-Haber Institute in Berlin, Germany where her father also researched several months each year in the summer. She was, of course, following in her father's footsteps. Irena, or Ira for short, was and is a renaissance person also. Out of many subjects, her all-round knowledge of painting, music, literature and all forms of art and culture is extensive.

She is also a universally acknowledged authority on the physical (material) aspects of the Dead Sea Scrolls. Over a good number of years past she has been researching the physical aspects, particularly the materials and inks used two thousand years ago, where they were stored over the centuries and the effect of the deterioration of these scrolls. She continues to do so. I could fill more than one page to describe her very passionate efforts in this field – so close to her heart – and pray for her success in all her efforts in this respect.

Ilana's young daughter, Julia (later Yael, now Yuli) had been only four years old when her family came to Israel. She went to kindergarten first and then attended the local primary school. Her scholastic achievements were not outstanding, not because she couldn't but rather because she wouldn't. I shall not elaborate on her secondary school career which was not particularly brilliant either – for the same reason. Nor will I elaborate on the various hormone-based episodes in this teen-agers life. Julia-Yael was very much a normal teen-ager, which made life very 'interesting' for her mother and for me. I may confirm that in most respects we were fairly normal, supporting parents. On more than one night, Julia was out till rather late, did we not sleep until she returned home, often going to the window whenever we heard a car stopping nearby to see if it was our beloved daughter. When it eventually was, and we heard the key in the lock, we returned to bed, pretending to be asleep, for reasons clear to all parents of teen-age daughters.

On leaving school she was conscripted into the army, as was usual in this country, to fulfil her national obligation. Here her tasks involved intelligence of a sort, keeping an electronic eye on our enemies all around us. She was in what was then called the Signals Corps, stationed in the Central Command H.Q. We had not a few sleepless nights at that time also. On concluding her military commitment, she decided to complete her studies toward her matriculation, having missed out on that while in High School. While studying, she took on employment of various kinds, including restaurant waiting at tables, telephonist, clerking, shop-saleslady, etc. She sat for and passed her matriculation and decided to continue her further, higher education. I will surely write more about her later.

Although her career in her primary school was not exceptional, she was very popular, always accepted by all, and a natural leader in her class. She learned ballet for some time and was very good at it. I also admired her drawings of ladies fashion. I do think she had a flair for that and excelled in it. As to her popularity, I recall that one of her male classmates (they were both about 9 or 10 years old at the time) sidled up to us one day and told us that we should expect, in a few years, to refer to him as our son-in-law.

I may have mentioned that she, Julia, as she still was, on meeting me for the first time, sent her mother out of the room to make us some tea in order that she could be left alone with me. She was only 6 years old at the time. Later, when she was alone with her mother, she appears to have told her mother that she should marry me – or have I mentioned this earlier?

What I have not yet described in detail is that when I decided to adopt this bundle of energy, the process took quite some time. We put in the application to the proper authority. It had to be 'we', not I, since Ilana, the mother of the child, naturally had to approve. Then we had personal interviews, some home visits (in the plural), tete-a-tete meetings with the child, who was by now eight years old and several attempts to obtain the biological father's consent. This was a vital part of the process and took some time, since the biological father was unwilling to endanger his position in what was still the Soviet Union and he feared to sign the required agreement. In fact, he never did, and the courts decided eventually to go ahead with the adoption process anyway. However, that was one of the main reasons that the adoption process took so long and brought us eventually and finally to our court hearing in front of the President of the appropriate court. At this last stage, the judge asked Julia if she wanted to be my daughter. Her reply was: "What? My daddy's?" That appeared to be sufficient for the judge, who granted the adoption order on the spot.

On leaving the army, Yael (an Israeli variation on her name that she started using in her teens), completed her matriculation studies – she had not done so while in school – working at various jobs while doing so. She continued to work while completing a general BA course in sociology at the Open University. Since then she married Natan ("Nati") whom she met in Tel Aviv while working there on leaving the army and completing her university studies.

Since he too was a Jerusalemite, they soon returned to the capital city. In due course she bore three lovely girls (twins – Mai and Shir - aged nearly 12 and Romi, who is 9 years - old). In addition to my wonderful two grandsons, Eitan and Tamir, Naomi's children, these three girls are my pride and joy – they are with us almost every day.

By this time, we have already reached the month of January 2016. Yael continues to work full-time in a central position – as Secretary for academic and student affairs - first at the Pharmacy School of the Hebrew University, and now in the university's Faculty of Dental Medicine which also forms part of Hadassah Hospital, Jerusalem, again on which I elaborated a little above.

Ilana herself, having completed her MA in librarianship at the University in Kiev, decided, on reaching Israel to change direction and learn another profession. When I asked her why she chose that particular subject for her MA course she replied because there were few other opportunities in the Soviet Union at the time for a Jewish girl.

The world is our oyster

And so, Ilana was set for a new profession, which brought her new friends, which included her 'boss', Esther. She quickly learned both restoration and conservation, dealing with books, scrolls and manuscripts dating back to as early as the 10th, or was it the 11th century. Bookbinding, also, played a major role in both preservation and restoration. It is a very specialized profession and she was fortunate that the laboratory 'boasted' having a volunteer whose specialty this was, and who chose to teach Ilana this profession also. Apart from actual restoration and preservation of ancient books and manuscripts the laboratory prepared selected and requested artifacts by museums and other places throughout the world to be put on exhibition. Frequently the items requested and sent had to be taken to the place of exhibition, there the proper display condition had to be assured, and the object or objects had to be returned by a qualified courier.

Ilana, when she became manager of the laboratory in due course, allocated these tasks in turn to one or another of the laboratory staff, including herself. This had also been the practice of her predecessor. It was my privilege and pleasure to be asked occasionally to accompany her. It usually was great fun, and this enabled me to visit a number of places. We usually managed to combine the official part of a visit to a particular town with a vacation not only in that town but to other cities in that country. For example, Ilana had to install a priceless object (book or document – parchment) in Seville. This enabled us to explore not only Seville itself but, by extending our stay in Spain, also Granada and Cordova. When she had 'business' (installation of items at an exhibition) in Madrid, we were able to visit places of interest to us in Toledo and other cities – possibly Alicante or Valencia. I really can't recall the other places – the memory does play tricks with one, especially an old one, although I have photographs of all the places we visited.

Then there was our joint trip to the USA. Ilana was there on her own at least twice without me. But I was able to join her on this one occasion because the people who requested the items for display, the Skirball Jewish Cultural Centre in Los Angeles, paid all her expenses (although not mine, of course). This included business class travel to and from the destination, and decent hotel accommodation. Since travel to such a distant place would then be more comfortable by travelling business class, I decided to join Ilana on this trip.

After installing the items, we had several days free in LA and, naturally, took the opportunity to see what we could in that time: the Getty museum, Santa Barbara, Beverly Hills, the Avenue where the Holywood Film Stars had their hand impressed Paving Stones. We also had the opportunity to meet some of Ilana's American relatives. They were nice people. Unfortunately, Chicago was rather a long way away, so we did not visit our niece (Ira's daughter) Tali.

In LA, however we did meet up with the boy with whom I was billeted in Ely in 1939 with the couple who owned the sweet shop. We had not met for 60 years, having been together not only for the few weeks with our Christian hosts but also in the hostel in Eli as well as in London also when we both belonged to the Habana youth movement and in the Jewish Brigade at the beginning of our army service. This was the last time we had seen each other until this visit to Los Angeles.

We took advantage of the fact that we were already in the Unite States to visit New York and Washington as well. As we had already come so far away from home, we thought we may as well make the most of it. Ilana had several friends in New York. One of these, Daria, had worked with Ilana in her laboratory in Jerusalem before settling in the USA. She now has her own laboratory in New York. Another of her friends was of longer standing, dating back to her youth and young womanhood in Kiev, Ukraine. In New York we wandered around in Central Park and visited the Metropolitan Museum. What an impressive place it was. We also visited the Guggenheim Museum, Times Square, and the Lincoln Centre. Then we just walked around letting the feeling of New York 'soak' into us. I do regret that we did not visit either the Statute of Liberty or Ground Zero (where the Twin Towers of the World Trade Centre had stood prior to being destroyed by Muslim terrorists, with the tragic loss of several thousand lives.

We also visited Washington DC where my old friend Bob Burka lives. The city is quite beautiful, and Bob took us for a car ride around the town, showing us Arlington (National) Cemetery, the Lincoln Memorial and a general tour of the city. We also 'gaped' at the White House from a suitable distance, visited the Capitol Building, where Congress sits, and also visited the Library of Congress. And we also went to see the Holocaust Museum and the Smithsonian Museum. In the evening, Bob treated us to a dinner at one of Washington's better - known restaurants. It was a very interesting and enjoyable visit.

As I already mentioned, in the fullness of time Ilana became the manager (or is it director) of that laboratory and only retired from her position on reaching the age of 60, the normal retirement age. She appears now to be busier than ever. Apart from her husband – me – her home, including our patio-garden (she had always yearned for her own garden where she could both use her energy and relax when work was done) , our daughter – Yael/Julia (I adopted her legally many years ago - 1978) born May28th, 1970, who holds a central post at the Hebrew University's Faculty of Dental Medicine, granddaughters – we have twin girls; Mai and Shir who are as of now almost 12 years old – approaching Bat-Mitzva rapidly (born April 14th, 2004) and the 'baby' (some baby) Romi aged 9 by now (born December 25th, 2006). There are also my children Simone the lawyer (formerly a police prosecutor in Jerusalem – now retired); born April 8th, 1955; David the author (published, of course, who lives in London) born March 15 – the Ides of March - 1957 and Naomi the public relations expert (with YadVashem in Jerusalem) born October 12th,1958 (this was in fact my 10 year anniversary to my marriage to Marion – according to the Hebrew calendar).

Then there are her mother, Zana, who now lives alone – and not alone, her father – Ilya – having died in 1989; he granddaughter Yael having bought a house which had an empty area on the ground floor had it converted to a one room flat – with all the trimmings – where she now lives, not far from us. There is also her sister –Ira (Irena) 9 years her junior– the scientist who lives in Berlin, who wrestles at long-range with the follies of those handling the invaluable and irreplaceable Dead Sea Scrolls (not her only scientific endeavour); her niece – Avital (Tali) born September 20th, 1980, who lives in Chicago, USA – a speech therapist by occupation and a consultant at one of Chicago's hospitals, I believe, who is by now the mother of two most beautiful children with her third ready to pop out anytime. Ilana maintains an assortment of friends and colleagues in Israel, Ukraine, Germany and USA – have I left out anyone and/or place? I could go on and on – but maybe later, or not.

Over the years, since we married, in 1978, we were fortunate to be able to visit many places in Europe. I have mentioned our one visit outside Europe, to the USA, already and will not refer to this journey again. Rather let me start with our travels from the beginning.

Even before our marriage, we visited the city of Zfat (Safed). The reason for this was first that we always liked the north of Israel, which is much greener than the rest of the country. Also, Ilana had friends there – people whom she had known in Kiev. And finally, because it contains an artists' colony that we were interested in visiting. About the last mentioned, I must explain that for years I have found it difficult to go into crowded and/or closed places. This has limited our visits to the artists' colony, which has spoiled the visits for Ilana somewhat.

Upon our marriage, we paid our first visit to London, a habit we developed over many years when we included London and England generally in our holiday itinerary every year. Sometimes we rented a car and toured. Sometimes we just enjoyed the sales, theatres, parks, and friends – not to forget my son David who returned to the UK. When touring in rented cars – Ilana always hesitated to drive in England, because in England they drive on the left side of the road rather than the right.

We visited Oxford and Cambridge. The latter was much more to our liking. Not only were the colleges an architectural delight but Kings College particularly offered us the opportunity once more to admire the chapel and listen to a rehearsal of the renowned boys' choir. The river Cam too was much prettier with its long punting boats, which I had already experienced during my sojourn in Ely (aged 12 to 14). Also, whereas Oxford is an industrial city as well as an academic one, Cambridge is smaller, more intimate and much more of a rural market town or at least still was at that time.

We also visited Stratford-on-Avon, the town always associated with The Bard – William Shakespeare. Anne Hathaway's cottage also is in the area. Stratford also has a Museum and a theatre where the Shakespeare festival is held annually. Warwick, situated in an altogether beautiful part of England, is also nearby. The Earl of

Warwick was known as the King maker during the time of the *Wars of the Roses*, the struggle for supremacy between the houses of York and Lancaster for the throne of England.

Bath, a World Heritage city with its dominant Georgian architecture, is a Spa town which has drawn visitors to regain their health for generations. The town dates back to before Roman times and has played an important part in English history. Gloucestershire, Torquay, Bournemouth, Brighton, Hastings and many other places were all on our itinerary on various visits – places too numerous to mention. We found many spots which reminded us of places mentioned in the numerous classic novels we had read – relating to pirates or smugglers as well as to the 'Houses' and estates of many a nobleman.

Ilana's former boss, Ester Alkalai, had meanwhile married Professor Gerhard Boyd and had gone to live with him in London where he was a professor of Organic Chemistry at London University. He was also a guest professor at the Hebrew University of Jerusalem. That is presumably where he met Esther. He was born in what was then Breslau, Germany and is now Wroclaw, Poland and came to England as a refugee in 1939. Esther and Gerhard invited us to join them on a week's holiday trip to the north of Scotland, via the Lake District. It was a magical journey, during which she and Gerhard warbled all the way. Ah well, even that did not spoil it for us – ha ha ha. As a matter of fact, it was rather amusing, and even enjoyable.

On stopping en-route at a resort by Lake Windermere, Ilana and I decided to climb one of the hills in the immediate area. (I was much younger then!) We enjoyed the climb, but unfortunately Ilana lost her gold bracelet, which I had bought her not much before that. We searched for hours but could not find it. We very much regretted this loss but did not let it spoil our vacation.

We holidayed in Berlin where our eight-year-old niece Tali was living with her mother Irena, Ilana's sister. This was Ilana's third or fourth visit to Berlin but my first and indeed only real visit there. I did not otherwise want to visit Germany and have not returned since, except passing through here and there. But on this occasion, I wanted to give Tali a traditional festival. To remind her of her heritage, we took with us a menorah, candles, a dreidel, and a compact disc with Chanukah songs, as well as some children's books in Hebrew. We lit the candles and sang the traditional songs for the occasion. Ilana taught Tali to make latkes (potato pancakes) and sufganiot (doughnuts) – the traditional foods for the festival.

Ira (Irena), took time off from work to show us the sights a bit. She gave us a very interesting car tour and we pottered about on Kurfurstendam and saw the Charlottenburger Tor, the bombed cathedral (or was it church). I think it was called the Gedenknis Kirsche in German (translated into English as the Church of Remembrance), in memory of the bombing of Berlin during World War II. I hope they also remember the *reason* for the bombing.

Because it was not only our Chanukah but also their Christmas, the city had market-like areas selling all sorts of Christmas fare. I am sure there are other things to remember, but I cannot recall them at present.

We had some friends in Stockholm who visit Israel frequently and usually find time to have lunch with us. (He is originally from Israel, where he was our neighbour for some years). They went on holiday one spring or summer and put their flat at our disposal to save us spending money on expensive hotels. We enjoyed that visit to Sweden very much, not confining ourselves to Stockholm but also visiting other places like Uppsala.

Our one visit to Copenhagen, Denmark was not particularly inspiring. The hotel was apparently ultra-modern, in the worst meaning of the phrase. Our room, in a mid-range class hotel, was more like a prison cell than a guest room. I remember two things only from that visit: the room and the statue in the harbour. The latter was mildly pleasing, the former was anything *but*.

In Holland, we were more at home and it was more to our taste and liking, by far. We visited the Rijksmuseum with its collection of old Dutch masters: Rembrandt, Franz Hals, Vermeer and many others. We also went to see many other museums, including the Anna Frank museum, which obviously was most moving. We saw the canals and took a river trip, something we were in the habit of doing in all large cities which we visited for the first time. And then there was the music at the Concertgebouw. All this and more in Amsterdam. The miniature city of Madurodam in Scheveningen was another attraction, as were other cities in Holland. In some cases, these were visits to places that I had already seen during my Jewish Brigade days, when I was stationed on Walcheren Island.

Belgium (Bruxelles) had some attractions too, although Ilana disliked the city. She tells me now that she only liked the market, which had an extremely large variety of flowers and an extensive selection of fish. I can't say that I recall the market here as I do the one in Barcelona. (We'll get there soon enough.) She did however concede that the chips she ate in that city were the best she ever tasted, before or since. This is not enough, however, to tempt her to revisit that city or country.

Austria is another country we visited, under circumstances other than army locations near where I was stationed many years earlier. I recall we flew to Munich where we took a car and left the same day first for Salzburg. Here we stayed for several nights, before leaving for Vienna. Passing through the Salzkammergut, with its collection of beautiful lakes and mountains, we decided to spend a night in one of the hotels on the shore of one of the lakes. It was quite heavenly. I don't remember if we took a boat trip on the lake; this is more than likely, since the place was quite magical.

The following day we continued our journey to Vienna, where we stayed several days in a charming hotel in one of the side streets in the centre of Vienna. I quite enjoyed our visit here, but Ilana did not. I don't know if it was the formality of the place or the local residents. But there it was – Vienna's loss.

One of the more enjoyable aspects for us both was the visit we paid to the Spanish Riding School where we were enabled to watch the Lipizzaner horses training session. These pure white stallions, and their becostumed riders, made a strong and lasting impression on me. I am sure Ilana also enjoyed the real McCoy *Sacher Torte* that we ate in the most popular coffee shop in the centre of Vienna. It was here, in Vienna, that we returned the car, and after a few days stay in Vienna – I think we cut our visit short because of Ilana's dislike of the city and left by train for Prague.

On at least one other occasion we came to Vienna, but I don't remember from where, nor indeed *to* where. My niece, Yochevet, lived at that time temporarily in that city while her husband, Avi, was attempting to establish himself as an orchestral conductor. Yochevet insisted we stay with her and her four year – old daughter – Ronnie. Her husband was away as a guest conductor, in Prague, I think. After putting down our suitcases we decided to take our first glimpse of Johan Strauss's city. A shock awaited us on returning to Yochi's flat. She was not at home, but Ronnie, her daughter, was. This very self-possessed young four-year-old informed us calmly that her mother had slipped, fallen and broken her leg and had been taken to the hospital. –We went with her by bus to the hospital, where we found Yochi with her leg in a plaster cast, confined to bed in the hospital. Ilana decided on the spot that we would stay and look after Ronnie. And so, we did for several days, until her mother returned home. I really don't remember where we went from there – Prague, probably.

Next in line in this long tale of journeys and or adventures was Hungary. Ilana and her boss and friend Tova, who had by then become the manager – or director – of the H.U. Conservation Laboratory, had to take some artefacts for exhibition in Budapest. One of their friends, who originated from that part of the world and still had many contacts there, recommended a suitable place to stay that was quite centrally located. I decided this would be a good opportunity to join Ilana and have a holiday. I let her go ahead with Tova to arrange and complete the business part of the journey and then I joined her some days later. Ilana met me at the still very primitive airport with the news that earlier that day her purse had been stolen while she was out walking with Tova. But we would not let this incident spoil our holiday. The flat we stayed in was large and comfortable. The bathroom, I remember particularly, was a huge room with a bathtub placed right in the centre of the room.

We went all over both Buda and Pest. We visited the museums, the churches and other centres of culture and of course the famous castle. While in Budapest we took a day excursion on a river boat, cruising along the Danube. I believe we reached Lake Balaton. I really can't remember how far up the Danube we actually sailed. Wherever it was, we stopped for lunch in a most charming restaurant in Szentendre, a gem of a place snuggled on the banks of the Danube. I think it was here that I learned about, and tasted, a very enjoyable and definitely eatable dessert to our meal: profiteroles. These were absolutely delicious.

(Actually, it may have been in Prague I learned about profiteroles – see below.)

And so we left Budapest for Vienna, picked up a car and drove to Bratislava, where we found what was listed as a 5-star hotel. We booked in for the night through a reception person, or possibly the housekeeper, who seemed to be living under the impression that the Soviets were still in charge. Her behaviour, at any rate, was definitely *Homo Sovieticus*. Not that this bothered us particularly. What *did* bother us was the discovery of giant cockroaches in the bathroom, the toilet and even the bedroom. It looked as if they dined better than most of the locals. I shudder at the memory.

We did not prolong our stay in Bratislava and the following morning made haste to leave for Prague via Brno. Now Prague was a very different kettle of fish. Not many years had passed since the Soviet Empire had collapsed. But the contrast between Bratislava and Prague was almost as the difference between night and day. Although Prague was still very much underdeveloped, there were all the signs of modernization and development to be seen everywhere, both on the face of the city and on the faces of its citizens. We were lodged in a suburb of the city. Tova, who had come with us from Budapest, took the smaller of the rooms and we the larger. Breakfast was included in the price. Much as Ilana had disliked Bruxelles, Vienna and Budapest, she found an immediate rapport with Prague.

We drove each day to the nearest subway station, took the train into town, returned by train and picked up the car for the drive back to the flat. It was great fun. Our visits to Prague – mine three times, Ilana's five times I think, saw the rapid development of this jewel of a city.

Our friend Jurek, one of Ilana's colleagues at the National Library,, had met a charming lady from Prague at one of the conferences he attended and been smitten by her. The feeling apparently was mutual and since he and Ilana had over the years become really close friends, he wanted her to meet this lady. I think he wanted the stamp of approval from someone whose opinion and regard he very much valued. Our next visit to Prague afforded such an opportunity and on the strength of his introduction we were able to meet Dana. Since she held a senior post in Prague's National Library we met her there. She very kindly showed us around, including areas not normally seen by the general public. It was a most enlightening tour. She was most charming, we found, and our friend's romance blossomed into marriage, He now lives and works in Prague.

Spain drew us like something of a magnet. The Iberian Peninsula had so many attractions, and so many historic connections to us as Jews, that we could not resist returning to one or another area of this part of the continent of Europe. The crown jewel for us however was always Barcelona. We took a day trip to Montserrat, high in the surrounding mountains, where we visited the church and monastery. Here, having timed it perfectly, we listened to the glorious voices of the boys' choir, who sang only at particular times.

The views from so high up were magnificent, and not only from the top. Every turn of our transport, going up or coming down, opened a different and fabulous view. In Barcelona too there was the Gothic Cathedral, the Picasso museum. Las Ramblas – the central boulevard where, on our first visit, our hotel was situated, the Gaudi buildings, the market (always an attraction) and oh so much more! Our Fodor travel guide referred us to one of the restaurants called Quo Vadis, just off the Ramblas, where we enjoyed the food so much that we returned there on subsequent visits to the city, even though we normally like to experiment and try different 'watering holes'.

Ilana did not like Madrid at first and was reluctant to revisit. The first time she went there was without me, on business. But I really wanted to visit Spain's capital city and managed to persuade her to visit there again. This time she began to see the virtues of the place – and those were numerous. We stayed in an excellent hotel called *The Wellington* which was almost across the road from the major park. Ilana and I very much enjoyed our daily tours to different parts of the city which included the Prada, where we gazed in wonder at the master works of Goya, Velazquez, El Greco and others. There were other museums and buildings. Being typical tourists, we took great delight on those warm and balmy early summer evenings to sit in one square or another, sipping Sangria or some other delight.

Can one imagine the fascination of Toledo or Seville, of Cordova and Granada – particularly the Alhambra? Each held its own particular fascination for us. The Jewish people's long history and close association with Spain and Portugal – attested to by the Jewish quarters in these places – stood out for me among the many other attractions. Our people had been expelled from Spain by the then ruling king and queen, Ferdinand and Isabella, yet our history is well-preserved in these places, as indeed they are in all the other countries in Europe, especially Prague – and we visited them all.

On one visit to Spain, we flew to Malaga, where we hired a car and drove to Torremolinos. We used this sea-side resort as our base for both rest and visits to various beauty spots in the area. From here too we took a one-day conducted bus tour to Gibraltar where we bought various tourist items. Our travels took us back to Malaga by car. From here we flew to Barcelona for another week's stay before returning home. There is much to write about our visits to Spain but enough is enough.

Perhaps this is the correct place to record our one-time visit to Portugal. Again, Ilana had to take an item for exhibition in Lisbon. With the help of the Fodor Travel Guide, we found a jewel of a hotel, high up and close to the customary castle. The view over part of the city from our balcony was spectacular. Here in Lisbon, one of the highlights of our visit was the Gulbenkian Trust, which included a museum which housed among its treasures paintings by Rembrandt, Rubens and other old masters and Impressionists. There was also the Moorish castle of Sao Jorge (St, George). We took an overnight trip to Porto, further north, which was also very interesting, especially the wine tasting.

Paris was another of our destinations where we visited not only once . The attractions of that city are well known. On one occasion I remember we took Julia-Yael first to London, where the sales were on, and then by Ferry across the English Channel. Both Yael and I felt very sea-sick on that crossing, but Ilana weathered it well. The train took us from Calais to Paris where we spent a week. Needless to say, we took the usual boat trip on the river Seine as well as a bus sightseeing tour of the city. This we were in the habit of doing in every city we visited for the first time. We visited the shops (naturally) and imbibed the air of this romantic city. It was our custom, in all cities we visited, to stroll through the streets and mingle with the 'natives'. Ilana and I have been to Paris since and visited the Louvre, Notre Dame, the Eiffel Tower, Champs Elysee, Arc de Triomphe, the Tuileries, Bois de Boulogne,

Versailles, many of the museums, and 101 or more other places of historic and general interest – too many to mention.

For some years now, we have not returned to England because the country, especially London, has changed and in our view not for the better. As a matter of fact, it was not so much the country, or London, but rather the demography – that is, the balance of the population. One heard and saw less of the locals and more, much more of the relatively recently arrived who brought with them a different culture and way of life. Yet, to confess, I hanker to return and visit all my old haunts – not just to visit David, although that is definitely on top of the list – but definightly to recapture my youth.

Our holiday travels have also taken us, sometimes with rented cars, more often without, to Rhodes, a not very large place where we spent almost all our time resting in a very comfortable luxury hotel. We should really go there again and see the sights of the Island.

Switzerland was another place on our itinerary in the earlier years of our married life. We visited Geneva, where we toured not only the city but the lake as well. Kleine Scheidegg was basically a skiing village but we visited in the summer. Still the views were spectacular. I think Schaffhausen was the place from where some of the best, and most expensive watches came . As it was located near Lake Constance, it was very pretty.

The Rhine Falls, too, were nearby affording a fabulous view of the surrounding area. These are the largest and most spectacular water falls in Europe. The lake too held many attractions, especially as the Rhine flows into it at one end and out at the other. The roar of the falls and the rush of the water, which are the cause, leave a memory long after leaving the place.

Lucerne, I had already visited with Marion but was not sorry to visit again with Ilana, and many other places, I am sure, the names of which escape me at present. In one of the cities – it may have been Lucerne – we witnessed a vintage car exhibition. In another, a flower show. There was never a dull moment. Regretfully, although Ilana does not particularly regret it, we never reached Basle and therefore did not see the famous balcony where Theodor Herzl stood – unlike, as I will record soon, the famous balcony in Italy referred to by Shakespeare, where Romeo wooed Juliet. Nor did we visit Zurich, famed in the world of banking, as the habitation of the Gnomes of Zurich – thus were the bankers of the city nicknamed. For Harry Potter fans the resemblance may be other than coincidental. We did, however, also visit Berne which we both found a lovely city and where we bought Ilana her black multi-zipped handbag which, incidentally, she still uses. I even remember the location of the shop.

Italy was and is another of our favourite haunts – one can assume that we visited and holidayed here more than once. Rome. What can one say about this glorious city? After all, they do say "all roads lead to Rome." The Forum, the Coliseum, the Vatican (in all its glory, including the Sistine Chapel), the Pantheon, Galleria Borghese, in fact the many palaces and museums, the Spanish Steps, the Trevi Fountain, Piazza Navonna, the food and flee markets, shopping malls, boutiques and a thousand and one other sights and delights. It was here, near the Trevi fountain, that two gypsy children, a boy aged maybe 12 or 13 and his younger sister, attempted to steal our wallets. They were not successful, largely because of an earlier experience I had in Venice.

We visited Venice in all its romantic glory where, on arrival in that beautiful city, we travelled on a Vaporetto – the Waterbus which is the main public transport here – carrying our not so light suitcase. My wallet (including all my money and 2 credit cards), which I carried in my hip pocket, was stolen by a very skilled pickpocket. We did not, however, let this spoil a wonderful holiday. Our hotel was just around the corner from Piazza San Marco with its beautiful Basilica, many museums, palaces and mansions, the Rialto bridge and all the highways and byways. Every time I think of our visit to Venice, I regret not having taken Ilana on a gondola, and I don't see really that it can still happen.

Florence – just the name inspires one, even if one remembers that at a certain period in history the Medicis ruled here. This city of outstanding beauty, which houses so many art treasures (especially the Uffizi Gallery), once suffered a devastating flood which caused havoc to the city. Of course, we did not miss out on, among other treasures, the exquisite Duomo, the fourth largest in the world and its attached Museum, nor Ponte Vecchio and its attached Palazzo, and again many, many other treasures, including the streets, alleys and shops. Padua (to where I think Romeo was banished after killing Juliet's cousin in a sword fight not of his seeking) is an ancient University centre dating back to 1220 in the civil calendar. It was here that Galileo also lectured.

Verona – and its Arena de Verona amphitheatre where in Roman times gladiatorial contests were held and where Christians were thrown to face wild and hungry animals for the entertainment of the local populace. These were the bread and circuses designed to keep the 'Plebes' happy. The arena now serves as a major centre for world renowned opera performances. Here we also found the balcony made famous by William Shakespeare where Romeo wooed Juliet.

Not very far away, the city of Vicenza is another World Heritage listed city, housing also the Olympic theatre as well as many palazzos, museums and squares. We did not, however, choose it for that reason. It served us rather as a base from where to visit a number of places of interest including our first visit to Lake Garda. After taking a leisurely boat tour around the lake, we saw advertised an exhibition of impressionist paintings. We later visited this exhibition, together with Ira, Ilana's sister who joined us for a few days. On another occasion we holidayed in Dezensano on Lake Garda, where we spent an enchanting week exploring some of the interesting towns around the lake – by boat, of course.

We holidayed in Tuscany where we stayed on one of the farms near Bucine and in our hired car explored many of the interesting places in the area including Arezzo, Montepulciano, Sienna and the other hill towns, including San Gimigniano and the wine growing (and tasting) routes. Other than that, once, on our way to catch our flight home from Rome Airport we stopped over in Orvietto, another charming Italian town.

Ilana visited Germany several times. Her sister, after all, lives there. She had also to go there on behalf of the National Library. I paid one visit described elsewhere, when Ilana and I decided, during year 2 of our niece Tali's residence in Berlin, to give her a break from the usual routine of work, work and more work. We decided to make this a pleasure trip only. Other than that, I passed through the Airport in Frankfurt once and Munich twice. On one occasion in Munich I think we may have stayed overnight and we had enough time to take our usual bus tour of the city, which we both found rather attractive.

We did not neglect visiting various parts of our own country. In the north we stayed in hotels, guest houses and/or Zimmerim on Kibbutzim and Moshavim. These are the communal or co-operative settlements where the residents had built bungalows to provide suitable accommodation for holidaymakers. We stayed with family in Haifa, with friends in Zfat and Nahariya, in Hotels in Tel Aviv, Ceasaria, Natanya, Acre, Tiberias, Metulla, Beth Lehem, Beer Sheva, Rehovot, Ashkekon and, it goes without saying, in Eilat. I recall visiting Massada and also the old city of Jerusalem including its Western Wall. I am a little vague about times, especially here: was it with Ilana? Was it before? I expect it was both, since I visited these places more than once.

There are numerous incidents during the course of my life which are all part of me and which I have not yet mentioned – probably because they are fleeting memories which are not always uppermost in my thoughts when I sit down to write this journal, but which are part of my personal saga. It is somewhat difficult, when they do spring to mind, to find the appropriate place where to insert them but with your indulgence and understanding I will relate some of them here, even if some items are repeated, as many have already.

The children

From an early age our children received a small amount of pocket-money with the intention that they should learn early on the value of money and how to handle it. They also had small amounts put into saving accounts for children. I was so determined for them to be prudent that on one occasion, when Simone wanted a rather expensive dolls parambulator we suggested she contribute one pound sterling to the cost. This was more than 50 years ago. The pram was a replica of what was termed the "Rolls Royce of prams" and the cost was somewhere in the region of 7-10 pounds. Were we right to do this? I don't really know. It was after all her birthday – her 7th, I think. She did, however, enjoy her gift, as did her younger sister also.

I mentioned David's independence and personal initiative earlier when I described his exploration on the Zim boat when we travelled to Israel for our working holiday (1960/1). To remind you, David, not yet four years old, decided to explore the boat from top to bottom, it seems.

Well, another example relates to him when he was 11 years old – practically an adult, or so he thought. London hosted many sporting events throughout the year, including wrestling. This particular event was in 1968 and took place in the famous Albert Hall named after Prince Albert, Queen Victoria's Consort (that was still in the 19th century: the prince, not the wrestling match). David, who was a great fan of wrestling, wanted very much to attend the competition but I would not or could not go. He insisted. We were obdurate – to the extent that we forbade him to leave his room. Relenting after a while we, or rather his mother went to his room, to comfort him, I think. Lo and behold, the room was empty. Our son had vanished.

We entered into panic stations. Since the window was open we assumed, rightly, that he had climbed through his bedroom window on to the landing outside and just left the building. Where could he be? The Albert Hall was right across London from where we lived. He had very little money, how would he get anywhere, let alone the Albert Hall, to where he was surely bound. We rushed to the nearest bus stop – no David. We raced to the nearest Underground station which was the most likely place to look for him. Here the man at the ticket-office remembered a young boy who asked for the correct underground train line to board for, you guessed it, the Albert Hall. The ticket collector remembered David a very short time before so we rushed down to the platform and watched the train just pull out of the station. We boarded the next one, of course. When we reached the Albert Hall we asked the attendant if they had seen this little boy. He affirmed that he had seen him enter, pointed out the section but advised that I sit with him and not make a scene, which would only alienate the child. I took his advice, entered, found my son and sat with him until that particular match was concluded. Then we went home and after discussing the matter concluded that "All's Well that Ends Well" (Shakespeare again).

Talking about David again brings to mind that he frequently played truant from his class at the Hasmonean Grammar School, particularly during certain lessons. I think the subjects may have bored him. He particularly avoided his physical exercise classes which he seemed to abhor: he always was more cerebral (is that the correct expression) than physical. On the other hand English, as a subject, was very much to his liking. He had particularly good teachers in this subject whom he liked. The teachers liked him too and encouraged his writing. There are other subjects also in which he did well and therefore liked. On reflection, his days of truancy must have coincided with the lessons he hated. Above all he, simply put, was extremely miserable and unhappy at that school also. In any case, as I've already indicated he was too much of an individualist who did not fit into any organized framework and school was, and had to be, an organized framework.

Still about David – chess is without a doubt a cerebral game, if game it can really be called. David, of course excelled at it from a very early age. It was perfectly natural for him to join his school's team and to be a member of the team which competed against other schools. I can't say he always won but he appeared always to enjoy it.

At 15 years old, I think it was then, he decided that he did not want to suffer the misery and unhappiness which he felt at that school any longer and decided to leave – the school, not the home. Try as we might, his mother and I, pleas, threats, cajolement, his mother's tears, the information that we, his parents not he himself, were liable to be fined or worse (the law required his attendance at school until the end of the school year on reaching his fifteenth birthday) had any real effect. His decision made nothing would budge him.

The antics all three of my biological children got up to were numerous – many I can't recall. Of those I can remember are their repeating something I recall from my own childhood – mentioned earlier when I wrote about Leipzig. In David's room he had a wardrobe low enough onto which they were able to climb. His bed was immediately below and tempted them to jump down onto – which they naturally did, repeatedly. Is genetics again playing a role here?

On other occasions they used our balcony, which was so situated that it overlooked the street (and entrance to our building) in order to bombard unwitting passersby with pellets from their pellet-guns. I do not want to make excuses, but I really did not know of their *delinquent* tendencies and would certainly have stopped them had I been aware of this at the time. Still, they were not bad children – in fact I always considered them rather good, and still do so.

Everyone knows that children, and not only they, argue often and sometimes quarrel. It may be in a game, or not; it may be intentional, or not. When you have three it is unavoidable that on occasion two 'gang-up' on the third. Frequently it happens that the middle child has to defend him/herself against the other two, but not always. It so happened that one time the two older ones decided to go against the youngest. I don't know if they quarrelled or maybe it started as a game. Certainly, there was no malice intended when Naomi went into the bathroom and the other two decided to 'imprison' her inside. I don't know whether they tied her up first, but they held the door shut and did not let her come out until...

Then there was this particular incident, with all three children, which cast me in the principal role of the villain, I fear – one of the actions for which I have not forgiven myself to this day, although I hope that I have atoned for it. Children, we all know, can be very noisy, especially when they quarrel. I don't know if they quarrelled at the time in question. I think Marion may have been out (not at home) at the time or I would probably not have been so distracted. I got into such a temper and lost control, and without thinking took Simone's favourite doll and threw it across the room.

To all our chagrin, mine most of all, the head of the doll cracked. What to do? We consulted, the four of us, and came to the conclusion that only an immediate operation could save the day. I became the surgeon; the three children were the nurses. I donned the equivalent of a doctors' gown and the children and I all donned masks (handkerchiefs, I think). The poor injured doll was placed on the table and the operation, which took some time, concluded with the scalp glued (stitched) together to the limited satisfaction of the family. In any event the operation was considered a miraculous success. The original offender was forgiven eventually, I think – I certainly hope so – and life returned to normal.

Having mentioned the 'moosies' drawings on their bedroom walls, with our reluctant permission, I must also mention that these drawings – was it their graffiti or their frescos – had rather nasty characters. The children therefore invented the 'goodies' to fight and defeat them in their verbal and written battles. These were, of course, the Shamir worms.

About Yael (Julia) – I can say that she left Kiev in the Ukraine when she was just 4 years old. I am told that even as a small child she had her more 'forceful' moments. People leaving this 'Communist Paradise' were in the 1970's permitted, it seems, to take out only personal items, which did not include, I think, valuables. This incident happened at the end of May or the 1st of June, 1974 on their aliyah to Israel. Ilana tells me that the searches conducted by the border police and custom officials were pretty thorough. It seems that when the female official at the airport wanted to examine Julia's abundant hair to see if any of the family's valuables were hidden there, this young tigress, being held in her mother's arms, lashed out and kicked the intruder in her chest or stomach. She was not arrested on the spot and sent to Siberia, fortunately, but landed safely in Israel after a very brief stay en-route in Vienna.

In Israel her mother had to work to support herself and her daughter. Julia, as she still was, was looked after by a 'minder' – Russian speaking of course, although the child quickly picked up the Hebrew language. At five she went to what the Americans call pre-school and like all children in Israel entered first grade school at the age of six. By this time she was already more Israeli than Russian and her Hebrew was as that of a native born Israeli. She had a natural charm and outgoing personality which brought her friends instantly – a trait which persists to this day. Her mother and I cannot go, with or without her, anywhere in Jerusalem without running into one or another of her friends or acquaintances. She was always very popular in school – a leader but not dominating.

I made her acquaintance first in late 1976, as I mentioned earlier, when her mother invited me to tea. She spent much time outdoors, frequently playing five-stones below one of our windows with her particular friend at that time. I imagine she played the usual games with all her friends from school. The school was practically right next door to where we lived. When school day was ended she was taken care of by one of the grandmothers – not necessarily her own – elderly ladies who did not go to work any longer and earned a little extra money in this way.

Later, after I married her mother in 1978 – with her enthusiastic approval, I would like to think – we arranged for her to learn English with one of these ladies who was an English teacher in Russia before her aliyah and which stands her in good stead still. We also sent her to various other extra-curricular groups, not only to keep her occupied but also to develop any talent of which she may be possessed. She was particularly fond of her ballet group and, indeed, was very good at it. In fact, her sense of rhythm is phenomenal, covering all kinds of dance (not only classical ballet). She also had, and still has an outstanding knack for women's clothes design. Her sense of fashion is a trend which the various female members of the family make use of still today.

Health – and other matters

In the course of a lifetime not everything always runs smoothly. Had I kept a diary all these years I would have been able to write down everything here in its correct time frame. Not having done so I must 'tell my tale' as best I can – and repeat some things already mentioned, in one way or another.

About Marion's illnesses (that is, her two major illnesses) I wrote in detail already, the second of which resulted, after more than two years of suffering, in her demise.

Ilana, the 29 years old girl whom I had the audacity to marry in 1978, three months before her 30th birthday, five years after losing my first wife, had a very serious operation about which I have not yet written. Sometime in the early part of 2007 (perhaps even in the later part of 2006) she started to have pains in her back. Stoicism is perhaps a thing to admire, but sometimes it is better to admit to oneself that one has pain and attempt to find a solution. I had learned from what happened to Marion, my first wife, that neglect can be fatal. (It was not really her neglect but rather her family doctor's lack of understanding or imagination – I don't wish to think of it as his ignorance).

Well, my Ilana suffered back pains for months and months until she finally succumbed and visited our doctor. You may well imagine my apprehension – thinking back to my first marriage. I won't go into all the details, including going to a chiropractor whose methods only caused her more pain and did nothing to help her and even made it worse. On one occasion, we even had to take an ambulance to take her to the Chiropractor.

Eventually, she went to an orthopaedic surgeon who ordered first, CT's and, not being satisfied with the results of that examination ordered an MRI examination. This last finally established that she had a growth on her spinal column which was pressing down on all the nerve ends and required an operation to remove it. I must confess that I started to imagine all sort of things, although I hope my fears were not apparent to those around me. We searched the internet and consulted whomever we thought may be able to advise, until we selected the neurosurgeon whom we considered most capable for this sort of specialist treatment –

privately, of course (not within the framework of the public health service). Ilana was operated on in October 2007. We were more than relieved to be told that the growth turned out to be benign fortunately and has not, to the best of our knowledge returned or affected her permanently.

So we come to the writer of these pages. I mentioned earlier being in an Army hospital somewhere in Europe with (double) Quinsy. I also mentioned the time I spent, five days, having a tube inserted into me at the Middlesex Hospital in London without discovering the reason and having no further 'trouble' there. I can now relate that I discovered suddenly in 1986 some problem with my 'innards'. Although never fond of doctor's visits – I tend to think that if I ignore the symptoms they will, sooner or later, disappear of their own accord – I decided on this occasion to go to my family doctor, wisely as it turned out. He referred me to a Gastroenterologist who, on examination removed a polyp from my intestines. The polyp was found to be cancerous.

An urgent appointment was made for an operation to remove the surrounding parts. We now had to make an important choice about which surgeon would operate. I had an old friend, Elliot Berry with whom I had prayed in the same synagogue in London before either of us came to Israel. I even remembered his Bar Mitzvah. He was also the doctor who kept us informed of Marion's progress during her first stay at the hospital in London after her cancer was discovered. He was now a Professor of Endocrinology at Hadassah hospital and we consulted him, asking for his advice. He recommended Professor Bertie Freund and also spoke to him about me. Professor Freund accepted me and, in fact, performed the operation, at the conclusion of which he told both Ilana and me, after I was released from the recovery room to the ward and could again hold a normal conversation, that it was his considered opinion that all the affected area was removed.

He appears to have been proved right since the operation took place in July 1986 and, praise the Almighty, no further problem has developed. I may add that Professor Freund made no charge for his services. However, this operation, and the reason for it, made it possible for me to retire from my position at the Hebrew University on health grounds in March 1987 although I had not yet reached the age of 60 – a number of years before the normal retirement age which at that time was 65.

I may add that the Department Head at the time of my retirement was Mickey Bavli, about whom (and about his family also) a great deal could be written. Among other tasks he served sometime as a deputy director of Israel's Ministry of Foreign Affairs, as Ambassador to Holland and currently represents the United Nations High Commissioner for Refugees in Israel in a voluntary capacity. Let it be noted that this is not UNWRA but rather the other one dealing with refugees from the entire world other than Palestinians. I will never understand why Palestinians require a separate United Nations Refugee organization to which most of the budget monies are diverted.

I coped, and worried on other occasions when my children, and more recently grandchildren, succumbed to one illness or another.

Marion's mother died, the result of another stroke, a little over a year after we came on Aliyah. I was not able to attend the funeral and truly regret my absence.

Sylvia, her second daughter, who was hospitalized at frequent intervals because of her continuing lapses into unreality when she imagined all sorts of things happening to her and to others – I referred to at least two occurrences earlier which, in my opinion, were major contributory causes to her illness.

Without going into details I must mention again the traumatic final few days in November 1989 in the intensive care unit at Hadassah Hospital, Jerusalem of Ilana's father, who had gone to the hospital's out-patients department for a routine check-up and did not leave the hospital again.

My eldest, Simone also had health problems one of which resulted in a major operation. She is now in good health and we hope will remain so, not only for us and her, of course, but also for her two cats (have I mentioned them before?) who are both getting on in years, are both not in the best of health and are much in need of her attention – as are we. (Both of her feline companions, have since died - each in their time. She has three others now).

Naomi, too, has had her problems. Suffice it to mention various health problems, especially during her visits to the USA. These visits were regular annual holidays before her eldest son, Eitan, was called for his military service. (She was not going to be far from him during his three

239

- year period of service.) At that time she, and her husband – who, incidentally, also has his health problems – encountered great resistance from the insurance company in the USA, about which I will say no more, except that these included problems during her pregnancies. Delays in treatment of other ailments may have led to one hip replacement, among other things and much pain and suffering in both. She does not let this interfere with her work at YadVashem.

David, the author who lives in London, brother to the girls (now women) – Simone, Naomi and Yael – has the usual 'ups and downs'. Once one problem, another time something else. Let me not go into that either except to record that although I am his father, I do not exaggerate when I say he had, and still has an excellent mind which should have led him to study – either Law or Physics or I don't know what. Still, writing was his love so that is what he concentrated on.

As to Yael – as all our children she too succumbed to this, that and the other. A hospital stay here, an operation there – all this in addition to the usual children ailments.

Finally …

To my wife Ilana, to whom I owe my reasonably good health and strength now I say, thank you for bearing with me for so long.

As Robert Browning wrote in his poem *Rabbi ben Ezra*:

"Grow old with me; the best is yet to be."

The Future Generation

If the children and especially the grandchildren would themselves write-up their life stories to date, I am persuaded they could easily fill an unimaginable number of pages. I, however, must confine myself to brief episodes only.

Naomi's and Barry's boys

Eitan turned 28 in November, 2018. He is my daughter Naomi's first-born.

His year of birth was 1990, one year and some months after Naomi married her lawyer/university lecturer husband in June 1989. (It is hard for me to accept that I was retired from work already more than two years)

244

Her wedding ceremony, incidentally, was conducted by my niece's husband, Avi who, in the fullness of time, served as the Israel Defense Forces' Chief Rabbi (he, Avi, is now head of the Yeshiva in his settlement).

Eitan's brother, *Tami*r, was born 3 years + later, in January 1994. They were, and still are, both lively and bright.

Both are now students in Tel Aviv University. As little ones they got up to many of the usual escapades. I remember them removing all the large cushions from the couch and armchairs in their salon and building castles, caves and shelters with them, as well as various other hiding places. When it came to entering the school stream, their parents decided to register them for the Experimental School which was an all age – 12 years education – establishment (from class 1 to class 12). The school laid more stress on the child's interests than on the formal curriculum – or so it seemed to me. But it educated its pupils in a way which enabled them, at the end of year 12, to sit for the matriculation exams.

Unlike school-leaving for youngsters in other Western-oriented countries our young people, on concluding their 12 year stint in school, were inducted into the Defence Forces – such was our security situation, and still is. Eitan served in a special unit while Tamir joined an Infantry division. On their discharge from the Defence Forces they both took some time to settle down, but as mentioned already both are now serious University students.

Yael's and Nati's girls

As mentioned already we are very happy to be grandparents also to three very boisterous granddaughters – the twins, Mai and Shir, and their young sister Romi. The twins were 13 years old in April 2017 and have now gone up to Middle School – class 7. Their young sister, now aged 10, will enter class 6 next school year, September 2017, the last year of primary school. How time flies.

Incidentally, I mention their **little** sister – this refers to years only, not height. She is actually very tall for her age. We see a good deal of these precious little 'monsters'. We, especially Ilana, are very involved with their development and education. They live a five minute car ride away and they are with us, or Ilana is with them, almost daily. We play with them, often take them to or from school (mainly Ilana), make sure they do their homework (again Ilana). *(And where did you hear of grade 1 and/or 2 doling out homework which they had in their time – almost a fulltime occupation.)* They eat lunch with us on weekdays and do their homework here, normally with Ilana's help because both their parents have full-time, very busy, jobs.

I suppose I could write much more about all my grandchildren but I'm trying not to be a bore.

I have so far come to the conclusion of this tale – so let me call this the first edition. I shall try to remember and/or keep notes of any item which pop into my mind regarding anything I may have forgotten, which may require revision or needs to be added. Should it be necessary and should I have the strength and sense of purpose I may yet produce a second edition. I can only repeat – in conclusion…

Man Proposes – G-D Disposes

Wonders will never Cease

I thought I had concluded the Memoire's personal and family history quite a long while back. However...

It is now January, 2019 and I have reached the age of ninety one and a half – and I thank the Almighty for all these years; especially in reasonable health.

As I have mentioned already – wonders and surprises never cease.

I have not mentioned it before because I was never aware of family relations on my father's side of which he may have known. We children were never aware of such. In fact, we – I certainly – often felt that there must have been other family. It was surely the custom in those days – the 1800th – for families, especially orthodox (Chassidic) families to have large families. Try as I might I was never able to find any, neither Kesslers nor Berggruens.

Now read this...

Early this month (January,2019) I received an e-mail from someone in Lakewood, New Jersey, USA. His name was Isaac Kessler and he thought we were related. From the information he sent me it became clear that we were definitely closely related. Isaac is 24 years old. He is married to Chana and they had their first child in August 2018 – a girl – whom they named Tzirel Esther. They, and all their very large family, are Bobover Chassidim. Isaac is a Yeshiva student. He has four brothers and four sisters. His brother, Avraham Yechezkel is expected to marry on February 7, this year – the civil date that Ilana and I married many years ago. Whereas Isaac lives and studies in Lakewood, his wife's family's residence, all his very large family lives in Borough Park, Brooklyn, New York. Apart from his brother Avraham Yechezkel his brothers are Solomon, Yisroel Aron and Eiiezer; his sisters are Hudes, Rochmie, Chana Mindel and Rochel Faiga.

His father is Meir Nussen who married Chaya Gitty (Gittel) Leser. As far as I can make out there are four siblings – two male and two female – Burech Shlomo and Avraham Chaim; and Miriam Charne and Chana Suri, all – except for Avraham Chaim, who lives in Israel – live in Borough Park. All are married and have large families.

250

Isaac's grandfather was Moshe who married Chaya Liba Hopstien. She was born in Israel, grew up in London and on her marriage in 1961 presumably moved to the USA. Again I have received names only of the Kessler siblings – probably not of all, Moshe's siblings are – males: Shulem; Matel (probably Motel), Shimon, Pesach, Duvid; female: Rishe, Mirel, Schprince, Necha. Again all have large families and live in Borough park – except for Necha who lives in Toronto, Canada and Mirel who lives in Manhattan, New York, USA.

Moshe's father, that is, Isaac's great-grandfather, was Yisroel Aron who was born in 1904. This was one year before my father, aged 10, came with his family to Munich in Germany. He, Yisroel Aron, was my father's cousin. His father – Yitzchak Isaac Kessler born 1865, being my father's uncle. My grandfather – Bezalel Salomon Kessler and Yitzchak Isaac Kessler were brothers, the sons both of Avram Hirsch Kessler who died 1876 and Chava Kessler nee Rosiner.

It thus turns out then that Yitzchak Isaac was brother to Bezalel Salomon (my Grandfather); Yisroel Aron was 1st degree cousin to Avraham Hirsch (my father) named for his grandfather Avram Hirsch; Moshe (Isaac's grandfather) is 2nd degree cousin to me – Bernard – and my siblings – Bezalel, Sara (Susi) and Dora (Dorle); Meir Nussen, (Isaac's father) is 3rd degree cousin to my children – Simone, David, Naomi and my adopted daughter Yulia (Yael); and Isaac Kessler – who started it all – is 4th degree cousin to Naomi's sons Eitan and Tamir and Yulia Yael's daughters – Mai and Shir (the twins) and Romi.

A family of whom we had not known actually existed. How wonderful. They came to the USA only in 1949, some years after WWII, having spent the whole time first in Galicia, Poland – and then, escaping from the Nazis when they attacked Poland, traversed the whole of the Soviet Union where they were arrested and sent to a camp in Siberia. They suffered greatly there, including loss of lives, but eventually – in 1949 – managed to leave there and reach the shores of the USA. If I manage to receive more details of all those years, I may be able to add more information about all the years in-between, and add details like wives, siblings, children, and full particulars for all. Meanwhile, this is it.

This is Isaac, aged 24 when he contacted me, on his Wedding Day two years earlier, with all his immediate family: his grandparents seated in front; his wife on his right; his mother next to her; his four sisters next; his father on his left; his four brothers next to his father.

To make life even more exciting February brought us news of the discovery of more family of whom we had no knowledge. This time it was a branch of the Sonnenblick family. They only reached the USA in 2016. Here too, part of the family managed to escape from Berlin in 1939 (they tell me it was actually 1940) and eventually wound up in Siberia in one of the Soviet "Re-education" centres. How they lived and survived there I can only imagine. When and how they managed to leave Siberia and the Soviet Union I have not yet discovered but some, at least reached the Holy Hand. Some were caught and lost their lives in the USSR and some in the Holocaust – too many, I fear. About one – David, one of Elimelech's and Rachel's sons – I wrote earlier, I am sure. He was of great help to my sister Susi, aged 15 at the time, when she passed through Turkey in 1940/1 on her way to Palestine. David and his family had managed to slip through the Nazis' fingers and reached Turkey on his family's way to Palestine also.

Let me start this again. In February this year – 2019 – only a month after hearing from Isaac Kessler – see above – I was contacted by Eli (short for Elimelech) Sonnenblick. I am sure you are aware that I have also created a Family Tree – in my case with My Heritage; in his through Ancestry. He discovered on his Tree about our existence and, as was to be expected, wrote to me. Naturally we commenced to communicate – and are still corresponding. We have much to learn about each other and about our families. I will try to outline what I have discovered so far.

Eli is named after his great-grandfather Elimelech Sonnenblick who married Rachel Krug from Lancut. Rachel was my grandmother Bluma Berta's sister. My grandmother, together with her whole family, came to live in Munich, Germany in 1905. Life in Poland became very difficult – especially for Jews. My grandparents, now in Munich, had bought a house which enabled Bluma Berta to invite her sister Rachel and husband Elimelech, with all their seven children, to come to live with them in Munich. This they did in 1913, the year before the first World War started. They stayed there until they moved to Berlin in 1920. Elimelech is thus Eli's great-grandfather after whom he was named. His grandfather, Shmuel, was Rachel and Elimelech's youngest son who came with them from Poland to Munich, Germany, when he was just a new-born baby.

He came to Berlin with his family when he was only seven years old. In 1938, being 25 years old, he was enabled to leave Germany and enter Switzerland for reasons of health. He suffered seriously from asthma and was allowed to live in Davos. Moving to Zurich, Switzerland he met and married his wife in 1945 and in 1946 bore here their first child – Eli's father, Moische Alexander. Not being residents officially they were obliged to leave Switzerland after WWII. They chose Nice, France as their home. Here they had two more children, Rita and Evelyn, who also married and have families. I am not sure where and how Eli's father – Moische Alexander – had met a Geneva born and raised girl whom he married. Being Swiss – she was of course allowed to live in that country. So, naturally, was her husband and they moved to Zurich, Switzerland shortly after. Here they had twelve children – all married, with families, except one. Eli, born in 1980 in Zurich married Esther who was born in Brookline, Mass USA in 1983. They have six children between the ages 11 and 1.

This leaves me to mention, briefly at least, Elimelech – after whom Eli is named – and my grandmother's sister Rachel. As mentioned, they moved to Berlin in 1920 where they lived 'till 1939/40. There they opened their own textile business. It is not clear how long they were permitted to own and use the enterprise after the Nazis came to power. At some stage they were of course obliged to flee via Poland and where else I know not.

They found their way through Poland and either Latvia, Estonia or Lithuania to the Soviet Union (Russia) from where they had hoped to reach Palestine. However, in the USSR they were arrested and sent to a camp in Siberia. Life was, no doubt, very difficult – I have no details – but after the war they managed to leave and eventually, somehow, reached Palestine/ Israel. Rachel, my grandmother's sister, already had died and was buried in Berlin in 1935. Elimelech, who had made his home in Tel Aviv, died in 1957 in Tel Aviv and was buried there.

One son – Moshe – and one daughter – Freda Yuta – with their spouses and children, lost their lives at the hands of the Nazis during the Holocaust. Sara Sala and David reached Palestine/Israel; Naftali – I know not; Goldie Lea died young, in 1939, after marrying her Haim Kessler; Shmuel is at the head of Eli's story. He, Shmuel is/was Elimelech Senior's youngest son, born in1913. He came to Munich with his family when he was just a few months old. He appears in the photo in the back row, second from the right. He is/was Eli's grandfather.

On his right is the groom, Moshe Wolf, then the Bride, Rita nee Sonnenblick, then, I think, Moische Alexander Sonnenblick, brother to both Rita and Evelyn. In the front, from the left is the very young Evelyn and Gertrude, mother of the bride. The others must surely be parents and siblings of the groom – but I can't tell who is who. The main thing is that they are the branch of the family from which Eli stems.

Lower row l.t.r. — Evelyn Sonnenberg Gerstel / Gertrude Sonnenberg-Hacker / unknown / unknown
unknown David Wolff / Erika Levi / Moshe Sonnenberg / Bill S Wolff / Malsenheel / Sam Ca.

Some of the people who have touched my life.

This was to have been the conclusion of my memoires, with possible corrections and changes in the existing text. However, on reflection, I have started to think of the many people I have known – the many interesting and some rather influential individuals - many of whom must have influenced my life in some way. Surely they have a place in my memoires even if my memory of some is more limited then of others. I shall try to keep them grouped in accordance with their relationship to one another rather than to their time in connection with me. My memory of some is more extensive then of others and I may then explain more of who they were, Well, here goes.

Leipzig

Herr Joffe – I don't know if that is how he spelled his name. Nor do I recall his first name – if ever I knew it. He is mentioned already in the appropriate place above where I expressed my regret at not knowing what became of him. He was my classroom teacher in school when I was about 10/11 years old, before our deportation to Poland. I remember him only vaguely – tallish (to me), strict but kind, well-dressed and always clean shaven, as was the custom for teachers in school.

Schwarzbard (I think he so spelled his surname) I believe his forename was Harry but am not altogether sure. His brother, who by the time I saw him in Israel had changed his name to Ze'ev Bard, was married to Janina. By the strangest coincidence they, with their two daughters, Naomi and Juliette, rented or purchased their flat opposite ours in East Talpiot. Ze'ev was a Building Engineer. Janina was something of a scientist, a biologist, I think.

Would you believe it? I cannot recall the names of any of the children in my class. There must have been a Fritz, a Willie, a Heinz, but I can't recall even one girl's name except perhaps a Rita.

POLAND

After our deportation by the Nazis from Germany to Poland in 1938 I spent 10 months here until, thanks to my parents' efforts we, my younger sister – Dorle – and I, were enabled to join the Kindertransport to England organised, I believe, by the Polish Refugees Committee. Here, too, I remember only a few names of adults and children at Otwock, near Warsaw, where we assembled. I do have a photograph which shows many of us who gathered there. Two members of the organising committee were *Messrs Esley (I think) Zeydlin* and **A.M.*Kaiser*** – I am not too sure of their forenames – nor their fate. They were both on the boat Warszawa with us, as were at least two young women who apparently were not Jewish, had no entry permits and were returned to Poland.

Esley Zeydlin was the Chairman of the Polish Refugee Committee; a lawyer by profession – in fact he was a Barrister and KC (King's Councillor). I was told by someone who had more contact with him than I had that he was rather dictatorial.

Aryeh Mayer Kaiser, on the other hand, was, I am told, very kind and helpful. He was a Yiddish author and journalist. He was born in Bjordanov (?) Poland in1896. I don't know when he came to England but he became a contributor to Yiddish journals. I must mention particularly the London journal "Unser (our)Tribune" which was edited by Zeev Jabotinsky and Moshe Grossman. Other journals included – Loshen und Leben; Die Yiddishe Shtimme which appeared in Kovno as well as in London; Letrzte neues which appeared in Tel Aviv, He wrote for many other Yiddish journals, He also wrote and published a number of books in Yiddish including Der Bandit fun Yerushalayim; Mir Zennen Hungerik; Bei uns in Weitchapel; and three shorter stories entitled Weitchapel lebt. There may be others but these are all I found.

The people I do remember from our Kindertransport were; ***Benno Katz; Herbert Haberberg; Booby*** (a nickname) ***Reich*** (I think his proper name was Jack and I think he now lives – with his wife – in Shoresh (not far from Jerusalem). I believe he had with him his sister ***Helen*** – and if I am not mistaken his son is called Alan. This would be the Alan who interviewed me in London a few years ago when he was preparing a film about the Kindertransport ; ***Jaques Reich; Ozzie Reich*** (who

called himself Michael later) and *Erich – later Sir Erich – Reich.* The
last three were not related to the first two named Reich; Jaques came on
the boat before ours because he was a little older than we were. Sir
Erich was only four years old at the time – the youngest, or one of the
youngest, so did not come with us to the Ely Hostel. He was placed in a
home for small children on arrival in England. Our group comprised 67
children, both male and female. I don't know where the girls all wound
up but we boys – at least those not collected, on arrival in London, by
families who had sponsored them – went to Ely with the Jews Free
School which, as many schools in the big towns, were evacuated to
country areas where the children would be less likely to suffer from
bombing attacks from the German Luftwaffe.

Benno Katz was not only in the Ely hostel with me (after being billeted
together with a local couple first – see above) and on leaving Ely for
London we both joined Habonim – a Zionist Youth Movement. We
both volunteered, then served in the Jewish Brigade – I in battalion one,
he in battalion three. In fact, whereas I arrived in Italy at the very end of
the war, still aged only 17 plus years old, he – my senior by three years
– arrived in Italy in time to participate in the battles on the crossing of
the river Sanio. On his discharge from the army he went to Palestine,
met and fell in love with Shoshana, married her and took her to
California, where he established a 'ball-bearing' factory. Shoshana died
some years ago; Benno is sill with us. On my one visit to California we
spent a lot of time with them and have been keeping up a
correspondence as well as phone contact.

Which brings us to *Gershon Growald.* Is it possible that I remember
him, and his wife Lilly, very well but can't recall from where? Was he
in the army with us? He too must have been in The Brigade and earlier
in Habonim in London. I just know we were, indeed are, good friends
whose wedding in London we attended – was it 1946 ? I just can't recall
where and how we first met. His wife, Lily, and he moved to Brazil
(Sao Paolo). We, too, are in touch fairly frequently.

I have always considered *Max Jotkowitz* my very best friend. Our
closest contact was in the Jewish Brigade, then the British army –
particularly the Interpreters Pool – since we both spoke German
fluently. On returning to civil life Max joined his father in his catering
business – to which I referred already above, especially in connection

with my own marriage in 1948. Max, too, married and went to live in Atlanta, Georgia. Both his wife and he have since died, leaving two sons with whom I have only very rare contact.

Freddy Kaye, formerly Katz, found his place in his appropriate part of the above memoire. Freddy did very well for himself, and for his family. As I already recorded he married his Boss's daughter after starting to work in 'the business'. Their wedding Marion and I also attended. Gertrude bore him three children. Eventually they came on Aliya where they settled in Natanya. Freddy is no longer with us. Gertrude lives in a very good old age village. One son, Michael and one daughter, Mimi live in Israel and the eldest, Linda lives in London still. They are all married and all have families

Herbert Haberberg is recorded in the main family memoire above, He was married to Milly - G-D Rest Her Soul - who, as Marion's best friend, first introduced me to Marion - G-d Rest Her Soul – the mother of my 3 biological children. He has always been active in local Jewish affairs, especially those concerned with his Synagogue. We are still in touch with one another.

The Jewish Brigade

Some of the above were also in the Brigade but of those not mentioned I remember one in particular – *Rafi Blumenthal*. He was from Palestine – my platoon sergeant in Tarvisio. As far as I am aware he studied and became an architect after his service , before and after the establishment of the State of Israel, in the Israel army. I have been told he was involved in the building of sections of the Givat Ram Campus of the Hebrew University of Jerusalem – particularly the National Library.

I may well remember others from my own army service like *Zigi Sattler*, who came to England from Vienna in 1939, served in the Jewish Brigade, came on Aliyah on leaving the British Army, in time to participate in Israel's War of Independence. He fought in the south of the country. When his unit was sent to capture hill 69 in the south of Israel – the Negev - they encountered very heavy attacks from the Egyptian forces and he was one of a number who lost their lives here on June 10,1948. His body was only recovered on October 18, 1949 when he was finally buried in the Kiryat – Shaul cemetery.

Joseph Fishbein was not on our boat to England from Poland as far as I remember but he also came from Leipzig. He was nine months older than I and managed to reach England also not, I believe, via Poland. He managed to complete his education in England before joining the British army. He fought in Italy, transferred to the Jewish Brigade when that was formed and participated with them in their battles in Italy. He, too, came on Aliyah on his discharge from the British army. On formation of the Israel Defence Forces he and his friend Zigi were both offered posts as instructors in the newly formed army. As did Zigi, he too declined, choosing to join a fighting unit. As his friend he participated in the battle for hill 69, and like him he also fell in that battle on the same day. In his case his body was only recovered in August 1950 and he was brought to rest in the Nachlat Yitzchak cemetery on the 31st of that month.

" MAY THEIR MEMORIES BE BLESSED AND THEIR SOULS REST IN PEACE"

Henry Stern could have been in "The Brigade" as well and probably was. From where else would I have known him? I don't recall him from Ely; probably from London where he was, no doubt, a member of one of the Youth Movements. I do know that he, too, reached Israel. The Youth Movement of which he had been a member was Brit Hanoar Shel Zeire Mizrachi – the religious Zionist Movement – and he went with them to join Kibbutz Lavi in Israel and served as that Kibbutz's internal secretary for many years. Come to think of it I most likely remember him as a member of that Movement in London and I arranged his Aliyah from there to Kibbutz Lavi together with his Garin (group).

I find it difficult to keep together all those belonging to a particular group, place or time so, as mentioned already, will record as memory brings a person to the fore.

Barry Mindell served for many years in London as secretary-general of Mizrahi/Hapoel Hamizrahi – the religious Zionist Movement mentioned above. In my aliya work I had very close contact with him – a friendship which continued loosely when Barry, as I, came on Aliya where he continued his work in the Mizrahi Movement in Israel organising the Movement's activities throughout the world. I, on the other hand, went in a different direction – workwise.

This may be the proper place to mention Abba Bornstein and the Mizrachi chairman – Manny Klausner – both of whom maintained regular contact with me concerning our mutual work,

Since I appear to be back in London working within the Zionist organisation, I will mention some of my colleagues in that framework.

I have already written about Dr. Shneuer Levenberg, Jewish Agency Representative in London. Did I mention Alf Shinewald, and Alex Gordon, Jewish Agency representatives in London (finance and organisation)? Or United Jewish Appeal representatives – Wally Gold; Harry Shine; Micky Barzilai; and many others.

SHLICHIM

There were also the representatives of the PATWA Association (PATWA stands for Professional and Technical Workers Aliya). Chairperson of the London Organisation at the time of my own Aliya was Pamela Assenheim with whom I had the closest contact (she also came on Aliya). I remember only two Slichim to PATWA – father and son. They did not, of course, serve at the same time. The father, Harry Sable came first. Later his son Robbie followed in his father's footsteps. My Marion worked with both in their time. I don't recall much of Harry's work other than working together. For Robbie I have much more to tell. First let it be known that Robbie is now a Professor at the Hebrew University's Faculty of Law. He was the Legal Representative of Israel's Ministry of Foreign Affairs and, as such, participated in the various discussions of that office with the "Palestinians", Americans, Syrians, Lebanese and others. He was and is a frequent interviewee on all subjects relating to our contacts with the world at large.

There is also a Pamela Sable – daughter to Harry and sister to Robbie – whose married name was, I think, Louvel. Her husband is joint owner of one of Jerusalem's most prominent estate agents. Pamela worked for many years as secretary and personal assistant to Abe Harman, President and later Chancellor of the Hebrew University of Jerusalem.

There is much to write about my time at the Hebrew University but, while still being with the Jewish Agency in England, I had better write something about the many Shlichim sent from Jerusalem to further Aliya from Great Britain and Ireland.

The first Shaliach to our office in London was – if my memory does not confuse me completely – a very senior government ministry official called Israel Gal-Edd who was with us for a rather short time – no more than a year, I think. I am not sure but I believe he too came on Aliya from the United Kingdom. (I may have mentioned in another place of the journal that he was from a Kibbutz- which may have been called Gal-Ed.) Such is the memory in old Age.

He was followed by a Deputy-Director of the Aliya Department Head Office in Jerusalem – Naftali Bar-Giora – who took complete control of our office from the day he arrived in London. Mona Woislavski, who had been the office's director, who had 'taken me on' as 'Chief Cook and Bottle Washer', as the local expression went, meaning doing all odd jobs required, remained director of the office officially. However, as mentioned already, Naftali immediately took over running the office. He soon appointed me as filing clerk, then as secretary, and had me working on all aspects of the various requirements necessary for the potential Oleh. This led to my eventual appointment some years later by the Aliya Department Head – Shlomo Zalman Shragai - as Executive Director.

Naftali had already served in the department as a wide roaming emissary. He had looked for, found and organised groups of potential Olim, so I have been told, from the Arab countries around us, and as far afield as Morocco, Tunisia, Algeria and other African countries. I cannot really vouch for every one of these places.

What does come to mind now that I am thinking back to that time is that my behaviour at that point was not what I now know it should have been, in connection with my relation to Miss Woislawski. I accepted what Naftali asked me to do, went to him when I required instructions, and almost ignored the formal director of the office. Today I know that this was most unworthy of me – and I regret it.

Apart from work in the department I can mention here our, particularly Marion's, custom to invite every new shaliach to our Shabbat meal on their first arrival in order to have them feel at home in a strange country. She always included their families – wives and children – if they too came to England. In Naftali's case who had come alone, at least at first, a minor tragedy occurred when our son David – accidentally I hope –

let his tie fall into Naftali's chicken soup – or was it Naftali's tie into David's soup. I do hope Naftali has forgiven him.

Who comes next. Shubi (ShearYashuv) Olswanger, if I remember correctly - I don't really recall all the Shlichim, certainly not in their order of arrival - was one of the most efficient. Son of the well-known Yiddishist, folklorist, renowned translator and firm Zionist, Dr Immanuel Olswanger, Shubi was a founding member of the Habonim Youth Movement in London. This movement spread not only to other towns in Britain but to many other countries. I believe I mentioned earlier that not only I but many of my friends, when coming to London in our youth, mainly from the Ely hostel – became members of that Youth Movement. Shubi, so we all called him, travelled all over England, Scotland, Wales and Ireland to meet Jewish communities and bring to them the information which might help those interested to reach the appropriate decision – Aliyah to what was then Palestine - with some measure of success.

On his return to Jerusalem he took charge of the Immigrants Club – a place where newcomers from all countries could meet, learn Hebrew, exchange information, help one another, and generally make new friends who may help each other (or moan to one another?).

Moshe Gan – an orthodox member of the Jewish Agency Aliyah Department in Jerusalem (I believe all officials in that department were religious) joined us in London with his wife – her name was, I think, Sara - and two daughters called Shlomit and Ruth. We became very good friends with them as did our children with theirs and on our visit to Israel one year at Succot spend some time with them in their Succah in Jerusalem. Their daughter, Ruth, on growing up, left the more orthodox religious community, joined the conservative stream, studied at the conservative Yeshiva and received 'semicha' (ordination) as a conservative/liberal Rabbi with her own community and Synagogue.

Moshe Carmon came to London with his family – wife and four children, I believe. We kept in touch for quite a while after his return to Israel but I have very little information about his work here. Whilst on shlichut with us he did his work well, meeting many potential Olim.

About Moshe Carmon, on the other hand, I know a little more. First he is a Jerusalimite. I wrote about him earlier, I am sure, concerning our visit to Israel before our aliyah. This Moshe was on loan to us from Israel's Ministry of Finance where he held a senior post with the Customs Authority Directory. His work with us included explaining customs and tax regulations in Israel for the newcomers. I know I mentioned already earlier about his taking us for an outing to Ein Fashcha on the Dead Sea but am not sure if I mentioned that when retiring he took a woodworking course. On hearing of Marion's death he crafted a Chanucca Menora which he dedicated to her memory.That Menorah is being lit today – the fifth candle light of Chanucca, 5779 (December 1918), when our family gathered in our home to celebrate and remember.

Moshe (again Moshe) Shamir is another 'kettle of fish' - as one might describe it. He is known for a variety of reasons. As one of Israel's best known and liked authors and playwrights his works – often at the top of Israel's best sellers list - are frequently used in schools as examples of outstanding writing. I believe when writing about my eldest daughter earlier I mentioned her winning a scholarship for writing a descriptive essay about one of his books, which earned her a 10 day holiday to Israel. (my mistake – Simone now reminded me that she won that prize for her essay on a book by Amos Oz) Shamir's works are basically biographical. philosophical and historical.

Moshe Shamir is a Sabra (native born in Zfat, Israel his father having come on Aliyah from the USA after World War 1. Moshe was a member of Kibbutz Mishmar HaEmek, was on the Editorial staff of Maariv – one of Israel's major newspapers, served as an officer in the Palmach and In Israel's Defence Forces, and sat in the Knesset – Israel's parliament - as leader of the party which he had formed. I must really add and I can't imagine why but unlike most of the other Shlichim to our office Moshe Shamir did not visit our home, as far as I remember; neither before nor after his wife and three children joined him in London. Maybe he did and I just don't remember. When, otherwise, did he promise Simone a library of all the books he had written – a promise which he never fulfilled – I am sure the reason was forgetfulness.

Yehuda Oron – what can I say about him (and about his wife -Ziva). I am in Israel 44 years already and they still contact me every Erev Pessach and every Erev Rosh Hashana. Yehuda, who was 29 years old when he joined us in London was and is a modern religious (kippa seruga – knitted scullcap) lawyer. His special assignment – modern religious professionals and business people who need up-to-date details of opportunities in The Holy Land and any specific problems they may encounter. He received his degree from the Law Faculty of the Hebrew University, Jerusalem, was legal adviser to several municipalities, before coming to London on Shlichut – all this after his army service (there is much to tell of his activities during the 6 - Day war,1967, but this is not the place). His wife – Riva – too had to leave her very interesting job at the ITIM News Agency in Tel Aviv where she held down the Executive – Secretary position with much success. By the way, Yehuda spent many years on regular reserve service with Israel's Defence Forces – first with his unit in the Tank Corps; later with the Legal Department as a prosecutor and finally as Judge in all areas where Israel's Forces held trials.

Speaking of a modern orthodox (kippa seruga) shaliach is, I think, the proper place to mention:

HaRav (Rabbi) Katzenellenbogen whose first name I don't remember. His wife, I think, was called Connie. His mission as an ultra-orthodox Jew himself was to show "Charedi" (ultra-orthodox) Jews that they, too, had a place in Eretz Yisrael. The more ultra-orthodox Jews came on aliya the more religion there would be in the Holy Land. There was a large "Charedi" community in Jerusalem as well as in Bnei Brak and there were Yeshivot and Kollelim all over the country.

Now that reminds me of a visit which Golda Meir paid to London some years earlier. At a well - attended meeting which she addressed groups of Charedim had penetrated the hall, holding several hundred people. They had placed themselves in various parts of the hall and interrupted Golda in her speech over and over again. The audience became very angry and wanted to throw out the interrupters but Golda would not let them. Instead she told them "If you want more religion in Israel come in large numbers, elect many members to the Knesset, and pass the appropriate laws". The audience approved; and so did the interrupters.

Yitzhak and Dinah Huberman– and their three children – were the most charming people we had come across. Not that all the others were not nice, pleasant, charming and friendly. They all were, of course. The

265

Hubermans just were 'heimish', if you know what I mean. I kept up contact with them for a while on our own Aliyah but the amount of work our settling in entailed didn't leave me much free time – if any. Our contact with one another regretfully payed the penalty.

Yitzhak, who started his Shlichut in January, 1967, was our organiser of parlour meetings where participants were able to raise their special problems and worries and by discussion often solve the problem and eliminate the worries. He had been a member of the same kibbutz which Levi Eshkol left to become Israel's Premier eventually – Degania Bet. Yitzhak's ambitions were apparently somewhat more limited. He, too, left the kibbutz, joined the Jewish Agency, where he became a senior official in the Information Bureau of that organisation. He completed studies in Social and Political Sciences and Economics.

Eli Teicher obtained his degrees in Law at the Tel Aviv University's Faculty of Law and at the McGill University in Montreal. His career, however, is in journalism and authorship. He was on the editorial staff of both the newspapers Davar and Haaretz. Eli was designated and sent especially to the British Aliya Movement which, in Israel, had existed for quite some time but as a Movement in Britain was established much more recently. I don't know how many Olim Eli brought to Israel. I am sure of one. Eli married Jill, She, obviously, came with him when, on his return to Israel after finishing his term in England, he returned to his home in Tel Aviv. Jill, at least in the beginning, found work with El Al-Israel Airlines, which at the time was located in Hayarkon Street – almost opposite the well-known Hotel Dan.

Paul Kohn – I know he came on aliya from England in 1949; which indicates that my office in London probably dealt with his aliyah arrangements. I don't remember knowing him before that or what his origin was. In Israel he worked as a military correspondent and as a reporter in Tel Aviv for the Associated Press, as well as a staff reporter in the Tel Aviv branch of the Jerusalem Post – the major if not the only English Language paper in this country. He was an active member of the original Hitachdut Olei Britania (HOB) and as such was able to help potential Olim with information based on his personal experience. In Israel he had also been a director of a Public Relations company which aided him in his activities during his shlichut by enabling him to establish contact with such organisation in England, - spreading the word about possibilities for newcomers to Israel.

Chaim Cohen was a 37 year old, Tel Aviv business executive who was enticed by the Jewish Agency Aliya Department to spend some time in Britain advising potential businessmen on opportunities in this newish and exiting, as well as developing country. Chaim was posted to our Manchester office but travelled over much of the midlands, meeting not only business people but all interested and potential Olim. As a former resident of Kibbutz Erez he was able also to advise potential settlers on joining agricultural settlements. His main task, however, was advising on Business Administration all interested in that line of activity.

In Chaim's letter of farewell, on leaving England to return home to Israel, he stresses that he does not want to sound like the proverbial Englishman who goes through the motions in order to do 'the proper thing'. His appreciation for the help and friendship Marion and I, and our children extended to their family on their arrival, and during their stay in England, when they needed all the encouragement possible, will never be forgotten.

Nadir Krongold, another Jerusalemite, was a senior employee with Amisragas when we, my children and I, came on Aliyah in 1974. I don't know his occupation prior to his Shlichut in London. His work in London was, as for all emissaries, advising potential immigrants to Israel about what to expect – language, housing, employment, bureaucracy, transport, climate, politics, and life in general in a completely different cultural environment. When we moved from the Katamon Absorption Centre to our permanent home in East Talpiot we were very pleased to discover that Nadir and his wife Noa, together with their children lived in their home, at that time, in North Talpiot which enabled us more easily to visit them (or have them visit us).

I only recently heard or read – I don't remember where – a most fascinating story relating to the Krongolds. Hearing a knock on their front door one day they found an elderly or old man, holding a parcel, wrapped up in what appeared to be a blanket of sorts. On unwrapping the parcel they discovered that it contained an old, old violin in a very dilapidated condition. The old man, who was in a similar condition, told them – to Nadir and to his sister – that the violin had belonged to their uncle, Shimon Krongold, their father's brother (it not being clear to me if they knew of his existence). Shimon Krongold was an outstanding violinist, and composer, well known in the musical world. His violin was an original Stradivarius or similar (I don't recall) worth more than its weight in gold, as the saying goes. During World-War II Shimon left Warsaw, fleeing from the Nazis in stages and, step by step, wound up eventually in Tashkent. Here he apparently met the man to whom he entrusted the violin prior to dying. He, the old man, wanted the violin returned to where he was sure it belonged but being poor himself asked for suitable recompense – which he was given. The violin was put into the hands of the best instrument maker and repairer in Israel at that time and was restored – very carefully – to its former glory. It reached the hands of the organisation which searched and collected instruments which escaped the greedy hands of the Nazis – 25 such instruments were found which eventually toured the world – another reminder of the Nazis' failure to eradicate the Jewish People.

I had read about this once only. My memory not being what it used to be there may be some variations to the actual events but I have not found again where I read of this. Should I find the article or video again I will make sure of the accuracy of the story.

Chaim Baram, son of Moshe and brother to Uzi, has been immersed in Israel politics from the day he was born. His father was a member of Mapai and served in Israel's Knesset as a member and as a minister. His brother Uzi, also a leading member of Israel's Labour Party, spend much of his life as a Knesset member and as Government Minister, until his retirement. Chaim, to the best of my knowledge did not enter the Knesset. This may be due to the fact that he was, and is, much more left wing in politics. As far as my memory goes this did not influence his missionary work as a Shaliach. He was very popular at the many group meetings he addressed.

Aharon Zachor: the best I can do to describe him is to quote part of the letter he wrote to me on returning to Israel with his wife and 3 children on the completion of his Shlichut. Aharon writes:

Dear Bernard,

Don't laugh because I am writing you this very personal letter. I do this on very egoistic grounds: to save myself a too lengthy goodbye!

In my whole career in administration I have never met such a loyal colleague as you have been to me.

I state this without any reservation or hypocrisy, and without any intention to appear polite. These are plain facts. And I want to thank you for all this.　…

This letter also stands as an ever-lasting open invitation to come and see us in Israel.

Yours in Friendship A.Z.

What more can I say?

Age has an effect on my memory. I may also mention two of the emissaries from the 'Agency's Economic Department – Uri Karin – for some reason he is referred to in some places as Director of my department in London. I do not recall him as such – but rather as shaliach of the Economic department – and Shlomo Chelouche, both of whom did excellent work during their missions.

There were a not inconsiderable number of other emissaries to our offices in Britain – too many to write lengthy individual accounts about each. Suffice it to mention Dani Bareli, who had been a senior Jerusalem Police officer; Mickey Shafir; Gideon Reicher who claimed the title of Chairman of the Association of Hypochondriacs; Aryeh Langer who, I think, was the security chief at the Jerusalem town hall; Simcha Glazer; Pesach Rifkin – deputy, I think, at Yemin Orde; Ulman (whose first name I don't remember – but I know that he was a Haifa lawyer); and there must have been female emissaries also – again, I cannot recall their names; apparently, as I said before, being 91 plus years old causes memory problems.

There is one more Shaliach about whom I must elaborate somewhat.

Yitzchak Meir was the main emissary of the department when my children and I went on Aliyah ourselves. He came to us from Yemin Orde. This was the Youth Aliya village named in commemoration of Orde Wingate – an officer in the British army during the time of Britain's mandate of Palestine – who used his military knowledge and experience to train members of Palmach and Hagana to defend our kibbutzim and villages against Arab marauders -in fact creating the origin of Israel's Defence Forces. All this without the knowledge of, I believe, and certainly against the wished of the British Mandate Authority.

To my surprise I just discovered that whereas Yitzchak spelled his Hebrew name in the usual way – מאיר - he spells his name in Latin as Mayer, not Meir. His full name is Yitzchak Mayer. There is much to be said about Ambassador, yes, Ambassador Mayer, some of which I may mention. First let me stress that his great love has always been education, in the widest possible field. For eighteen years he served as Director of the Yemin Orde Youth Aliya Village. Apart from diplomat and educator he has been – and indeed still is a commentator and author, invited frequently to schools, synagogues, community centres and other organisations. In 1979 he was offered the diplomatic post as Consul General in Zurich. The following year he was transferred to Montreal where he stayed 'till 1983. In 1991 he was sent as Ambassador to Belgium and Luxembourg and from 1997 to 2000 he was Ambassador to Switzerland, He has published novels – both fiction and non-fiction – as well as plays, essays and poetry. He is still very active as a Senior Advisor at the Natanya Academy and is working to develop Kiryat Yam as a World Chess Capital. A very active person.

ISRAEL

Shlomo Zalman Shragai was the head of my department in Jerusalem. A wonderful man – let me tell you a little about him. He was born in Poland in 1899. His father was not only a member of Hovevei Zion but also of Mizrahi – one of the earliest Zionist Movements, orthodox, of course. He himself, still as a youth, founded Ze'irei Mizrahi in his city and published a religious Zionist newspaper called Tehiyah. He was a founder of the He-Halutz Ha-Mizrahi training farm and a leader of Mizrahi in Poland. He settled in Palestine in 1924 and soon held various positions in the Hapoel-Hamizrahi leadership. In 1946 Shragai became a member of the Jewish Agency Executive in London and may well have sat in the 'Max Nordau' chair in the office which, in later years, became mine. On Israel's establishment he returned home as a member of the Agency's Executive. In 1950 he was elected mayor of West-

Jerusalem, a post he held until 1952, and 2 years later returned to the Jewish Agency Executive as Head of the Aliyah Department.

In this capacity, and because he was one of the leaders of orthodox religious Zionism in Jerusalem, he received the Aram Tzova in the early fifties when the Chalabi Rabbis had it sent to Jerusalen during the Arab riots in Syria. In the course of time the document left Shragai's possession when it was deposited with the Ben Zvi Institute where, and only the Allmighty knows, what happened to the many pages which later were found to be missing– but that is another, very interesting but sad story.

He laboured in this position until 1968. Amongst his fervent efforts after WWII was to find and bring to Israel the holocaust survivors and find ways, often by endangering his own safety, travelling, clandestinely, to many Arab and African countries to bring home Jewish groups who were always in danger in their countries of birth.

It only remains for me to record my own personal relationship with that fervent and religious, Jerusalem-loving Zionist. I can best demonstrate that by quoting what he wrote to me on retiring from his post as Aliyah Department Head at the Jewish Agency in Jerusalem:

מר קסלר הנכד

עם פרישתי מההנהלה ומתפקידי בענייני עלייה, קבל נא את הכרתי ו

המשותפת,הנאמנה והמסורה האחראית והמדוייקת שהיתה בינינו במשך עשרים שנה כמעט

יודע אני להעריך את מסירותך נאמנותך לענייני עלייה על הבנתך המליאה לנפשו של המועמד

לעלייה ועל העמל הרב שהשקעת כדי שענייני העלייה מאנגליה יתנהלו כשורה ובסדר הראוי למופת.

היה ברוך ומבורך מתוך בריות גופה להמשך עבודתך בהצלחה .

ש.ז.שרגאי

In a free translation – for those who know not Hebrew:

Dear Mr Kessler,

On my retirement from the Executive of the Jewish Agency, and from my tasks in the Aliyah Department, please accept my blessings and appreciation for your loyalty, dedication, and sense of responsibility and preciseness in the work we shared for some 20 years.

Well do I know to appreciate your devotion and loyalty to the Aliyah Enterprise, your full understanding of the Aliyah candidate's 'soul', and all the hard work you invested, in order to ensure that Aliyah from England is handled smoothly and in admirably good order.

Be doubly blessed, to enable you to successfully continue in your endeavours.

S.Z. Shragai

Baruch Duvdevani was I believe, the department's Director-General during most, if not all the years that Shlomo Zalman Shragai headed the Aliyah Department. Like Sharagai he, too, was very orthodox but I am not sure if he too was active in in the religious Zionist party – Mizrahi/Hapoel Hamizrahi.

Baruch was, however, also born in Poland, 18 years after Shragai, in 1917. His family was closely connected to the Hassidic community in his town of birth yet unlike many others they were also very Zionist oriented. The family- father, mother, grandfather and 12 year old Baruch came on Aliyah in 1929. On his arrival he first started to study in the "Etz Chaim" yeshiva. Then entered the "Mercaz Harav" yeshiva established by the renowned Rabbi Kook who exercised a profound influence on young Baruch, which remained with him all his life.

As one of the leaders of the religious youth section of the Etzel – Irgun Zvai L'Umi – the resistance movement against British occupation led by Menahem Beigin – who years later became Israel's Prime Minister – his activities caused him to be arrested 3 times by the British occupying power and he sat in prison in Saraf and, Jerusalem and Latrun. The end

272

of WWII when many survivors found themselves in displaced refugee camps he volunteered, in 1946, to join Unwra and that year the Jewish Agency sent him to Italy where he was put in charge of a refugee camp of 4000 survivors. He used this opportunity to send many 'illegally' to Palestine. 1949 saw him in Libya from where he managed to send 30 thousand Jews to the recently established new State. From 1950 on he was Mr ALIYAH who traversed not only much of Europe but crossed – from end to end – Morocco, Algeria, Tunisia. Persia (Iran) and the various South American countries were also in his itinerary. One must add his devotion to Jerusalem to the development of which he spent much time and effort and to his special regard for Religious – Zionist education.

On returning from a conference in Zfat (Safed) he lost his life in a fatal car accident.

Yehuda Dominitz took over as Director-General from 1978 to 1986 after Baruch retired from the Jewish Agency. His parents had sent him to Palestine in 1939 from Czechoslovakia when he was 13 years old and thus saved his life. He did not see his family again who all lost their lives in the Holocaust. His early work with the Jewish Agency was as a Youth Aliyah Shaliach to Italy. Here he laboured from 1946 to 1948. He worked with orphan children who had survived the Shoah (holocaust) preparing them for a new life in Youth Aliyah villages in Israel. On returning to Israel he transferred to the Aliyah Department where he fulfilled many important functions. His tasks were confined not only to The Jewish Agency and they took him to many places including Europe, America and other parts of the world. As his predecessor – Baruch Duvdevani – and, indeed, the Head of the Department – Shlomo Zalman Shragai – he 'travelled the world over'.

He was involved very much in arrangements for the transfer of Jews from Ethiopia having doubted at first about their suitability because of the problem of their Jewishness but put his efforts into it once it was decided to go ahead with their Aliyah. What engaged him even more was the thought of large -scale Aliyah from what still was the Soviet Union. He put his heart and soul into his effort to fulfil what may have been his greatest hope – perhaps his dream, which he saw fulfilled in the years that followed.

Moshe Yakir was my main personal contact with our head office. I don't think that he visited London more than once during my time at the Jewish Agency, Aliyah Department there (1949 t0 1974). I did, of course, spend much time with him on my visits to Israel in those years. Our correspondence was almost daily, one might say, and I am sure he corresponded with all the world-wide offices as frequently. On the personal side I do remember particularly that Simone, my daughter on leaving for Israel (before her Aliya, I think) asked his advice about what Tefillin to buy for me. In the end we did not buy them, I may still do so.

My memory is so limited that although I remember many people I can't recall their names or particulars. Such is the case with the Jewish Agency, the World Zionist Organisation, the Hebrew University, the British Zionist Federation, Keren Hayesod and Keren Kayemet and others. Like Moshe Rivlin, Aryeh(?) Dulczin, Gabriel Turner (who at some stage became Mayor of the Negev capital - Beersheva; or am I mixing him up with Yaacov Turner – a completely different person). When I knew Gabriel (or Gabby) he headed the Bureau for the promotion of Immigrant Projects; M.Haskel (J.A. Treasury) Eran Laor (J.A. rep in Geneva) ? Sabato (Aliyah Dept). and many, many more whom I will add if they come to mind again; as they often do.

There is one, while we are still with the head office of the 'Agency' Aliyah Department, who cannot be forgotten – Uzi Narkiss. I imagine I could fill a whole page about Uzi – but I won't. I will try to give a relatively brief outline about this interesting character who was my boss – head of my department- for the last six years of my time in London before our own Aliyah – 1974., a post he held until 1978. His parents came to Palestine from Poland - from where else? He was born in Jerusalem, in 1925 – where else? and died in 1997, also in Jerusalem I am sure, having spent a lifetime of 72 years serving this country.

Already at the age of four he felt the importance of Jerusalem for our people and our country. He recalled his earliest memory at that age finding places to hide during the Arab risings in 1929. This, according to him, shaped his outlook of the world – as my early life, especially the deportation from Germany to Poland, did mine. At the age of 16 he joined the Palmach and Haganah and was heavily involved in all their

274

action – in defence against the Arab marauders and against the British Mandatory Power. Early in 1948 he led the attack on Katamon , liberating the San Simon Monastery, which was considered a key strategic position.

During the early years of the State He spent several years in France, first as a student at the well-known Military Academy and later as military attache, - being awarded the Legion de Honneur. In 1965 he became the first Israel National Defence College director. In the Six-Day-War Narkiss, as during all his military endeavours, was responsible for combating the Arab Legion of Jordan which led to the liberation of the Old City of Jerusalem, held till then by the Jordanians. Which, of course, led to the re-unification of our capital city and, eventually, to returning the US embassy to the Holy City. A pity that Uzi's death did not enable him to witness the return of the Embassy to his beloved Jerusalem.

His work for the Aliyah department brought him to many parts of the world, including Britain where, apart from our meetings in Israel, I met him whenever he came to us. To my great disappointment he was unable to offer me what I considered a suitable position in his department on my Aliyah in 1974.

However, as Ilana, my wife, always tells me, what is meant to be will be and I very quickly found a suitable position at the Hebrew University where I then worked for 12 years plus and which, incidentally, led to my meeting Ilana – and to our marriage five years after losing my first wife – Marion – so tragically.

If I remember others from my work in the Jewish Agency's Aliyah Department I may add them here, if possible.

Meanwhile let me now put on record information about some of my colleagues and friends – both senior and junior – from my work at the Hebrew University of Jerusalem, some of whom I wrote about above – in the main memoire.

Avraham Harman – or Abe, as he is known to everyone – was born in 1914 in London, United Kingdom. He is described very briefly as an Israeli diplomat and academic administrator, having immigrated to Mandate Palestine in 1938, aged 24y, about a year before the outbreak of WWII. It was also the year of our deportation from Leipzig, Germany to Poland. He had already received his Law degree in 1935 from Wadham College, Oxford.

On Israel's independence he worked in Israel's Ministry of Foreign Affairs for 20 years, till 1968. During that time he was deputy director of the Press and Information Division; then was appointed Israel's first consul-general in Montreal; in 1950 he was part of the Israeli delegation to the United Nations, where his wife Zena, also born in England, held a responsible position as well. Incidentally, I believe she also sat in the Knesset at one time as did her daughter, Naomi Chazan. Back to Abe Harman now. 1953 to 1955 saw him in New York still, now as Israel's consul-general. He was appointed Israel's ambassador to the United States- a post he held from 1959 to 1968.

A change in his career was called for it seems, and on being offered the position of President of the Hebrew University of Jerusalem Abe accepted - at once, I imagine. So - in 1968 - Abe, following in Abba Eban's footsteps, took up his position in Jerusalem, a position he filled from 1968 to 1983 during which he expanded the University – especially the Mount Scopus campus which had been returned to us following the 6 – Day war in 1967. After 1983 he was appointed Chancellor of he University.

Honorary degrees were heaped on him by universities the world over, including his alma mater, Wadham College, Oxford, who named him an honorary fellow.

I just want to mention two of Abe's notes to me:

I enjoyed very much the method, style and content of your donor reports and want to congratulate you on your good work.

The other was:

Dear Bernard,

Many thanks – I would like to express my deep appreciation to you for all your devotion and for the personal relation between us. I send you my best wishes for the future and I do hope that we shall stay in touch. With kindest regards and appreciation.

Abe Harman

Who's next? Why – Bernard Cherrick, of course! Like Abe Harman Cherrick was also born in 1924. His birthplace was Dublin, the capital of Ireland but he, too, grew up in England from where he immigrated to what still was Mandate Palestine in 1947. In England he studied in a yeshiva where, at some stage, he was granted his S'micha (ordination) and became, formally, a Rabbi. He studied at The London School of Economics for his first degree and earned his Master degree from the University of Manchester in 1937. At the start of WWII he served as a Rabbi with the British Expeditionary Force in France and may have been among those rescued from the beaches of Normandy. During those years he was also Rabbi to the New Synagogue in North London's Stamford Hill – which I attended in my young days – and as a director of both the Jewish National Fund and United Israel Appeal. On his arrival in Israel in 1947 he joined the public relations department of the Hebrew University in charge of fund raising. He was made vice-president of the university in 1968 and remained as such until almost his death in December 1988.

As vice-president he persuaded Frank Sinatra to endow the construction of the Frank Sinatra International Student Centre. and subsequently invited Hollywood celebrities like Billy Crystal, Gregory Peck, Barbara Streisand, Helen Mirren, Elisabeth Taylor, Kirk Douglas and many others to encourage fundraisers on campus.

Now to mention – and I mean just mention in passing – some of the people with whom I worked in the Hebrew University particularly, and in other places – both before and after coming on Aliyah.

Eliyahu Honig – I am pretty sure that I wrote about Eliyahu in the more personal part of my memoires

And don't need to add anything else. (It was he who accepted me to work in his department when he was Director of the Public Relations Department of the University. I really must add that whereas I have been fully aware that it was Eliyahu, as Benard Cherrick, who often took important visitors round the H.U. campuses I only just discovered about his promotion to Vice-President, probably on Bernard Cherrick's death.

Micky Bavli took over from Eliyahu Honig as Director of the Public Relation Department which by now was called The Department of External Affairs and it was during his term that I retired in 1987 as Head of The Reporting Unit of the Hebrew University,

Micky was a well-known participant to Israel's Radio Music Quizz as well as one of the main contributors to the musical recordings to that program. He left his position at the Hebrew University, I was informed, on being offered a diplomatic position as Israel's Ambassador to Holland but have not found any confirmation of this. I had lost touch with him by then and don't know what else he did thereafter.

Sinai Leichter – the love of his life was, surely, Yiddish, and especially Yiddish folksongs and music. I don't know what else he published but he was the principal collector and Editor – apparently – of all seven volumes of the Anthology of Yiddish Folksongs which were all published by Magnes Press. Sinai presented me with the first 4 volumes – subscribed to me - where Abba Kovner is mentioned as a co -editor. He, Sinai, really was a good friend.

I am not too sure what all his functioned in our department were; certainly fundraising in Israel itself was a main part.

Yehuda Kavish, whose position I filled when joining the university, was now responsible for fundraising in Europe. The USA had a well-established Friends organisation – as did Britain.

Rahamim Dayan, Mordechai Mizrachi, Edna and others fulfilled various functions which I need not elaborate on.

Judi Argaman nee Rabinowitz became my first secretary/personal assistant. She had come on Aliyah from the USA where her father was the Rabbi of what was one of the largest and earliest established Conservative synagogues – Adas Israel – in Washington. While working with me – and she was an excellent PA – Judy studied to become one of Israel's foremost experts on early childhood education.

Since I started mentioning my office staff at the Hebrew University I will try to remember as many of the girls/women – young and not so young – I will insert here all I recall at present. Anette, whose family

278

name was I think Freeman replaced Judi. She lived in Tekoa, several kilometres from Herodian, of King Herod fame. Tami Cohen was the Hebrew language typist who, on her marriage moved to Maale Adumim. Vicky Maharshak was one of my English secretaries. She hailed from Venezuela and dealt with reports and correspondence to Latin America and Spain. On my retirement she obtained a senior post in the Sam Rothberg School for Foreign Students at the University. I had one secretary – a linguist, who was originally from Portugal, I think. She dealt with all correspondence and reporting in Spanish. and Portuguese – taking care of Spain, Portugal and Brazil.

There were several more, whose names 'escape' me at present – old age, I expect – which I will add, if I remember. Two were reporters of research of various fields – one lived in a village on the old road leading to Ramle whose name was Frieda; the other – a Jerusalemite – who I recall was a specialist car driver who, in the past, had participated in the Sahara Desert race. For me she had to be satisfied with research reporting; but she was very good at that also.

One, who was with me before Anette was the wife of one of our diplomats and mother to a mathematics teacher at the school next to the University. I have left my filing clerk to the last – and not because she was of least importance, Dorine (or Doreen) Kehila was my filing clerk for all the time that I worked at the Hebrew University. As such she was of supreme importance to us all. (We all know what 'mixed-up' filing can do) She also happened to be the wife of the university's Head of the Workers Council – they were the body responsible for negotiations with the University on all matters relating to employer/worker relationship.

Avraham Kehila was the Univerity's Workers Council chairman for many years There comes a time, however, when one is either forced to or wants a change. In Avraham's case I believe it was the latter. He stood for election to the Jerusalem Municipality. He won, and on election became a Deputy Mayor. I don't recall for how long he held that position nor what followed.

Alan Baker was born in 1947 to a traditional family in Britain. Before coming on Aliyah in 1969 he completed his Bachelor of Law degree at University College, London and went on to study for his Master of Law in International Law at the Faculty of Law at the Hebrew University of Jerusalem.

Two years after graduating he became a Military Prosecutor and advanced steadily in the Military Advocate General's Unit until 1979. After some years in private practice he returned to public service in 1985 when he was seconded to the United Nations serving as senior legal adviser until 1988. The International Criminal Court was his task in 1995 and the Rome Diplomatic Conference demanded his attention.

During the years he participated in negotiations with Egypt, Jordan, Lebanon and the Palestinians, focusing mainly on international law. Alan fulfilled many important functions, including four years as Ambassador to Canada, far too many to mention here. Just another brilliant career, on behalf of Israel, of an immigrant from the United Kingdom.

Harav Shlomo Goren – not exactly my personal friend. I did, however, spend some interesting time with him and found him a man to be admired.

He was born in Poland in 1917 and immigrated to Palestine with his family in 1925 – aged eight. At the age of 12 he was enlisted at a yeshiva – I don't know which – but was soon recognised as a prodigy, He published his first religious article when he was only 17 years old. In 1936, when just 19 years of age, he joined the Haganah. When questioned on religious matters arose in the army he was often turned to for solutions.

This caused the Chief Rabbis to recommend him as Chief Chaplain to the Israel Defence Forces – the first I believe in this position. A brave soldier himself he frequently accompanied the troops into battle, even by parachute, and often behind enemy lines, to bring back dead soldiers for burial at home. He reached the rank of Brigadier – General. On retiring from the army in 1972 he was elected Ashkenazi Chief Rabbi, a post he held until 1983. He was sent on a mission to the U.K. in 1978 when I travelled around with him on behalf of my department. I recall he was a vegetarian. I also recall that he used to rise in the mornings at 4 a.m. or soon after, to study the Talmud, before commencing the day's work.

Morele Bar-On can best be described as a historian. He was born in Tel Aviv in 1928, during the Mandate of Palestine – long before the Establishment of Israel. On that auspicious occasion, in 1948, he became a member of the IDF's first officer training course. On graduating he became first a platoon commander, then company commander, in the Givati Brigade. In 1954 he established the Academic Pool in the army and the following year became Head of the History Department of the General Staff before his appointment as head of the Chief of Staff's Bureau. He then became Chief Education Officer in the Education and Youth Corps until his demobilisation in 1968. In that year he was sent to the U.K. to help raise funds for Israel and promote Aliyah Thus my contact with him. He was elected to the Knesset in 1984 but resigned.

Samuel Kassow, about whom I wrote in the family history, when I described our meeting and it's result, needs me to add some factors not mentioned earlier. Sam was born in a displaced persons camp in Stuttgart, after his mother and sister survived the holocaust. His father was arrested by the Soviets and spent the duration of WWII in a Soviet prison. After WWII the family reached the USA and Sam grew up in New Haven, Connecticut. In 1966 he earned his B.A. at Trinity College, Hartford, and in 1968 was awarded his M.Sc. at the London School of Economics – when we made our first acquaintance. His Ph.D. he earned from Princeton University in 1976.

A brilliant historian Sam was the Charles Northam Professor at Trinity College until his retirement not so long ago. He authored a number of major books dealing with Tsarist Russia, and with East European Jewry, His most outstanding work – which was made into a film -is called "Who will Write our History. It is based completely on the hidden – buried – publications of Jews in the Warsaw Ghetto during the Nazi Occupation, and its final destruction. This book is a "MUST Read".

I could write a complete page, at least, about Sam Rothberg who by many was called Mr Hebrew University – a title which speaks for itself. I personally had very little direct contact with him – I think he barely knew me by name although he was chairman of that institution from 1968 to 1981. I had more direct dealings and regular contact with Sam's successor – see below.

Harvey Krueger who, on hearing that I was about to retire early in 1987, wrote to tell me that he enjoyed our meetings and cooperation, which he hopes will continue.

He was raised in New Jersey and became legendary in Israeli business circles. He was the first banker to bring Israel to international capital markets. A graduate of Columbia University and Law School, he eventually, became a Vice Chairman of Lehman Brothers and of Barclays Capital. The number of posts and the many organisations – not only charitable – which benefitted from his participation and often leadership are too numerous to mention here. He holds honorary degrees from several higher education institutions and was a great supporter of his Synagogue.

He was, as I indicated in the last chapter, Chairman of the Hebrew University's Board of Governors. He was also Chairman of the University's Friends Organisation which was led, most efficiently, by its Executive Director,

Seymour Fishman with whom I had frequent contact by regular correspondence concerning detailed reports to donors of scholarships and research funds.

I believe Seymour was actually born in Poland and only luckily was rescued before WWII. Seymour's uncle Sam apparently lived already in Canada, as best as I can make out. In 1938 he went back to Poland to convince his family still living there to leave Europe while they still had the chance. Most of the family – which was quite large I think - fell victim to the holocaust. Mendel, Sam's brother, his wife Goldie, and their son Seymour survived. With Sam's help they were able to reach Canada after the war.

Joel Alpert was in charge of the Hebrew University Rector's Office for many years during which we had very close relations. Indeed, we became good friends in all that time. From 1983, I think, he was on shlichut from the University in the Canadian "Friends" office in Toronto, Ontario and returned to the University in Jerusalem in 1987. I don't know what position he filled on his return.

Nehemia Levtzion was the Bamberger and Fuld Professor of The History of the Muslim People. When I got to know him he was Dean of the H.U. Faculty of Humanities. In that capacity I had frequent contact with him which developed into a friendship which continued after he relinquished that position. Apart from African history, especially Islam on that continent, he was very active in higher level educational institutions like the Open University, the Van Leer and Ben Zvi Institutes and others. Modest as he was, he was a welcome, very knowledgeable participant in study and research activities, as well as conferences, at many Universities all over the world and received many honours. One could fill a whole page or 2 at least of his achievements if room allowed but...

In my work at the J.A. Aliyah Department in London we had 5 doctors on call – all approved, and used also, by the Israel Embassy in London. Their job was to medically examine all potential immigrants to Israel. The chief doctor, who had to confirm all exam results, was Thilla Krikler with whom I was in almost daily contact. Thilla had herself suffered from a most serious illness, had been cured, gave birth to two more children – against her own doctor's advice – and served our department for many years. Her illness eventually returned after a number of years and she died relatively young leaving a husband and four young children. She visited our home during Marion's illness and on one occasion told us "It is not how long you live – it is rather "How you live". I admired her very much.

Aharon Keidar was the principal researcher of the Dinur Research centre, concerned very much with Zionism in Germany and 'Brit Shalom' which was established in Germany in 1925. I know very little of that time except that many prominent persons were involved. My office was in close touch with Aharon and his research, and he expressed his close association in a warm letter to me on my leaving the university. I will, however, not quote it for lack of space.

Malachi Beit Aryeh expressed his appreciation of our close relation when he was Director of the National Library – or was he?

Amram Ashri, Jacob and Rachel Liss Professor of Agronomy also acknowledges our regular contact about his research at the Faculty of Agriculture in Rehovot.

Dr. Avraham Kraizer, who was the Deputy Dean at the School of Pharmacy of the Faculty of Medicine at Beit Hakerem, met with me on the friendliest terms on regular occasions in connection with our mutual work.

Raphael Mechoulam, The Lionel Jacobson Professor of Medicinal Chemistry wrote me in his letter on my retirement that he cannot imagine the HU administration without me and that he will always remember the efficiency, good humour and pleasant ways in my dealings in all our mutual matters.

Professor Natan Kaufman of the HU – Hadassah Hospital School of Nutrition wrote to tell me of his regret that the university will no longer benefit from my 'blessed' work, as he called it.

Rivka Inbal – was it in relation to her work at the University Comptroller's office that I first met her when she came to inspect our books and files – as well as our work methods? Did she then leave that office to become Deputy Dean in one of the Faculties? A pleasant person with whom to work.

What can I say about Benny Mushkin – and there is much one could write of his work at the University. There was also much outside the university which attracted his attention and participation. I will confine myself here by saying only that he was a friend.

Dr.Hillel Raskin was, for many years, head of the Howard and Mary Edith Cosell Centre for Physical Education, Leisure and Recreation at the Givat Ram Campus of the Hebrew University in Jerusalem. He was also one of the main fundraisers for the Centre. He was also a good friend,

Rachel Shitrit directed the Special Projects Division of Keren Hayesod in Jerusalem and we also worked together in my field of activity.

Yisrael Ro'i became my good friend early in our relationship over a good many years, in his work as – eventually -Deputy Dean of the Rothberg School for Overseas Students on the Mount Scopus campus of the University.

Israel J. Herman of the School of Applied Science and Technology,was one more academic with whom I had not only contact but very friendly relations, as well.

So was Prof. David Levy of the Levy Eshkol School of Agriculture, Faculty of Agriculture, Rehovot.

The Institute of Philosophy and History of the Faculty of Humanities brought me into regular contact with Shlomo Slonim with whom I established a very friendly relationship.

I mentioned the American and Canadian Friends already, so let me now add the London, U.K. Friends. We, Ilana and I, visited that office on a number of occasions where we became good friends with Charlotte and, - was it Sabina? The London offices had a flat attached where Ilana and I stayed when we visited London during the early years of our marriage. St. Johns Wood, where the Friends were located, was close to Regents Park – a favourite place of ours. Even nearer was Lords Cricket Ground – I think we could actually watch, from the flat, that game – cricket – being played.

Jumping about from place to place let me now mention the Deputy Director of the Jerusalem Municipality's Education Department, Moshe Cheshin, who dealt especially with Higher Education. We had regular contact about scholarship arrangements which developed into very friendly work relations,

Dare I mention someone to whom I can hardly refer as a friend – but very friendly he was with both Marion and me in the short time of our contact. It would seem he was much impressed with both our devotion to Zionism and especially to our Aliyah activities – including dealing with his own. That was Rabbi Solomon David Sassoon. He was scion to the widely known Sassoon family – a long line of Rabbis before him – and followed as such by his son – who originated in Baghdad (and India, I think) He made original contributions to linguistic analysis, philosophy, physiology and Biblical criticism. He was held in such high esteem by all that he was twice offered the post as Sephardi Chief Rabbi of Israel – in 1953 and 1964. He declined on both occasions, such was his modesty. A pity I am unable to find his letter to Marion and me on his aliyah. I do have his letter of condolences to me, sent from Israel, on Maron's demise. He, himself, died in 1985. I can, however, add remarks from a letter from Mr. David Elias who was Honorary Secretary and Welfare Officer of the Ohel David Eastern Synagogues - which had

285

branches in Golders Green, Stamford Hill and East London – which read " On behalf of the President, Rabbi S.D. Sassoon and the Eastern Jewish Community, I wish to express to you and all the members of your family, our deep sympathy in the loss you have sustained".

I have letters of friendship also from Friends Organisations: Mexico – Anita Viskin; Brazil –Leon Herzog; South Africa – E. M. Udwin; and a good many others.

Tour VeAleh – the Unit which dealt with the promotion of Immigration Projects, was led by my good friend Gabby Turner, referred to earlier, assisted by Aryeh Chapman. Aryeh, whose Aliyah from England I had arranged, was by the purest chance on his way to Israel on the boat my family and I travelled on when were on one of our visits to Israel. As most children they found their way to the swimming pool aboard. Aryeh enjoyed playing with them by taking each, one by one, on his back and swam around the pool with them. All this on our earliest family visit when the children were very young.

I have not yet mentioned the Hitachdut Olei Britania, or was it the Volunteers Union, which was established in Britain also. Its Organising Secretary was Rona Hart – who I later met in Israel, before she returned to London (She has since returned to Israel and is now resident in Haifa)

I think Pamela Sussman, now Mrs Lewis, was also active in that organisation, both here and in England. So was Josef Kissinger. Both Marion and I were closely associated with both organisations – and with the active members of those organisations.

Beatrice Barwell was active in the Zionist Federation; Mickey Barzilai in the U.I,A,; Norman Oster, a barrister in England but for many years an advocate in Tel Aviv, Israel who was most active before his Aliyah in PATWA, ZF, HOB - a good friend.

The girls in my office in London -Lynn Stock; Sharona Joffe; Tzilla Lavie; Haggy Dattner; Rachel Mordechai; Ahuva Cohen; - of course Freda Miller and Anita, it goes without saying. Anita found herself a nice Israeli husband – or rather was found by ???? whom she married and came to live in Israel. I don't know if she is still here – we lost touch long ago. Freda remained in London and married there. Some of

286

the girls mentioned were Israeli and returned to their respective homes while others are not mentioned by name because my memory is such that I cannot recall how they were called.

As I mentioned earlier, at least I think I did, potential immigrants to Israel had to be medically examined before being issued with their visa to Israel. The Israel Consulate had on approval a number of doctors in London who were naturally also approved by The Jewish Agency. I mentioned the Chief Medical Officer Thilla Krikler, to whom all results of the various doctors were submitted for approval. The others were – Dr.B.Hermann; Dr.M.H.Zim; Dr.S.David Moss; Dr.D.Feldman; and there was, of course, Dr.Donald Phillips. I remember him especially since I first met him when I underwent an 'operation' of sorts at the Middlesex Hospital in London where he was one of the resident doctors. What keeps him in mind is that following my stay at the hospital Donald offered his home for my convalescence. He and his family lived in Stock, Essex which is out of London, near Chelmsford. He took his wife and children away on a two weeks holiday so that they could put the whole house at our – Marion and I and our three children – disposal. A really good friend.

Judith Barnett, Freddy's sister, and her husband Bob were always close friends.

As was Estelle Roith who was a sort of relation to us since her sister was married to my cousin Zvi and divorced only some years after giving birth to Cygal – I think that is how she spells her name.

Michael Shine, a friend from London, came on Aliyah and joined the Law firm of Gideon Hausner in Jerusalem, He was also an excellent Chazan, having an outstanding tenor voice.

Celia Goodman- what can I say about Celia (and her husband). When we both still lived in London we both attended the large Stamford Hill Synagogue. I do remember having a 'crush' on Celia but 'though she was always kind she wouldn't have me. When we came on Aliyah ourselves we discovered that she and her husband had a shop in Shlomzion Hamalka street in Jerusalem which, naturally, we visited. It was nice to see her – but the passion was there no longer. After all, some 30 years or so had passed.

Joe Ezekiel was Hon.Secretary of the Association of Friends of Hitachdut Olei Britania. Needless to say, we had mutual interests which brought us in contact often.

Tova and Stuart Cohen relate already to our membership of the Central Synagogue in the centre of London, when I was no longer a youth and was married with children of my own. We had been close friends for many years, but lost touch here in Israel. If the address I have, which dates back to 1973, is still the same I shall attempt to re-establish contact.

I found him today – December 26, 2018 – and just spoke with him and was very glad that he expressed his delight at our re-established contact. He now lives in Modiin, which is about half-way between Jerusalem and Tel Aviv. We may even meet – here or there.

Ruby and Ezra Shamash, on their Aliyah, moved into a flat in Jerusalem's Tschernichovsky Street. Again, I lost contact. Pity. I may be able to re-establish contact with them also.

I am beginning to find it difficult to find where to insert all those I remember into their proper places. The only thing to do under the circumstances is write where I am and insert where and when I can.

So – here goes.

Maria Beck was a Health Visitor when our children were young. We became good friends as the years went by – a friendship which continued over the years.

Reverent Avraham Rosenfeld – a friend of many years in London when he was not only a Chazan in one of the North-West London Synagogues but was most active with the JNF and JPA in fund-raising as well as aliya activities. He even went as far as Wellington in New Zealand where he served not only as Chazan in their Beth El synagogue but was much involved with the Wellington Hebrew Congregation as a whole.

This is, no doubt, the appropriate place to mention his son, Lionel – and Lionel's wife Natalie. This charming couple lived not far from us in East Jerusalem (Armon Hanatziv). Lionel was a Chartered Accountant by profession and was employed by one of Israel's leading firms. During our High Holidays he acted as Chazan to Prayer Services in

Minyanim and Batei Knesset in various places – first in Israel then on invitation at one of the main synagogues in Central London. Here he was eventually persuaded to take on the position of Chazan and Rabbi permanently. Natalie, his wife, was an English teacher. Most important, 'though, is the fact that Lionel acted as Chazan at Ilana's and my Wedding Ceremony at which Rabbi Paul Lederman, an American Oleh, and another good friend in our neibourhood, officiated.

Sid Gilbert was an active member of all Zionist activities in London. He worked with me for a time. So, when asked for my recommendation as my successor, I suggested Sid as possibly suitable. And so it was – but not for long. Sid did start in my office but for reasons unbeknown to me to this day he remained in the post for a short time only.

Donald Silk and Sidney Shipton followed one another as Secretaries – General of the Zionist Federation of the United Kingdom of Great Britain and Northern Ireland, of which Lord Janner of Leicester was President. I had frequent contact with them about Aliyah activities.

Rabbi Solomon David Sassoon, mentioned earlier, may or may not be related to Vidal and Ivor Sassoon but I thought I would mention it. Whether or not he was – as is most unlikely - the two last mentioned were brothers who both had very problematic childhoods. Vidal, who became the most renowned Hairdresser, who dressed the hair of most of the famous film stars in his time, had no personal contact with me. The contact we do claim, Ilana and I, is that on our second (1979?) or third (1980?) visit to London Ilana decided to have a Hairdo in Vidal's establishment. She was not treated by the Master himself but by one of his assistants. I am not sure if Permanent Waves were his invention but that is what she had – and looked absolutely gorgeous (what's more, I have her photograph).

All this in order to record our firm and long-standing friendship with his brother Ivor and his wife – Ivor's – Carmella. My memory being what it is now (aged 91y) I do not remember what his/their occupation was. However, in 1973 They were in Londonderry, Northern Ireland, where they both attended The New University of Ulster – either as students or as teachers. I don't know about Carmela, but Ivor died relatively very young – may his soul rest in peace, (Incidentally, Vidal died aged 84, I believe)

The Chief Rabbi of Great Britain and the Commonwealth in the time before my immigration to Israel was still, I think, Rabbi Dr Immanuel Jakobovits who, on his retirement, was made a Baron in the Queen's New Year Honour List. I had no direct contact with him. I did however have frequent regular contact with Moshe Davis, who was director of the Chief Rabbi's Office, and with whom I became firm friends.

Another friend, perhaps not quite so close and frequent, was the Reverend Dr I Levy O.B.E., T.D. who was the Director of the Jewish National Fund. He was more closely associated with Marion (my wife) who worked at the J.N.F. for Dr Herbert Freeden.

Levy Gertner was director of the London Office of the World Zionist Organisation – and the Jewish Agency- Education Department. Naturally, we had much to discuss in our mutual tasks.

Earnest Frankel, like Michael Sacher, was a Business-man, not an employed person. His association with the Zionist Federation, Jewish Agency and J.P.A – later J.I.A. -was strictly voluntary. He was one of the active Honorary Officers of those organisations. Over the years he has always been most supportive and helpful to me personally, as well as to the organisations he served.

I may add that his son – whose first name escapes me at present, - came to live in Israel where he became a lecturer or professor ((I am not sure) at the Hebrew University where I worked.

The Secretary of the Central Synagogue, about which I believe I wrote earlier, was Mr Ehrlich. This was our regular 'shul' and we attended services on Shabbat and Festivals regularly. I think I wrote already about Rabbi Cyril Shine and his lovely wife Sylvia and about the splendid – widely known – Chazan Shimon Hass and Elaine, his wife. Let me add that the synagogue's Secretary was always most helpful. So was the Shamash – Mr Wosner – and Mr Dugan, the caretaker and his wife.

There was also "aunty" Rosie whose pockets were always filled with sweets for the children and, of course – Vivienne Simons who lived in Grosvenor Square, near the American Embassy, sitting where Marion and the girls sat in a place where she and they could see David and me – and vice-versa.

I shall not mention Isaac Woolfson, whose synagogue this was – after all, he had it built so he would not have to walk too far from home to synagogue.

Shmuel Lowenstein was involved with most Zionist efforts, apart from his business activity. He lived in Edgware, a largely Jewish neighbourhood many years ago. Now it is partially occupied by "many newcomers" – Hindus and Muslems , mainly from India. The kosher shops are still open as are the restaurants.

My son David does not have to go so far since he can still go to Golders Green if he wants nice and kosher food for Shabbat.

Haim Pinner was the Executive Director of Bnai B'rith District Grand Lodge of Great Britain and Ireland. We were in touch quite often – I don't remember why but probably about our mutual Zionist interests.

Lille Myer was General Secretary of Children and Youth Aliyah in Britain' but my regular contact was principally with the Secretary of the Organisation – Mina Tym. Even when I came to represent the organisation and dealt with their Childrens' Aliyah arrangements I had no real contact with Honorary Officers such as Lady Woolfson, Lady Brodie, Lorna Wingate and others at their level.

The Reverend Reuben Turner was General Secretary of Mizrachi – Hapoel Hamizrachi Federation of Gt, Britain and Ireland. He was also Director of the Zio9nist Federation Schools Orgenaisation – of which there were nine, I believe. Also he edited the Federations journal – The Gates of Zion. We had regular contact – as I did with Howard Cohen, Seretary of Bnei Akiva of Great Britain and Ireland. The Federation of Women Zionists was also one of the organisations with which I remained in contact, 'though not so regularly.

Without going into personal details about each individual I would like to name a number of those who were in central positions in either the Israel office of Britain's Zionist Federation, or the Aliyah Department or Children and Youth Aliyah whom I had to consult or to whom I had to report on occasion. The Z.F. office in Israel -Eric Lucas; Moshe Dubski; I already mentioned Ralph Hadani and Miriiam Zaffran as well

292

as Shlomo Temkin; Keren Kayemet (JNF) - Moshe Rivlin; Jewish Agency, Aliya Department - Harav Mordrchai Kitshblum; Dov Landkutson; Chaim Shteinmitz; Children and Youth Aliya – Klarman, Director-General 1968; Shraga Adiel, Director-General 1971-1974; Shimon Tuchman, Treasurer; There was also the Head of that department – Moshe Kol- with whom I met occasionally.

Sam and Betty Boxer were friends from our synagogue in London – The Central Synagogue – where we met every Shabbat and Chag, They lived not far from there in what in London was known as the central residence of specialist doctors, all very expensive and used, therefore, by private patients who could afford their charges. I don't know his or her occupations.

The principal and largest Jewish newspaper in Britain and Commonwealth was the Jewish Chronicle. One of its senior journalists, George Garai, was most concerned with the many Jewish organisations in Britain. I had frequent contact with him about our work, which led to our becoming fairly good friends.

Zena Klein was just a friend, whom we had 'inherited' from Marion. I really don't know what occupied her time.

Rabbi Dr. Litvin, edited the Zionist Federation journal called "The Gates of Zion" until his death, I believe; the journal represented the 'Federation's widespread involvement with it's schools and synagogues which were much under the watchful eye of Rabbi Dr, Litvin.

I mentioned much earlier about the Rabbi I met in Bloomsbury Square while waiting for Marion to join me for lunch and his lesson about a successful marriage. Dr. Litvin's message to me was rather different. His words were, and I quote – and this was only a few years after WWII and the Holocaust – "How many children have you now? What – only one boy and two girls? Every Jewish couple should have 10 boys, at least; girls as many as you like – to make up what we lost. He had two children, but then, he was considerably older than we. In the time which passed his wish to be reburied in Israel was fulfilled and his grave is now in the Givat Shaul cemetery in Jerusalem.

His place as editor of the journal was filled many years ago by The Reverent Reuben Turner, Secretary-General of Mizrachi, about whom I wrote some paragraphs earlier.

Dr L. Shafler, for some years – I think – editor of the Jewish Observor and Middle east Review, and I.J.Miller – an administrator – were senior members of the Zionist Federation, with whom I kept in regular touch.

Wally Gold of the JPA/JIA – have I mentioned him before? He also came on Aliyah and lived in Tel Aviv.

Reuven Yannai was a Shaliach to our office in Manchester with whom I corresponded in Ivrit.

K. Pestka represented the Zionist Federation in Liverpool.

Joseph Shine was the Shaliach in Copenhagen, responsible for all of Scandinavia.

Asher Blake was the U.K. representative of Israel's Discount Bank who kept in touch in the hope that we would recommend his bank to potential Olin – at least, I think that was one of the intentions.

Rudi Freedman – was he from the J.N.F in London? Was he the one who was 'renowned' for always shouting at his secretary – who dealt with that by stretching out her arms wide and answering " I made a mistake ? – so shoot me". I hope I have not maligned him and I apologise here if I have.

Barnet Litvinoff, was Marion's 'Boss' for a good many years. I don't know exactly if this was principally in connection with her and his Zionist activities or mainly with his writing. She certainly was much involved with his authorship activities – as secretary/personal assistant and typist. Barnet wrote and had published many books. The Story of David Ben-Gurion (a biography); and about 12 books dealing with Chaim Weizmann's letters and papers are only a small example

I may not have mentioned all he wrote but felt I wanted to mention these. We were very, very good friends.

I have known, and been in contact with, many more interesting people –
at least a hundred to two hundred more. Each person will have had
some influence on me, but…

ENOUGH is ENOUGH.

44015070П001GG

Printed in Poland
by Amazon Fulfillment
Poland Sp. z o.o., Wrocław